The Other People

ALSO BY MEG WILKES KARRAKER

Diversity and the Common Good: Civil Society, Religion, and Catholic Sisters in a Small City (forthcoming, 2014)

Global Families, 2nd edition (2013)

Families with Futures: A Survey of Family Studies into the Twenty-First Century, 2nd edition, with Janet R. Grochowski (2012)

The Other People

Interdisciplinary Perspectives on Migration

Edited by Meg Wilkes Karraker

palgrave
macmillan

First published in 2013 by PALGRAVE MACMILLAN® in the United States—a division of St. Martin's Press LLC, 175 Fifth Avenue, New York, NY 10010.

Where this book is distributed in the UK, Europe and the rest of the world, this is by Palgrave Macmillan, a division of Macmillan Publishers Limited, registered in England, company number 785998, of Houndmills, Basingstoke, Hampshire RG21 6XS.

Palgrave Macmillan is the global academic imprint of the above companies and has companies and representatives throughout the world.

Palgrave® and Macmillan® are registered trademarks in the United States, the United Kingdom, Europe and other countries.

ISBN: 978-1-137-29695-5

Library of Congress Cataloging-in-Publication Data

Karraker, Meg Wilkes.
    The other people : interdisciplinary perspectives on migration / Meg Wilkes Karraker.
        pages cm
    Includes index.
    ISBN 978-1-137-29695-5 (hardback : alk. paper)
    1. Emigration and immigration—Cross-cultural studies. 2. Emigration and immigration—Case studies. I. Title.

    JV6035.K37 2013
    304.8—dc23   2012046088

A catalogue record of the book is available from the British Library.

Design by Scribe Inc.

First edition: May 2013

D 10 9 8 7 6 5 4 3 2

To the person pictured on the cover, an emigrant from Sudan awaiting the bus to adult education classes on a snowy January morning in St. Paul, Minnesota, USA

Contents

Acknowledgments

In spring 2011 I returned from a conference in Oxford, England, greatly inspired by a body of scholarship on "the other people" that spans disciplinary boundaries. At that conference, I also became enmeshed in a new network of colleagues. As editor, my first thanks goes to the organizers of the Oxford Roundtable and to that first set of contacts, now friends: Anthony Gray, Bruce Einhorn, Richard Morgan, and Marcella Myers.

Beyond that first group, this volume brings to a broader audience the original scholarship of Jennifer Blank, Veronica Deenanath, Joanna Dreby, Patti Duncan, Øystein LaBianca, Dung Mao, Marianne Noh, Susan Smith-Cunnien, and Zha Blong Xiong. I extend special thanks to Jan Orf, Susan Smith-Cunnien, and Mathew Vicknair, contributors with whom I share the privilege of working at the University of St. Thomas.

Wing Young Huie, award-winning photographer (and visual sociologist), provided the evocative image that graces the cover of this book. Use of that image was made possible by a grant from the Center for Faculty Development at the University of St. Thomas.

Along the way, we gathered advice and encouragement from the Palgrave Macmillan team, including editorial assistants Leila Campoli and Sara Doskow, editorial director Farideh Koohi-Kamali, and production associate Richard Bellis, plus project manager Sarah Rosenblum and her team at Scribe, as well as colleagues at our respective institutions and (of course, not to be missed) our friends and families.

PART I

Migration Studies in the Twenty-First Century

CHAPTER 1

Introduction: Global Migration in the Twenty-First Century

*Meg Wilkes Karraker**

If they were a country of their own, migrants would constitute the fifth most populous nation in the world. According to the International Organization for Migration (IOM), a partner with the United Nations on migration-related issues, at 214 million, international migrants represent 3.1 percent of the world's population. The percentage of migrants varies widely by country, from a high of 87 percent in Qatar and 70 percent in the United Arab Emirates, to below 1 percent in Nigeria, Romania, India, and Indonesia.[1] Although the global recession has substantially dampened immigration to developed countries, one-quarter of the world's migrants live in Western Europe alone.[2] In Australia, Canada, and the United States, respectively, 21.9, 21.3, and 13.5 percent of people are foreign born.[3]

Between the middle of the nineteenth and middle of the twentieth centuries, international migration was primarily within Europe and between Europe and the Americas. Today, migration is increasingly a worldwide phenomenon fueled by great disparities between wealthy, developed countries and poor, less-developed countries, as well as national and regional conflict. Today, the largest migration streams are (1) from the Caribbean and Latin America to the United States, Canada, and Western Europe, (2) from South Asia and Southeast Asia to the United States, Canada, and Australia (with some to Western Europe), and (3) from North Africa, the Middle East, and Southern Europe to Northwestern Europe (with some to the United States and Canada).[4]

---

* Address correspondence to Meg Wilkes Karraker, PhD, Department of Sociology, University of St. Thomas, 2115 Summit Avenue, Mail #4048, St. Paul, MN 55105-1096, USA. Email: MWKarraker@StThomas.edu.

Reflecting on one country's long history of emigration, Michael D. Higgins, ninth president of Ireland, summarizes the reciprocated effects of migration, for those who leave and those who stay, as well as their societies.

> Those emigrants who left solved two pressing problems: their own and their people's. By moving out, they very often secured the chances of greater material comfort, not just for themselves but for those who remained. Had they stayed, some would doubtless have been creative contributors, but many for want of employment would have been a drain on the public kitty. Ireland today would look a lot more like an underdeveloped country if the one in two who left since 1841 had remained. And places like North American and Australia might not be quite so interesting or so prosperous.[5]

Immigrants often face racial, ethnic, and national prejudice and discrimination as they enter new societies, and they and their new countries encounter a myriad of challenges such as social inclusion and integration. At one extreme, until the end of the twentieth century, South Africa's apartheid represented brutally unequal pluralism among divergent groups. These groups included (1) indigenous black Africans from several tribal groups as well as black African immigrants from other African nations (approximately 80 percent of the population), (2) British, Dutch, French, and German white settlers who began arriving at the end of the seventeenth century (approximately 9 percent of the population), (3) mixed-race ("coloureds"; another 9 percent), and (4) Asians, primarily immigrants from India and China (just over 2 percent of the population). At the other extreme, ethnically diverse countries like the United States and Australia have often presumed an assimilationist ideal for immigration, with mixed success in real practice. In contrast, Brazil is often cited as an example of not assimilation, but amalgamation, while some countries like Canada are moving toward a more egalitarian, pluralistic ethnic ideology.[6]

Emigrants leaving their home countries under the pall of war, genocide, and other horrific circumstances may feel they have "come from a fire into a fire."[7] For some emigrants, even as they weigh the economic, political, religious, social, and other benefits of leaving the familiar behind, migration remains an equivocal experience. On the one hand, immigration heralds freedom and opportunity. On the other hand, emigration threatens "native identity and intercontinental exile,"[8] and reveals a "hole in their hearts, culture shock, the discomfort of the unfamiliar and the fact [of not being] at home anymore."[9] Many emigrants have written of the importance of "home" and the nostalgia associated with such feelings.[10] Some of the most evocative images of the pain or grief associated with leaving are reflected in memoir and folklore. For example, the story told of the *madrileño* (Spaniards arriving in Argentina), crying as they sailed on the ship crossing the Atlantic, saying, "Good-bye Madrid! Nobody lives there anymore!"[11]

The Other People seeks to capture the human and social context of the experience of global migration. To set the stage for the chapters that follow, this Introduction commences with observations regarding the structure of global migration in the twenty-first century.

The Structure of Global Migration

Even dramatic statistics such as the IOM's size of the migrant population worldwide do not paint the full picture of migration. Not all migrants are crossing national borders. In fact, the number of internal migrants is almost four times the number of migrants who have moved to another country. Of those who do move across national borders, over a third move from a developing to a developed country; however, most of the world's international migrants move between developing countries or between developed countries.[12]

The stories of human migration are of voluntary (more or less) emigration but also of forced displacement. The IOM estimates the number of internally displaced persons (IDP) in the world at 27.5 million. Sometimes called de facto refugees, uprooted people, externally displaced persons, or just displaced persons, the IOM defines IDPs as "groups of persons who have been forced or obliged to flee or to leave their homes or places of habitual residence, in particular as a result of or in order to avoid the effects of armed conflict, situations of generalized violence, violations of human rights or natural or human-made disasters, and who have not crossed an internationally recognized state border."[13]

The year 2011 was a record year for such forced displacements, with 43 million people newly dislocated.[14] In the same year, fueled by cataclysms in Republic of Côte d'Ivoire (the Republic of the Ivory Coast), Libya, Somalia, Sudan, and elsewhere, eight hundred thousand people became refugees, the highest number since 2000.[15] The United Nations High Commission on Refugees (UNHCR) defines a refugee as someone "who owing to a well-founded fear of being persecuted for reasons of race, religion, nationality, membership of a particular social group or political opinion, is outside the country of his nationality, and is unable to, or owing to such fear, is unwilling to avail himself of the protection of that country."[16]

Still other migrants call no distinct nation home. The largest minority group in Europe is the Roma (sometimes referred to by the pejorative term "gypsies"). The Roma have lived and traveled across Europe for centuries, confronting discrimination and suffering poverty wherever they settled. European Union (EU) countries like France have engaged in the forced return of Roma to Bulgaria and Romania (which have large Roma populations and both of which joined the EU in 2007), drawing charges that France is compromising the rights of Roma as EU citizens to free movement within the EU.[17]

To further complicate the picture of migration in the twenty-first century, the migration experience itself is changing. For most of human history, migration has been a journey of no return. Emigrants departed their country of origin never again expecting to see loved ones they left behind. In the late 1860s, when nearly one out of every seven Irish-born persons emigrated from the starvation and poverty that had beset the nation, Irish Catholic country folk had a ritual for this "breaking of earthly ties."[18] Signifying that the emigration of a loved one was the equivalent of death, kin and neighbors came together around what they called "American wakes" to share food and drink, singing and dancing, "a seemingly incongruous mixture of grief and gaiety."[19]

In the twenty-first century, migration is less likely to be a one-way passage. Intra-and intercontinental travel has never been more frequent nor, some would say, more convenient. Dangers remain, as witnessed by repeated maritime disasters involving "boat people" trying to reach Australia, the United States, and other countries where they seek refugee status.[20] Still, transglobal information and communications technology (ICT) has effectively reduced separations of time and space for many. For migrating persons and those they leave behind, ICT systems like e-mail, Skype, and cellular telephones make ongoing contact a reliable certainty, at least for those who can afford the technology. Although a technology gap remains, one-third of the world's population uses the Internet and an increasing number of ICT users are in developing countries. In fact, in 2011, 62 percent of the world's Internet users were in developing countries, where 25 percent of the homes have a computer and 20 percent have Internet access. Moreover, between 2008 and 2010, the cost of ICT services dropped 18 percent globally, while in developing countries the cost of fixed broadband technology dropped by 52.2 percent.[21]

For some, the passage between receiving and sending country is involuntary. Such is the case with the recent rush of children—an estimated three hundred thousand between 2005 and 2010—who moved south as their Mexican parents chose to return to Mexico or were deported from the United States. These transnational children may struggle with school, peers, and simply fitting in: "I dream, like, I'm sleeping in the United States, but when I wake up, I'm in Mexico." Marta Tienda, a sociologist at Princeton University and herself born to Mexican migrant laborers, has said, "These kinds of changes are really traumatic for kids. It's going to stick with them."[22]

Those who can or do return to their original homes, voluntarily or otherwise, may experience a sense of normlessness, what sociologists call anomie. Award-winning British-Indian author Salman Rushdie (who became the subject of a *fatwā* for what some fundamentalist Muslims considered his blasphemy) describes both the provocations and connections experienced by people like himself who move between adopted countries and the country left behind. Rushdie recounts his experience of revisiting his "lost city" of Bombay (now Mumbai) and of being "haunted by some sense of loss, some urge to reclaim, to look back, even at the risk of being mutated into pillars of salt. But if we do look back, we must do so in the knowledge—which gives rise to profound uncertainties—that our physical alienation from India almost inevitably means that we will not be capable of reclaiming precisely the thing that was lost; that we will, in short, create fictions, not actual cities or villages, but invisible ones, imaginary homelands, Indias of the mind."[23]

Recent shifts serve as reminders of the dynamic nature of emigration and immigration. After four decades and 12 million immigrants (an estimated 51 percent of whom who entered illegally), the net migration flow from Mexico to the United States has come to a halt and may have even reversed. On the American side, reasons for the dramatic shift include weakened employment markets, stronger enforcement of the US/Mexico border, more deportations, and greater dangers associated with illegal border crossings. However, some of reasons for the change also include improving economic conditions in Mexico, as well as a long-term decline in the country's birth rate.[24]

Asians have now passed Hispanics as the largest group of new immigrants to the United States. Such trends in immigration in developed countries will affect every institution in both developed and developing societies. In the words of Paul Taylor, executive vice president of the Pew Research Center, "Immigration is the engine that makes and remakes America. It is also a riveting personal and societal drama, one that unfolds in a complex interplay of social, economic, religious, political and cultural transformations—among the immigrants and their descendants, and within the nation as a whole."[25]

Immigration and Cultural Diversity

One of the most profound transformations attending immigration is cultural diversity. This diversity is perhaps nowhere more evident than in the languages spoken in a country. Even in a city like Minneapolis, Minnesota, with a population of less than four hundred thousand, more than eighty different languages and dialects are spoken at home by children in the public schools. While English is the home language for 69 percent of students and Spanish for another 16 percent, 6 percent of children speak Somali, 5 percent speak Hmong, and still other students speak German, Oromo (from Ethiopia), Tagalog (from the Philippines), Ojibeway (a North American First People language), and more than 72 other languages and dialects.[26]

Immigrant children's academic success is related to the ability to navigate educational systems, either in their language of origin or through language programs that develop skills in the host country's language. Beyond primary and secondary education, fluency in the spoken language of the host country is one of the gateways to socioeconomic attainment and social participation, including higher education, employment, and income, as well as access to important services. In Australia, perhaps the most linguistically diverse nation in the world, only 55.8 percent of those not proficient in English can drive, compared to 86.1 percent of those proficient in English.[27] Some receiving nations such as Canada endorse and support the preservation of foreign languages and enhance their status and continued use through legal provisions such as the Canadian Multiculturalism Act and the Official Languages Act.[28] In nations where English is the dominant language, immigrant languages tend to disappear by the second[29] or at least by the third generation[30] in favor of English. At least in Canada, groups such as those that speak Spanish, Chinese, or Punjabi are more likely to maintain their languages than immigrants in other countries.[31]

Financial and labor market issues reveal another "riveting personal and social drama" revolving around migration. For example, remittances (monies earned or acquired by nonnationals that are transferred back to their country of origin[32]) are a significant force in global economics, while also serving to maintain connections between emigrants and those left behind. The World Bank estimates that, across the world in 2010, migrants sent US$440 billion back to their home countries. The actual amount of remittances, including unrecorded flows through both formal and informal channels, is estimated to be significantly higher. Of those remittances, US$325 million flowed back to developing countries. Not surprisingly, rich countries are the primary source of remittances. With US$48.3 billion recorded in 2009, the United States is by far the largest source of remittances, followed by Saudi Arabia, Switzerland, and Russia.[33]

In the economies of developed societies like the United States, immigrants represent a major component of collective human capital. The US Bureau of Labor Statistics estimates that, in 2011, foreign-born workers comprised 15.9 percent of the civilian labor force. Foreign-born workers are more likely than native-born workers to be employed in service occupations (24.6 versus 16.4 percent), especially in food preparation and serving and in cleaning and maintenance. Foreign-born workers are also more likely to be employed in production, transportation, and material-moving occupations (15.8 versus 11 percent); and in natural resources, construction, and maintenance occupations (13.5 versus 8.5 percent).[34] However, a recent report from the Fiscal Policy Institute revealed that, although they compose 13 percent of the population and 16 percent of the labor force, at 18 percent, immigrants are over represented among small business owners in the United States.[35]

Receptivity to immigrants often reflects economic climate. Societies like Australia, Ireland, Spain, and the United Kingdom, which had welcomed immigrants in the economic boom years of the early twenty-first century, experienced a sort of "buyer's remorse" when faced with the Great Recession of 2008. In Spain, where the foreign-born population rose from 8 percent in 2006 to 12 percent in 2007, the construction industry came to a standstill and the economy ground to a halt in 2008, unemployment hit 11.3 percent overall and 17.5 percent among foreign-born workers.[36] At the same time, research sponsored by the Partnership for a New American Economy, a bipartisan group of US mayors and business leaders, revealed that more than 40 percent of the 2010 *Fortune* 500 companies were founded by immigrants or their children.[37] Furthermore, immigrants to the United States are involved in three out of four patents held at the nation's top research universities.

Yet even such innovators, many of whom have trained at American universities in science, technology, engineering, and math (the "STEM" fields considered to be drivers of job growth), may seem to face insurmountable hurdles with remaining in the United States.[38] While the Pew Research Center reported a "modest decline" in anti-immigrant sentiment among Americans surveyed in 2012, 46 percent agree with the statement, "The growing number of newcomers from other countries threatens traditional American customs and values," down from 51 percent in 2009. Still, 69 percent of those surveyed in 2012 agreed with the statement, "We should restrict and control people coming to live in our country more than we do now," down from 73 percent in 2009.[39] A collection of original research published in a recent issue of the *Annals of the American Academy of Political and Social Science* offers compelling evidence that immigration and the ensuing cultural diversity has not produced "conflicts of culture" in American society, nor has immigration increased violence or social discord. In fact, over the last two decades, crime is down and cities and poor neighborhoods, as well as small towns and rural areas, have grown in population and become more robust economically.[40]

Arguments regarding what Julia Preston of *The New York Times* calls "the fierce debate over immigration policy" are fodder for presidential campaigns and state and national legislation. Such was the case of Arizona SB 1070, a law that some said would effectively curb illegal immigration, yet others said would separate families and drive illegal immigrants further underground.[41] In June 2012, the US Supreme Court rendered a split decision on SB 1070. The Court upheld the law's "show me your papers" provision, which requires law enforcement officials to determine the immigration status of anyone they stop or arrest if they have reason to suspect the individual may be in the United States illegally. The Court overturned parts of the legislation that imposed criminal penalties associated with illegal immigrants seeking employment.[42]

Clearly then, one of the most provocative issues in contemporary government in developed nations is the challenge of buffering national borders. While seeking "a global approach to migration,"[43] governments like the EU wrestle mightily with "irregular migration" (while difficult to measure accurately, estimated to be five hundred and seventy thousand across the EU in 2009), especially the detection and prosecution of criminals involved in human trafficking (both prostitution and forced labor). "Greater mobility brings with it opportunities and challenges. A balanced, comprehensive and common migration policy will help the EU to seize these opportunities while tackling the challenges head-on. This policy—currently under development—is built upon solidarity and responsibility."[44] Current EU efforts are working to simplify and standardize migration procedures for diverse categories of migrations: highly qualified workers, students, and researchers; long-term residents and families desiring reunification; seasonal workers and intracorporate transferees.

The EU is certainly not alone. After underlying contested national borders is dispute over broader cultural issues, including cultural responses to immigrants. Are they newcomers to be welcomed, or strangers to be feared? These are the themes the contributors to *The Other People* address in the following chapters.

Plan of the Book

As a measure of the significance of migration studies within academia, by the late twentieth century, immigration had achieved status as a special topic across a wide range of disciplines, from the humanities to the social sciences. Since then, the number of courses devoted to migration studies has exploded. Virtually every four-year liberal arts college as well as all large universities offer one and sometimes more courses that address immigration and the migration experience. Some offer entire majors and minors. Likewise, as they increasingly must consider migration and migrants in their respective fields of endeavor, professionals involved in education, health care, justice and peace, law, social welfare, and other fields have taken a keen interest in migration.

The Other People provides a testimony that migration's challenges can best be understood by holding up a variety of disciplinary mirrors to issues faced by people making global exits and entrances. Taken together, these chapters affirm that migration offers opportunities for examining both terrible risk and impressive resilience, including the common good of migrants themselves as well as the communities in which they reside. The authors also aim to provoke scholars and citizens to think more broadly about contemporary human rights and social justice and how to engage others around those issues.

The Other People grew out of an Oxford Roundtable at Lincoln College in the spring of 2011. The contributors to this volume include five participants in that conference. They are joined by other scholars from across social science and professional disciplines. Together, they serve anthropology, criminology and criminal justice, economics, family social science, legal studies, library science, nursing, political science, social welfare, sociology, and women's studies. Their university affiliations and degrees include Australian, Canadian, English institutions, as well as universities from coast to coast in the United States. Throughout, the chapters include original research by the authors. Many of us have lived professional and personal lived experience across borders.

The chapters in *The Other People* explore new questions in migration and approach some familiar issues from original angles. Beyond a keen interest in the scholarship of global migration, what unites the authors of the chapters that follow is the ardent desire that scholarship contributes to the common global good. One of the first arenas where that process can begin is in places where we engage one another, teaching and learning. In the chapter that follows this Introduction, anthropologist Øystein LaBianca and political scientist Marcella Myers, both of Andrews University in Berrian Spring, Michigan (who wrote their chapter while on site in Petra, Jordan, studying on a Fulbright grant in Germany, and teaching in Kenya), reflect, in Chapter 2, on "Teaching and Learning about 'The Other' in Immigration."

In Part II, "Everyday/Everynight Immigrant Lives," scholars from women's studies, criminology, sociology, family studies, sociology, and political science elucidate important ways in which immigrants are situated in twenty-first-century societies. The six chapters in this section consider issues related to the feminization of migration, human trafficking, migration as a family-focused experience with effects on women and their children and parent/child relationships, identity and conflict, and distributive effects in the welfare state.

The Feminization of Migration

The first two chapters in Part II recognize that, while emigration has historically been a young man's game, international migration is increasingly done by women. Today, women represent a growing proportion (49 percent) of migrants worldwide, so we are quite correct in speaking of the increasing feminization of international migration.[45] The reasons for migration, use of varying migration channels, and distinct migration experiences all differ from women to men. Some researchers are beginning to explore how gender shifts in transnational migration patterns can change family structures and dynamics, including triggering renegotiations in the household division of labor in traditionally patriarchal societies.[46]

The IOM recommends that gender issues be considered when formulating migration policy around family reunification, labor migration, resettlement, asylum,[47] as well as the reproductive and other health needs of migrant women, human trafficking, and other forms of violence against women and girls. Women's studies scholar Patti Duncan of Oregon State University explores this theme in Chapter 3, "Gendered Migrations: Transnational Feminist Perspectives."

Perhaps nothing illustrates how profoundly gender intersects with migration than one of the great scourges of modern society: human trafficking. Defined as "recruiting, transporting, transferring, harboring, or receiving a person through use of force, coercion, or other means for the purpose of exploiting them," human trafficking qualifies as a crime against humanity. Every country in the world is affected by human trafficking, if not as a country of origin, then as a transit or destination for victims. Human trafficking occurs not only cross-border but also within a country and for a range of exploitative purposes, sexual and otherwise. Trafficking victimizes not only women but also men and children, and it may take place with or without the involvement of organized crime groups.[48] The underground nature of the crime, as well as the misidentification of situations involving trafficking, mitigates against reliable estimates of human trafficking. However, the United Nations conservatively estimates the number of victims of human trafficking at 2.5 million at any given time and the profits for criminals at tens of billions of dollars per year.[49]

While human trafficking includes not only the sexual exploitation and the prostitution of others but also forced labor, slavery or similar practices, and the removal of organs, the United Nations Office of Drugs and Crime has identified 79 percent of human trafficking as involving sexual exploitation. Victims of trafficking can be of any gender; both victims and criminals of sexual trafficking are disproportionately women. In Chapter 4, "Human Trafficking, Migration, and Gender: An Interdisciplinary Approach," Jennifer Blank, a criminologist trained at Middlesex University in London, takes an integrated, interdisciplinary approach to those subjects, drawing on her original research in which she interviewed men involved with the business end of sex trafficking.

Migration as a Family-Related Process

Some of the classic work on immigration (e.g., Thomas and Znaniecki's masterwork *The Polish Peasant in Europe and America*) addressed family issues. Joining the feminization of migration is a second revolution in migration studies: greater recognition of the extent to which migration is a family-related process.[50] Recalling the earlier discussion of language, the most important factor in origin-language transmission is the speaking of indigenous languages in the home.[51] Thus a greater prevalence of immigrant families in countries like Canada in the last half of the twentieth century contributes to the retention of immigrant languages in those communities, at least into a second generation.[52]

The Other People illustrates the family processes of migration in two contrasting chapters. In Chapter 5, Joanna Dreby (sociologist at the University of Albany–SUNY and award-winning author of *Divided by Borders: Mexican Migrants and Their Children*[53]) offers findings from her research on transnational parents and their children. She poignantly illustrates some of the everyday/everynight effects of migration on families in "The Ripple Effects of Deportation Policies on Mexican American Women and Their Children."

In Chapter 6, Zha Blong Xiong, Veronica Deenanath, and Dung Mao, family social scientists at the University of Minnesota, describe "Parent-Child Relationships in Hmong Immigrant Families in the United States." They argue that Hmong immigrant families face significant acculturative stress and experience drastic changes in parent-child relationships due to previous agrarian lifestyle, immigration history, and lack of exposure to the Western culture prior to their settlement in America.

Identity and Conflict in the Immigrant Experience

Writing in the twentieth century, Robert Ezra Park wrote of cities wrestling with exclusion and inclusion. Park and his colleagues at the Chicago School examined racially, ethnically diverse cities in the United States, especially those like his own Chicago, facing what must have seemed like an onslaught of immigrants from Eastern and Southern Europe, Central and South America, as well as Asia and Africa.[54] In the last two chapters of Part II, two social scientists explore relations between majority and minority immigrant groups in the twenty-first century. In Chapter 7, "From Model Minority to Second-Gen Stereotypes: Korean-Canadian and Korean-American Accounts," Marianne Noh, a sociologist with an appointment in the School of Nursing at the University of Western Ontario, carries us beyond Park's conceptions of competition, conflict, accommodation, and assimilation in an archetypical twenty-first-century direction. She reveals how, within the persistence of racial and ethnic stereotypes, second generation immigrants appear to be appropriating the "model minority" into the "second gen."

Chapter 8, "Social Exclusion and the Welfare State: Effects of Distributive Conflicts on Immigrants in Germany," the final chapter in this section, reminds us of the continued pertinence of Park's first three concepts: competition, conflict, accommodation. Political scientist Marcella Myers describes the challenges faced in Germany, where 30 percent of the population agrees that foreigners come to Germany to exploit the welfare state, that there are too many foreigners in Germany, and that the number of foreigners is dangerous.

Immigration, "the Other," and Social Justice

How then are societies to respond to xenophobia and challenges to justice embedded in migration? On the one hand, hospitality toward "the stranger" and especially the immigrant is deeply embedded in many cultural traditions, including the three Abrahamic faiths, Judaism, Christianity, and Islam. The Torah and Old Testament[55] include both negative and positive commandments regarding the stranger: "You shall not wrong or oppress a resident alien, for you were aliens in the land of Egypt" (Exodus 22:21), and "You shall also love the stranger, for you were strangers in the land of Egypt" (Deuteronomy 10:19). In the New Testament, Jesus instructs his disciples: "For I was hungry and you gave me food, I was thirsty and you gave me something to drink, I was a stranger and you welcomed me" (Matthew 25:35). Likewise, the Qur'an compels Muslims to extend charity toward the hungry, poor, and those in need.[56] Two of the five pillars of faith for Muslims, *sawn* (fasting) and *zakat* (giving alms), are inextricably linked to solidarity with the disadvantaged. *Sawn* and *zakat* are intended to contribute to the "just circulation and distribution of wealth in society" and to "establishing social conditions for basic human dignity described in the Qur'an."

Many societies wrestle with internal cultural contradictions implied by their refusal to admit or decisions to deport people fleeing oppression and hardship in home countries. For example, Israel, with its patrimony as a nation formed by refugees but now a destination for those fleeing across the Sinai, struggles mightily as a "crackdown on migrants tugs at [the] soul of Israel."[57] Likewise, US president Barack Obama's executive action issued in 2012 to permit undocumented immigrants who came to the United States before age 16 to remain in the United States was met with unbridled joy by some, but called an election-year stunt that exceeded presidential authority by others.[58] Other societies with racist, xenophobic legacies may be becoming more willing to embrace citizens with immigrant backgrounds. In a year in which 59 racial incidents during the Italian soccer championship resulted in fines of more than €400,000 (over half a million USD), Italians have embraced soccer hero Mario Balotelli, who was born in Palermo to Ghanaian parents before being adopted by an Italian family.[59]

Immigration is a primary factor in increasing ethnic diversity in most developed countries and, at first glance, "the other" is rooted in minority group status, especially around ethnicity. In the long run, immigration and the ethnic diversity it creates promise cultural, economic, and other benefits for receiving countries. Writing of diversity and community in *E Pluribus Unum*, Robert Putnam argues that "ethnic diversity is, on the balance, an important social asset."[60] At least in the short term, immigration appears to auger lower social solidarity, which is reflected in lower trust and rarer action for the common good on the part of individuals and their communities. However, Putnam, who has invested more than three decades probing civil society, argues that the crucial commission of twenty-first-century societies facing increasing diversity is inclusion, "to create a new, broader sense of 'we.'"[61]

Few scholars would discount the challenges diversity poses for society. Speaking from a paper titled "Entering the Realm of 'the Other,'" Juan Moreno offered, "The changing demographic characteristics of our society as well as the increasingly global nature of all enterprises are rapidly propelling us into ever more frequent close encounters of the cultural kind with persons quite dissimilar from ourselves. We are largely unprepared to adequately cope with this quiet but significant revolution taking place in our society and our world."[62] The revolution for which the receiving countries are so unprepared is embodied in the escalating volume and complexity of contact, competition, conflict, accommodation, and assimilation wrought by international migration. Hence the last portion of *The Other People* turns to the matter of human rights and social justice for these "others" around global migration.

The four chapters in Part III, "Toward Justice," acknowledge these challenges. In Chapter 9, "Somewhere over the [Rainbow] Nation: Zinbabweans in South Africa," Susan Smith-Cunnien (professor of sociology and criminal justice at the University of St. Thomas in St. Paul, Minnesota) describes the mixed success of efforts to bring Zimbabweans into South African society. Smith-Cunnien, who brings several years of teaching and research in African countries to the table, describes the escalating migration of Zimbabweans to South Africa and the exclusionary environment they find upon arrival. While the government there formally decries the xenophobia behind the recent violence against immigrants, it is also accused of fomenting that xenophobia. Smith-Cunnien concludes that the more migrant-centered consideration of the issues that is promoted by several South African scholars may allow the nation to deal more justly with the neighbors who cross its borders.

Anthony Gray (professor of law at the University of Southern Queensland, Australia) considers, in Chapter 10, the extent to which "Comparative Religious Freedom: The Right to Wear Religious Dress" is accommodated in select jurisdictions around the world. He finds that courts have been surprisingly willing to accept intrusions on the right of an individual to express their religious views through dress, based on other interests claimed to be incompatible with religious freedoms. The specific current context of bans on dress often associated with Islam provides the focus for a conclusion that jurisdictions need to accommodate an individual's right to express their religious views more strongly than what currently appears to be the case.

In his powerful essay in Chapter 11, "We Are All Children of Babel," Bruce Einhorn (professor of law and director of the Asylum and Refugee Law Clinic at Pepperdine University School of Law in Malibu, California) considers how the fair adjudication of asylum claims in the United States is made more difficult by the cultural dissonance between the immigration judge or other government adjudicator and the foreign-born litigant. Using case law and his experience as a US Federal Immigration judge, Einhorn considers differences in language, understandings of time and chronology, and differences in ethnic background, all factors that combine to create a disconnect between legally trained American lawyers and judges, and non-Western asylum seekers.

Finally, in Chapter 12, Richard Morgan (assistant professor of social welfare at Stony Brook University in New York) applies his experience with social work, as well as his training in theology to reflect on human rights and immigration in "Life, Liberty, and the Pursuit of Happiness: Human Rights and Immigration." Drawing on the writings of philosopher Amartya Sen, Morgan unites themes from the previous chapters, maintaining that a case for the rights of migrants must be predicated on a vision of human rights as adhering to all people because of their common humanity and, therefore, as existing prior to membership in any particular social order.

In exploring new questions in migration and approaching familiar questions from original angles, *The Other People* seeks to answer Knoll's question: "And who is my neighbor?"[63] Collectively, the contributors apply interdisciplinary perspectives to narrate a deeper understanding of migrant lives and the challenges facing the societies that receive them, what the US Conference of Catholic Bishops called "Welcoming the Stranger among Us."[64] Scholars new to the field will find support for additional study in an appendix, "Resources for Research on Global Migration," coauthored by Janice Orf (reference librarian), and Mathew Vicknair (undergraduate student in sociology and economics), both from the University of St. Thomas in St. Paul, Minnesota.

The contributors to *The Other People* include award-winning photographer Wing Young Huie. His evocative photograph of a person from Sudan awaiting a bus to education classes on a snowy Minnesota morning graces the cover of this book. Heartened by that image and the chapters that follow, *The Other People* hopes to stimulate creative and compassionate thinking about that most complex global concern: migration.

Notes

1. International Organization for Migration, "Facts and Figures," accessed May 31, 2012, http://www.iom.int/jahia/Jahia/about-migration/facts-and-figures/lang/en.
2. Martin N. Marger, *Race and Ethnic Relations: American and Global Perspectives* 9th edition, Belmont, CA: Wadsworth, 2012).
3. United Nations, "International Migrant Stock: The 2008 Revision," Department of Economic and Social Affairs, 2009, accessed June 30, 2012, http://esa.un.org/migration/p2k0data.asp.
4. Marger, *Race and Ethnic Relations*.
5. Michael D. Higgins with Declan Kiberd, "Culture and Exile: The Global Irish," *New Hibernian Review (Iris Éireannach Nau)* 1 (1997): 11.
6. Marger, *Race and Ethnic Relations*.
7. Mary Pipher, *The Middle of Everywhere* (Orlando, FL: Harcourt, 2002), 21.

8. Thomas Dillon Redshaw, editor's notes to *The New Hibernian Review* (*Iris Éireannach Nau*) 1 (1997): 5.

9. "The Left and Bereft," Columbans Ireland, accessed June 4, 2012, http://columban .com/ssc/index.php?option=com_content&view=article&id=556:the-left-and-bereft&catid=96:viewpoints&Itemid=283.

10. Jan Willem Duyvendak, *The Politics of Home: Belonging and Nostalgia in Western Europe and the United States* (Hampshire, UK: Palgrave Macmillan, 2011).

11. Story recounted by Paola Ehrmantraut, an Argentinian, as told by her grandmother.

12. United Nations, "Overcoming Barriers: Human Mobility and Development," Human Development Report, 2009, accessed June 28, 2012, http://hdr.undp.org/ en/reports/global/hdr2009.

13. International Organization for Migration, "Key Migration Terms," accessed May 31, 2012 http://www.iom.int/jahia/Jahia/about-migration/key-migration-terms/ lang/en.

14. United Nations High Commissioner for Refugees (UNHCR), "A Year of Crisis: Global Trends 2011," accessed June 21, 2012, http://www.unhcr.org/4fd9e6266 .html.

15. UNHCR, "A Year of Crisis."

16. UNHCR, "Refugees: Flowing across Borders," accessed May 31, 2012, http:// www.unhcr.org/pages/49c3646c125.html.

17. Kristi Severance, "France's Expulsion of Roma Migrations: A Test Case for Europe," Migration Policy Institute, accessed June 7, 2012, http://www.migrationinformation .org/Feature/print.cfm?ID=803.

18. Peter McCorry, "The Lost Rosary; or, Our Irish Girls, Their Trials, Temptations, and Triumphs," in *The Exiles of Erin: Nineteenth-Century Irish-American Fiction*, ed. Charles Fanning (Notre Dame, IN: University of Notre Dame Press, 1984), 154.

19. "American Wakes," *Encyclopedia of Irish History and Culture,* (Detroit: Macmillan Reference, 2004), 15.

20. Matt Siegel, "130 Rescued after Shipwreck South of Indonesia," *New York Times*, June 27, 2012, accessed June 28, 2012, http://www.nytimes.com/2012/06/28/ world/asia/boat-with-asylum-seekers-sinks-near-indonesia-report-says.html?_r=1.

21. United Nations International Telecommunications Union, "The World in 2011: ICT Facts and Figures," accessed June 30, 2012, http://www.itu.int/ITU-D/ict/ facts/2011/index.html.

22. Damien Cave, "American Children, Now Struggling to Adjust to Life in Mexico," *New York Times*, June 18, 2012, accessed June 20, 2012, http://www.nytimes. com/2012/06/19/world/americas/american-born-children-struggle-to-adjust-in -mexico.html?_r=1&pagewanted=all.

23. Salman Rushdie, *Invisible Homelands: Essays and Criticism, 1981–1991* (New York: Penguin, 1992), 10.

24. Jeffrey Passel, D'Vera Cohn, and Ana Gonzales-Barrera, "Net Migration from Mexico Falls to Zero and Perhaps Less," Pew Hispanic Center, accessed June 5, 2012, http://www.pewhispanic.org/2012/04/23/net-migration-from-mexico-falls -to-zero-and-perhaps-less/?src=prc-headline.

25. Pew Research Center, *The Rise of Asian Americans*, accessed June 21, 2012, http://www.pewsocialtrends.org/files/2012/06/SDT-The-Rise-of-Asian-Americans-Full-Report.pdf.

26. Minneapolis Public Schools, "Over 80 Languages Spoken in the MPS School District," January 2009, accessed June 30, 2012, http://ell.mpls.k12.mn.us/uploads/Languages_Spoken_in_Mpls_Public_Schools_2.pdf.

27. National Disability Alliance, "People with non-English Speaking Background with Disability in Australia: What Does the Data Say?" accessed June 30, 2012, http://apo.org.au/research/people-non-english-speaking-background-disability-australia-what-does-data-say.

28. René Houle, "Recent Evolution of Immigrant-Language Transmission in Canada," *Statistics in Canada*, accessed June 8, 2012, http://www.statcan.gc.ca/pub/11-008-x/2011002/article/11453-eng.htm#a3.

29. Alejandro Portes and Richard Schauffler, "Language and the Second Generation: Bilingualism Yesterday and Today," *International Migration Review* 28 (1994): 640–61.

30. Richard Alba et al., "Only English by the Third Generation?: Loss and Preservation of the Mother Tongue among the Grandchildren of Contemporary Immigrants," *Demography* 39 (2002): 467–84; Rubén G. Rumbaut, Douglas S. Massey, and Frank D. Bean, "Linguistic Life Expectancies: Immigrant Language Retention in Southern California," *Population and Development Review* 32 (2006): 447–60.

31. Martin Turcotte, "Passing on the Ancestral Language," *Canadian Social Trends* 80, no. 4, Statistics Canada Catalogue no. 11-008. (2006): 23–30.

32. International Organization for Migration, "Key Migration Terms."

33. International Organization for Migration, "Fact and Figures."

34. United States Bureau of Labor Statistics, "Foreign-Born Workers' Labor Force Characteristics–2011," accessed June 5, 2012, http://www.bls.gov/news.release/pdf/forbrn.pdf.

35. Fiscal Policy Institute, "Report Breaks New Ground on Immigrant Businesses," accessed July 10, 2012, FPI-release-immigrant-small-business-owners-20120614 http://www.fiscalpolicy.org/FPI-release-immigrant-small-business-owners-20120614.pdf.

36. Migration Information Source, "'Buyer's Remorse' on Immigration Policy," accessed June 7, 2012, http://www.migrationinformation.org/Feature/display.cfm?id=710.

37. Partnership for a New American Economy, "The New American *Fortune* 500," accessed June 28, 2012, http://www.renewoureconomy.org/2011_06_15_1.

38. Partnership for a New American Economy, "Patent Pending: How Immigrants Are Reinventing the American Economy," accessed June 28, 2012, http://www.renewoureconomy.org/index.php?q=patent-pending.

39. Pew Research Center, "Partisan Polarization Surges in Bush, Obama Years," accessed June 5, 2012, http://www.people-press.org/2012/06/04/section-8-values-about-immigration-and-race.

40. John MacDonald and Robert Sampson, eds., "Immigration and America's Changing Social Fabric," *The Annals* 641(2012).

41. Julia Preston, "Mexican Immigration to U.S. Slowed Significantly, Report Says," *New York Times*, April 23, 2012, accessed June 5, 2012, http://www.nytimes.com/2012/04/24/us/mexican-immigration-to-united-states-slows.html?_r=1.

42. Adam Liptak, "Blocking Parts of Arizona Law, Justices Allow Its Centerpiece," *New York Times*, June 25, 2012, accessed June 28, 2012, http://www.nytimes.com/2012/06/26/us/supreme-court-rejects-part-of-arizona-immigration-law.html?pagewanted=all.

43. European Commission Home Affairs, "A New Impetus to the EU External Migration Policy: The Global Approach to Migration and Mobility," accessed June 30, 2012, http://ec.europa.eu/home-affairs/news/intro/news_201111_en.htm#20111118a.

44. European Commission Home Affairs, "Toward a Common European Union Migration Policy," accessed June 6, 2012, http://ec.europa.eu/home-affairs/policies/immigration/immigration_intro_en.htm.

45. United Nations, "International Migrant Stock."

46. Lan Anh Hoang and Brenda S. A. Yeoh, "Breadwinning Wives and 'Left-Behind' Husbands: Men and Masculinities in the Vietnamese Transnational Family," *Gender & Society* 25 (2011): 717–39.

47. International Organization for Migration, "Migration and Gender," accessed June 30, 2012, http://www.iom.int/jahia/Jahia/gender-migration.

48. United Nations Office on Drugs and Crime, "Human Trafficking," accessed June 30, 2012, http://www.unodc.org/unodc/en/human-trafficking/what-is-human-trafficking.html?ref=menuside.

49. United Nations Office on Drugs and Crime, "Human Trafficking."

50. International Organization for Migration, "Facts and Figures."

51. Erika Hoff, "How Social Contexts Support and Shape Language Development," *Developmental Review*, 26 (2006):55–88.

52. Houle, "Recent Evolution of Immigrant-Language."

53. Joanna Dreby, *Divided by Borders: Mexican Migrants and Their Children*, University of California Press, 2010.

54. Robert E. Park, Ernest W. Burgess, and Robert D. McKenzie, *The City* (Chicago: University of Chicago Press, 1967); Robert E. Park and Herbert A. Miller, *Old World Traits Transplanted* (New York: Harper Brothers, 1921).

55. Biblical passages are taken from the New Revised Standard (Anglicized Edition). Oremus, "Bible Browser," 2011, accessed June 6, 2012, http://bible.oremus.org.

56. See for example, *The Cow*, Qur'an 2:215.

57. Isabel Kershner, "Crackdown on Migrants Tugs at Soul of Israelis," *New York Times*, June 18, 2012, accessed June 18, 2012, http://www.nytimes.com/2012/06/18/world/middleeast/crackdown-on-african-immigrants-tugs-at-israels-soul.html?pagewanted=all.

58. Julia Preston and John H. Cushman Jr., "Obama to Permit Young Migrants to Remain in the U.S.," *New York Times*, June 15, 2012, accessed June 15, 2012, http://www.nytimes.com/2012/06/16/us/us-to-stop-deporting-some-illegal-immigrants.html?pagewanted=all.

59. Elisabetta Povoledo, "A New Hero Challenges Notions of Italianness," *New York Times*, June 30, 2012, accessed June 30, 2012, http://www.nytimes.com/2012/06/30/sports/soccer/30iht-balotelli30.html?_r=1&emc=tnt&tntemail1=y&pagewanted=print).

60. Robert D. Putnam, "*E Pluribus Unum:* Diversity and Community in the Twenty-First Century, The 2006 Johan Skytte Prize Lecture," *Scandinavian Political Studies* 30 (2007): 138.
61. Putnam, "*E Pluribus Unum,*" 139.
62. Juan C. Moreno, "Entering into the Realm of 'the Other": A Few Suggestions for Crossing Boundaries of Human Difference" (paper presented at the annual meeting of the *Minnesota Council of Family Relations,* St. Paul, Minnesota, December, 2002, 1).
63. Benjamin R. Knoll, "'And Who Is My Neighbor?' Religion and Immigration Policy Attitudes," *Journal for the Scientific Study of Religion* 48(2009):313–31.
64. United States Conference of Catholic Bishops, "Welcoming the Stranger among Us: Unity in Diversity," 2000, accessed June 28, 2012, http://nccbuscc.org/mrs/welcome.shtml.

Bibliography

Alba, Richard, John Logan, Amy Lutz, and Brian Stults. "Only English by the Third Generation? Loss and Preservation of the Mother Tongue among the Grandchildren of Contemporary Immigrants." *Demography* 39 (2002): 467–84.

"American Wakes." *Encyclopedia of Irish History and Culture,* I. Detroit: Macmillan Reference, 2004.

Cave, Damien. "American Children, Now Struggling to Adjust to Life in Mexico." *New York Times,* June 18, 2012. Accessed June 18, 2012, http://www.nytimes.com/2012/06/19/world/americas/american-born-children-struggle-to-adjust-in-mexico.html?_r=1&pagewanted=all.

Duyvendak, Jan Willem. *The Politics of Home: Belonging and Nostalgia in Western Europe and the United States.* Hampshire, UK: Palgrave Macmillan, 2011.

European Commission Home Affairs. "A New Impetus to the EU External Migration Policy: The Global Approach to Migration and Mobility." Accessed June 30, 2012, http://ec.europa.eu/home-affairs/news/intro/news_201111_en.htm#20111118a.

———. "Toward a Common European Union Migration Policy." Accessed June 30, 2012, http://ec.europa.eu/home-affairs/policies/immigration/immigration_intro_en.htm.

Fiscal Policy Institute. "Report Breaks New Ground on Immigrant Businesses." Accessed July 10, 2012, http://www.fiscalpolicy.org/FPI-release-immigrant-small-business-owners-20120614.pdf.

"The Gospel vs. HR 4437." *New York Times,* March 3, 2006. Accessed April 4, 2012, http://www.nytimes.com/2006/03/03/opinion/03fri1.html?_r=1.

Higgins, Michael D., with Declan Kiberd. "Culture and Exile: The Global Irish." *New Hibernian Review (Iris Éireannach Nau)* 1 (1997): 9–22.

Hoang, Lan Anh, and Brenda S. A. Yeoh. "Breadwinning Wives and 'Left-Behind' Husbands: Men and Masculinities in the Vietnamese Transnational Family." *Gender & Society* 25 (2011): 717–39.

Hoff, Erika. "How Social Contexts Support and Shape Language Development." *Developmental Review,* 26 (2006): 55–88.

Houle, René. "Recent Evolution of Immigrant-Language Transmission in Canada." *Statistics in Canada.* Accessed June 8, 2012, http://www.statcan.gc.ca/pub/11-008-x/2011002/article/11453-eng.htm#a3.

International Organization for Migration. "Facts and Figures." Accessed June 30, 2012, http://www.iom.int/jahia/Jahia/about-migration/facts-and-figures/lang/en.

———. "Key Migration Terms." Accessed June 30, 2012, http://www.iom.int/jahia/Jahia/about-migration/key-migration-terms/lang/en.

———. "Migration and Gender." Accessed June 30, 2012, http://www.iom.int/jahia/Jahia/gender-migration.

Jones, Robert P. *Progressive & Religious.* Lanham, MD: Rowman & Littlefield, 2008.

Kershner, Isabel. "Crackdown on Migrants Tugs at Soul of Israelis." *New York Times*, June 18, 2012. Accessed June 18, 2012, http://www.nytimes.com/2012/06/18/world/middleeast/crackdown-on-african-immigrants-tugs-at-israels-soul.html?pagewanted=all.

Knoll, Benjamin R. "'And Who Is My Neighbor?' Religion and Immigration Policy Attitudes." *Journal for the Scientific Study of Religion* 48 (2009): 313–31.

"The Left and Bereft." Columbans Ireland. Accessed June 4, 2012, http://columban.com/ssc/index.php?option=com_content&view=article&id=556:the-left-and-bereft&catid=96:viewpoints&Itemid=283.

Liptak, Adam. "Blocking Parts of Arizona Law, Justices Allow Its Centerpiece." *New York Times*, June 25, 2012. Accessed June 28, 2012, http://www.nytimes.com/2012/06/26/us/supreme-court-rejects-part-of-arizona-immigration-law.html?pagewanted=all.

MacDonald, John, and Robert Sampson, eds. "Immigration and America's Changing Social Fabric." *The Annals* 641 (2012).

Marger, Martin N. *Race and Ethnic Relations: American and Global Perspectives.* 9/e, Belmont, CA: Wadsworth, 2012.

McCorry, Peter. "The Lost Rosary; or, Our Irish Girls, Their Trials, Temptations, and Triumphs." In *The Exiles of Erin: Nineteenth-Century Irish-American Fiction*, edited by. Charles Fanning, 153–59. Notre Dame, IN: University of Notre Dame Press, 1984.

Migration Information Source. "'Buyer's Remorse' on Immigration Policy." Accessed June 7, 2012, http://www.migrationinformation.org/Feature/display.cfm?id=710.

Minneapolis Public Schools. "Over 80 Languages Spoken in the MPS School District." Accessed June 30, 2012, http://ell.mpls.k12.mn.us/uploads/Languages_Spoken_in_Mpls_Public_Schools_2.pdf.

Moreno, Juan C. "Entering into the Realm of 'the Other': A Few Suggestions for Crossing Boundaries of Human Difference." Paper presented at the annual meeting of the Minnesota Council of Family Relations, St. Paul, Minnesota, December 2002.

National Disability Alliance. "People with Non-English Speaking Background with Disability in Australia: What Does the Data Say?" Accessed June 30, 2012, http://apo.org.au/research/people-non-english-speaking-background-disability-australia-what-does-data-say.

Oremus. "Bible Browser." 2011. Accessed June 6, 2012, http://bible.oremus.org.

Park, Robert E., Ernest W. Burgess, and Robert D. McKenzie. *The City*. Chicago: University of Chicago Press, 1967.

Park, Robert E., and Herbert A. Miller. *Old World Traits Transplanted*. New York: Harper Brothers, 1921.

Partnership for a New American Economy. "The New American *Fortune* 500." June 28, 2012. http://www.renewoureconomy.org/2011_06_15_1.

———. "Patent Pending: How Immigrants Are Reinventing the American Economy." Accessed June 28, 2012, http://www.renewoureconomy.org/index.php?q=patent-pending.

Passel, Jeffrey, D'Vera Cohn, and Ana Gonzales-Barrera. "Net Migration from Mexico Falls to Zero and Perhaps Less." Pew Hispanic Center. Accessed June 5, 2012, http://www.pewhispanic.org/2012/04/23/net-migration-from-mexico-falls-to-zero-and-perhaps-less/?src=prc-headline.

Pew Research Center. "Partisan Polarization Surges in Bush, Obama Years." Accessed June 5, 2012, http://www.people-press.org/2012/06/04/section-8-values-about-immigration-and-race.

———. *The Rise of Asian Americans.* Accessed June 21, 2012, http://www.pewsocialtrends.org/files/2012/06/SDT-The-Rise-of-Asian-Americans-Full-Report.pdf.

Pipher, Mary. *The Middle of Everywhere.* Orlando, FL: Harcourt, 2002.

Portes, Alejandro, and Richard Schauffler. "Language and the Second Generation: Bilingualism Yesterday and Today." *International Migration Review* 28 (1994): 640–61.

Povoledo, Elisabetta. "A New Hero Challenges Notions of Italianness." *New York Times*, June 30, 2012. Accessed June 30, 2012, http://www.nytimes.com/2012/06/30/sports/soccer/30iht-balotelli30.html?_r=1&emc=tnt&tntemail1=y&pagewanted=print.

Preston, Julia. "Mexican Immigration to U.S. Slowed Significantly, Report Says." *New York Times*, April 23, 2012. Accessed June 5, 2012, http://www.nytimes.com/2012/04/24/us/mexican-immigration-to-united-states-slows.html?_r=1.

Preston, Julia, and John H. Cushman Jr. "Obama to Permit Young Migrants to Remain in the U.S." *New York Times*, June 15, 2012. Accessed June 15, 2012, http://www.nytimes.com/2012/06/16/us/us-to-stop-deporting-some-illegal-immigrants.html?pagewanted=all.

Putnam, Robert D. "*E Pluribus Unum:* Diversity and Community in the Twenty-First Century. The 2006 Johan Skytte Prize Lecture." *Scandinavian Political Studies* 30 (2007): 137–74.

Redshaw, Thomas Dillon. Editor's notes to *The New Hibernian Review* (*Iris Éireannach Nau*) 1 (1997): 5.

Rumbaut, Rubén G, Douglas S. Massey, and Frank D. Bean. "Linguistic Life Expectancies: Immigrant Language Retention in Southern California." *Population and Development Review* 32 (2006): 447–60.

"Rushdie Knighted in Honours List." *BBC News*, June 15, 2007. Accessed June 7, 2012, http://news.bbc.co.uk/2/hi/uk_news/6756149.stm.

Rushdie, Salman. *Invisible Homelands: Essays and Criticism, 1981–1991.* New York: Penguin, 1992.

Severance, Kristi. "France's Expulsion of Roma Migrations: A Test Case for Europe." Migration Policy Institute. Accessed June 7, 2012, http://www.migrationinformation.org/Feature/print.cfm?ID=803.

Siegel, Matt. "130 Rescued after Shipwreck South of Indonesia." *New York Times*, June 27, 2012. Accessed June 28, 2012, http://www.nytimes.com/2012/06/28/world/asia/boat-with-asylum-seekers-sinks-near-indonesia-report-says.html?_r=1.

Turcotte, Martin. "Passing on the Ancestral Language." *Canadian Social Trends* 80, no. 4, Statistics Canada Catalogue no. 11-008 (2006): 23–30.

United Nations. "International Migrant Stock: The 2008 Revision." Department of Economic and Social Affairs, 2009. Accessed June 30, 2012, http://esa.un.org/migration.

———. "Overcoming Barriers: Human Mobility and Development." Human Development Report, 2009. Accessed June 30, 2012, http://hdr.undp.org/en/reports/global/hdr2009.

United Nations High Commissioner for Refugees (UNHCR). "Refugees: Flowing across Borders." Accessed May 31, 2012, http://www.unhcr.org/pages/49c3646c125.html.

———. "A Year of Crisis: Global Trends 2011." Accessed June 21, 2012, http://www.unhcr.org/4fd9e6266.html.

United Nations International Telecommunications Union. "The World in 2011: ICT Facts and Figures." Accessed June 30, 2012, http://www.itu.int/ITU-D/ict/facts/2011/index.html.

United Nations Office on Drugs and Crime. "Human Trafficking." Accessed June 30, 2012, http://www.unodc.org/unodc/en/human-trafficing/what-is-human-trafficking.html?ref=menuside.

United States Bureau of Labor Statistics. "Foreign-Born Workers' Labor Force Characteristics–2011." Accessed June 5, 2012, http://www.bls.gov/news.release/pdf/forbrn.pdf.

United States Conference of Catholic Bishops. "Welcoming the Stranger among Us: Unity in Diversity." Accessed April 4, 2012, http://www.usccb.org/issues-and-action/cultural-diversity/pastoral-care-of-migrants-refugees-and-travelers/resources/welcoming-the-stranger-among-us-unity-in-diversity.cfm#summary).

CHAPTER 2

Teaching and Learning about the Other in Immigration

Øystein S. LaBianca and Marcella Myers*

From the perspective of global history, migration has been a constant that in its inevitable wake has been accompanied by variously challenging encounters between peoples who are not the Same, where "the Same" refers to people who we view as being like us. In recent times such encounters have become more frequent, as Meg Wilkes Karraker points out in Chapter 1, the opening chapter to this volume: "If they were a country of their own, migrants would constitute the fifth most populous nation in the world." This increased rate of encounter among people who are not the Same has led to heightened awareness in the general population and among politicians of the demands for hospitality, generosity, and integration generated by an expanding population of "other people." This, in turn, has made teaching and learning about the Other—that is, those who are not like us—an urgent priority in many different settings, not the least colleges and universities. The present volume is another testimony to this reality—an academic response to a societal need.

While the connection between migration and curiosity or angst about the Other is easy to understand, we must not forget that in this age of global connectivity, the construction of the Other is not primarily something we do as individuals as a result of our personal encounters with immigrants. As important are the narratives about the Other propagated by traveler's accounts, the printed word, the fine arts, and most of all today, electronic media. Thus as

* Address correspondence to Øystein S. LaBianca, professor of anthropology, Andrews University, Berrien Springs, MI 49104-0030. Email: labianca@andrews.edu. We thank Jonathan Koch, our undergraduate research assistant, for his hard work and the Office of Scholarly Research at Andrews University for funding and support of undergraduate research.

we undertake to develop ways to teach and learn about the Other, we seek an approach that encompasses all these purveyors of curiosity and angst.

Course Design Considerations

An approach to teaching and learning about the Other that focuses on a single discipline does not do the topic justice. The Other has today become a core concern of a wide range of disciplines, including communication, history, literature, media studies, philosophy, political science, religion, sociology, and social work, to mention just a few examples. In our view an approach that incorporates multiple disciplinary perspectives is thus preferred over a single disciplinary one.

Another consideration when teaching and learning about the Other is that coming to know ourselves—our particular way of being human—is absolutely fundamental to understanding about other ways of being human. To understand how the Other sees us, we need to know something about the values and patterns of behavior that set us apart. In the case of the authors of this book and the courses we teach, we devote considerable time and effort to learning about who we are as Westerners and as North Americans.

Finally, in our view, to successfully teach about the Other, instructors should "fight in their own armor." Teachers should design the course in such a way that it capitalizes on their own personal experiences and academic background when deciding on readings and topics to include in the course. For example, LaBianca, who is an anthropological archaeologist, draws on his experience working in the ancient Near East when explaining about the role of civilizations in shaping understanding of the Same and the Other. His research in archaeology has inspired a definition of the concept of civilization that he shares with his students: "A civilization is a luminous constellation of radiant attitudes, beliefs, institutions, great and little traditions and works of art, artisanry and architecture that emanate from an epicenter such as Thebes, Nineveh, Persepolis, Athens, Rome, or Constantinople."[1] This definition provides a foundation for discussions throughout the semester not only of the Other but also of us.

Types of Others

In our case, the previous considerations inspired an approach to teaching and learning about the Other that looks at various types of Others. Among the various types of Others that we discuss are the oriental, exotic, utopian, rebel, demonized, and immigrant. First, we begin with an articulation of how the Other relates to the Same.

The Same and the Other

A leading figure in the contemporary discourse about the Other is the philosopher and holocaust survivor Immanuel Levinas. Levinas offers a radical ethical perspective that insists on an all-or-nothing approach to dealing with the Other as a means to overcome the tendency to want to make the Other become the Same.[2] When we encounter those not like us, our natural tendency is to try by whatever means to grasp them as if they were somehow the same as us. In so doing we end up not really getting to know the Other but instead dominating or controlling them. Such domination and control is dangerous as it may lead to contempt for the Other.[3] Levinas calls for an approach to the Other that is totally devoid of any effort to make the Other become the Same. He calls for an absolute acceptance of the Other, to the extent that when we embrace this call, we glimpse the Divine.[4] This is the transcendental aspect of Levinas's teaching—the idea that by accepting the Other as they are, we open ourselves up to experiencing the presence of the Divine.

Orientalism

Edward Said's seminal book *Orientalism* provides another key resource in teaching and learning about how we, in the West, have come to see the Oriental Other.[5] Said has had an enormous influence on nearly all disciplines concerned with the study of the Other. The importance of Said is found in his detailed analysis and documentation of the West's project of manufacturing an image of the East, or the Orient, which is more a reflection of Western hubris and fear than an accurate portrayal of the East. Any teaching around the topic of the Other would be incomplete without including a critical examination of Said and his work. Perhaps more than any other twentieth-century scholar, Said was a pioneer in researching ways in which two centuries of Western literature, social science, and media have managed to make the East into the Other.

One application of such an approach is embodied in Mark Twain's *Innocents Abroad*. That work details Twain's and his fellow travelers' encounters with and reactions to the Other. This classic in American literature is rich in detail and humor while providing a great illustration of orientalist attitudes and beliefs.[6] As students engage in this book, we ask them to look for examples of various "terms of engagement" with the Other on the part of Twain or his companions, including admiration, annoyance, demonization, dishonesty, ethnocentrism, exploitation, fear, loathing, humor, idealization, ignorance, impoliteness, kindness, mistreatment, misunderstanding, politeness, prejudice, stereotyping, and suspicion.

The Exotic Other

Clifford Geertz's *Interpretation of Cultures*[7] is an analysis of the social significance of the betting that accompanies illegal cockfights among Balinese men. Geertz's analysis shows that by their pattern of gambling, the men reify the prevailing social order in Balinese society. He also includes a discussion of how cock owners come to see themselves in their animals. The consequence is that the owner of a winning cock experiences a great ego boost, whereas the owners of losing cocks experiences deep shame and humiliation. Not only does the article serve as an illustration of the exotic Other, but it also provides an exemplar of ethnographic fieldwork—starting with the process of entering the community and gaining trust. Geertz illustrates how, by focusing on a particular public event, insights can be gained into the workings of other cultures.

The Utopian Other

The utopian Other links in important ways to Levinas's call for a radical ethic of accepting the Other. Such is the case when considering the various Anabaptist traditions as examples of the utopian Other. These have in common with Levinas a vision of humanity in which the natural tendency of individuals to privilege their own self-interest must bend to the greater good of accepting the Other and, in the case of the utopian Anabaptists, prioritizing the good of the group over that of self. As in Said's analysis, such a conceptualization sees denial of the self as a condition for experiencing the transcendental Other—the Divine.

We recommend selections from Robert Kraybill's *The Riddle of Amish Culture*.[8] Kraybill's work is an excellent exposition of the ideals that animate the Amish way of life and the reasons behind their day-to-day practices. Especially valuable regarding the Amish and other Anabaptist traditions are that these people live within our borders. In many ways, their utopian ways are a direct contradiction of the core values for which America stands: above all, the freedom and the responsibility of the individual to be the artist of his or her own lives.

The Rebel Other

A good example of "the rebel Other" is Bob Marley and the Rastafarian religion that inspired his message and lyrics.[9] What makes this such a good case study is that while most students are likely well acquainted with and many are great fans of reggae music, very few know much about Rastafarianism and its influence on Marley's career and songs. Rastafarians and Marley are rebelling against the inequities and consumerism that have accompanied the expansion of capitalism and the global rat race. Marley's music and lifestyle—dreadlocks and all—are present in nearly every major capital in the world, a powerful testimony to the power of reggae music as a vehicle for dissent against the established order around the world. The study of Rastafarianism provides a convenient segue to examination of global processes that link to the rise of identity and resistance movements, each with its particular otherness.

Islam and the Demonized Other

Of all the Others, few can match Islam when it comes to being feared, misunderstood, and misrepresented by the American public. In our view, the topic of Islam as the demonized Other must be included in any teaching dealing with the Other. We have found Mark Sedgwick's *Islam and Muslims* to be an excellent text in highlighting the many commonalities that Christianity and Islam share while also explaining the salient differences and how they are understood by members of each faith.[10] Sedgwick knows both traditions. In addition to being an Oxford-trained Middle East historian and a student of Sufi mysticism, he spent many years living among Muslims in Egypt while teaching at the American University of Cairo.

We also emphasize the many ways in which Islam provides believers with a strong sense of belonging, a purpose for living, and a template for how to be a good human being. In our experience most of the information about Islam and Muslims that we provide in lectures and assigned readings is new to our students. Learners come to better understand that the narratives by which Islam and Muslims are demonized are manufactured and sustained in the West. At the same time they acquire a deeper understanding of how Islam is deployed by extremists to legitimize and mobilize anti-Western rage among their cobelievers in the Middle East and beyond.

The Immigrant Other

Finally, we turn to the immigrant Other. A good resource for teaching and learning about the immigrant Other is the life story of Richard Rodrigues.[11] The son of Mexican immigrants in the United States, Rodrigues explores the emotional losses that accompany assimilation into a new culture. In order to succeed as an immigrant academic, mastery of English is crucial. With this mastery comes a *hunger of memory*—the awareness that communication with family in any language other than Spanish is somehow not the same. Rodrigues has become a controversial character in higher education circles. He takes a strong stance against immigrant children in the United States being taught in their native tongue in schools and the use of affirmative action to open doors for minorities to attain places in higher education institutions and work places. Rodrigues thus offers plenty of grist for discussion pertinent to the immigrant Other.

Beyond Teaching and Learning about the Other

The extent to which the current discourse about the Other is relevant to understanding international relations and politics is highlighted by Harvard political scientist Samuel Huntington's "clash of civilizations hypothesis."[12] First posited in 1992 in an article in *Foreign Affairs*, which was later expanded into a book-length volume, the clash of civilizations hypothesis argues that future conflicts around the globe will occur along civilizational fault lines rather than along national borders. In other words, cultural differences will play a larger role in future conflicts than squabbles between nations. Following September 11, 2001, Huntington's thesis went viral. For ten years before the assault on America, Huntington's thesis had identified the fault line between Islam and the West as one of the most conflict-prone fissures of the new world order. This thesis was cited by some in President George W. Bush's administration as justification for the war on terror and the invasion of Iraq. Huntington's argument is tantalizing due to its simplicity—initially providing a compelling explanation for many current conflicts in the world today.

According to Edward Said[13] and other critics, Huntington's hypothesis is vastly reductionist because of its simplistic understanding of the nature of civilizations. In Huntington's view, civilizations are static and uniform. In reality, the opposite is the case: civilizations are constantly changing, made up of multiple, often conflicting centers of elite and local power. Thus there is thus no such thing as a fixed civilizational identity because individuals within any given civilization today typically have multiple identities that they express in different ways, depending on their backgrounds and perceptions of which identity they wish to present. In Said's view, the clash of civilizations hypothesis is a sad return to the days of the Cold War. What he suggests is a new global consciousness—a global humanity perspective that recognizes our interdependence as members of the global village that is the modern world.

A new global consciousness means negotiating multiple identities. Multiple, sometimes competing identities pose a problem for politicians, governments, and those attempting to exercise power but not in the way the Huntington argued. Multiple identities put emphasis on the role of the state in the definition of the identity of citizens and feelings of solidarity and loyalty that are consolidated around a single political community.[14]

People identify themselves in many ways and adopt alternative identities, depending on the context in which individuals finds themselves. For governments identity is important due to the political cleavages that emerge based on religious, linguistic, ethnic, or cultural considerations.[15] Management of the ensuing political cleavages is potentially one of the most difficult challenges for government. The term cleavage indicates not merely political and social differences and diversity but divisions that are deep and lasting between clearly defined groups in society.[16] Yet in the end, governments must manage these cleavages to maintain long term stability.[17]

Because we teach in an American context, we return to the question of identity as Americans respective to others. What makes us "the Same"? This question is universal and raises again the question of how we identify ourselves and the Other. We use as a point of departure for this discussion Samuel Huntington, this time in his most recent publication *Who Are We?*[18] According to Huntington, what makes us uniquely Americans is that we are not, first of all, a nation of immigrants but a nation of settlers and, more precisely, a nation of settlers with an Anglo-Protestant cultural core. It is this core that gives us our "American creed," which includes among its central ideas "the essential dignity of the individual human being, of the fundamental equality of all men, and of certain inalienable rights to freedom, justice and a fair opportunity."[19] In the Declaration of Independence, Jefferson wrote of the equality of man, inalienable rights, and "life, liberty, and the pursuit of happiness." We revisit notions such as the idea of an American civil religion, the American dream, American exceptionalism, and American universalism. The stage is thus set for a lively discussion of what it really means to be part of the Same in America.

Teaching and learning about the Other is about how we construct our understanding of who we are as part of the Same and how we/our society manufacture notions of the Other, whom, of course, are the people who are not the Same.

Notes

1. Øystein LaBianca and Kristin Witzel, "Nomads, Empires and Civilizations: Great and Little Traditions and the Historical Landscape of the Southern Levant," in *On the Fringe of Society: Archaeological and Ethnoarchaeological Perspectives on Pastoral and Agricultural Societies*, ed. Benjamin A. Saidel and Evelyn J. van der Steen (Oxford: Archaeopress, 2007), 65.
2. Emanuel Levinas, *Alterity and Transcendence* (New York: Columbia University Press, 1999).
3. See Erich Fromm, *Escape from Freedom* (New York: Holt and Company, 1994).
4. Emanuel Levinas, *Alterity and Transcendence* (New York: Columbia University Press, 1999).
5. Edward W. Said, *Orientalism* (New York: Vintage Books, 1978).
6. Mark Twain, *The Innocents Abroad* (New York: Dover Publications, 2003).
7. Clifford Geertz, *Interpretation of Cultures* (New York: Basic Books, 1973).
8. Donald B. Kraybill, *The Riddle of Amish Culture* (Baltimore, MD: Johns Hopkins University, 2001).
9. Barry Chevannes, *Rastafari: Roots and Ideology* (Syracuse, NY: Syracuse University Press, 1994); Ennis B. Edmonds, *Rastafari: From Outcasts to Culture Bearers* (Oxford: Oxford University Press, 2003).

10. Mark Sedgwick, *Islam and Muslims* (Boston: Intercultural Press, 2006).
11. Richard Rodrigues, *Hunger of Memory* (New York: Bantam Books, 1982).
12. Samuel P. Huntington, *Clash of Civilizations* (New York: Touchstone Books, 1996).
13. Edward Said, "The Myth of the Clash of Civilizations" (lecture, University of Massachusetts Amhurst, 1996), accessed September 13, 2012, http://www.youtube.com/watch?v=boBzrqF4vmo.
14. Riva Kastoryano, *Negotiating Identities: States and Immigrants in France and Germany*, trans. Barbara Harshav (Princeton: Princeton University Press, 2002), 7.
15. Richard Gunther and Anthony Mughan, "Political Institutions and Cleavage Management," in *Do Institutions Matter? Government Capabilities in the United States and Abroad*, ed. R. Kent Weaver and Bert A. Rockman (Washington, DC: Brookings Institution, 1993), 272–301.
16. Arendt Lijphart, Ronald Rogowski, and R. Kent Weaver, "Separation of Powers and Cleavage Management," in *Do Institutions Matter? Government Capabilities in the United States and Abroad*, ed. R. Kent Weaver and Bert A. Rockman (Washington, DC: Brookings Institution, 1993), 302.
17. Gunther and Mughan, "Political Institutions and Cleavage Management," 272.
18. Samuel P. Huntington, *Who Are We?* (New York: Simon and Schuster, 2004).
19. Gunnar Myrdal, *An American Dilemma* (Piscataway, NJ: Transaction Publishers, 1944).

Bibliography

Chevannes, Barry. *Rastafari: Roots and Ideology.* Syracuse, NY: Syracuse University Press, 1994.

Edmonds, Ennis B. *Rastafari: From Outcasts to Culture Bearers.* Oxford: Oxford University Press, 2003.

Fromm, Erich. *Escape from Freedom.* New York: Holt and Company, 1994.

Geertz, Clifford. *Interpretation of Cultures.* New York: Basic Books, 1973.

Gunther, Richard, and Anthony Mughan. "Political Institutions and Cleavage Management." In *Do Institutions Matter? Government Capabilities in the United States and Abroad*, edited by R. Kent Weaver and Bert A. Rockman, 272–301. Washington, DC: Brookings Institution, 1993.

Huntington, Samuel P. *Clash of Civilizations.* New York: Touchstone Books, 1996.

———. *Who Are We?* New York: Simon and Schuster, 2004.

Kastoryano, Riva. *Negotiating Identities: States and Immigrants in France and Germany.* Translated by Barbara Harshav. Princeton: Princeton University Press, 2002.

Kraybill, Donald B. *The Riddle of Amish Culture.* Baltimore, MD: Johns Hopkins University Press, 2001.

LaBianca, Øystein, and Kristin Witzel. "Nomads, Empires and Civilizations: Great and Little Traditions and the Historical Landscape of the Southern Levant." In *On the Fringe of Society: Archaeological and Ethnoarchaeological Perspectives on Pastoral and Agricultural Societies*, edited by Benjamin A. Saidel and Evelyn J. van der Steen, 63–74. Oxford: Archaeopress, 2007.

Levinas, Emanuel. *Alterity and Transcendence.* New York: Columbia University Press, 1999.

Lijphart, Arendt, Ronald Rogowski, and R. Kent Weaver. "Separation of Powers and Cleavage Management." In *Do Institutions Matter? Government Capabilities in the United States and Abroad,* edited by R. Kent Weaver and Bert A. Rockman, 272–301. Washington, DC: Brookings Institution, 1993.

Myrdal, Gunnar. *An American Dilemma.* Piscataway, NJ: Transaction Publishers, 1944.

Rodrigues, Richard. *Hunger of Memory.* New York: Bantam Books, 1982.

Said, Edward. "The Myth of the Clash of Civilizations." Lecture, University of Massachusetts Amhurst, 1996. Accessed September 13, 2012, http://www.youtube.com/watch?v=boBzrqF4vmo.

———. *Orientalism.* New York: Vintage Books, 1978.

Sedgwick, Mark. *Islam and Muslims.* Boston: Intercultural Press, 2006.

Twain, Mark. *The Innocents Abroad.* New York: Dover Publications, 2003.

PART II

Everyday/Everynight Immigrant Lives

CHAPTER 3

Gendered Migrations
Transnational Feminist Perspectives

*Patti Duncan**

In her work, "Genealogies of Community, Home, and Nation," feminist scholar Chandra Talpade Mohanty suggests that questions of home, nation, and belonging are profoundly complicated and increasingly political, particularly for those who migrate. "What is home?" she asks. "Is home a geographical space, a historical space, an emotional, sensory space?"[1] The very notion of home invokes ideas of belonging and community. The narrative of her desire to claim a history of anticolonialist feminist struggle in India is juxtaposed with the recognition of her connection to a larger South Asian community in the United States and the creation of a strategic space she calls "home."[2] Mohanty's work highlights the ways in which a consideration of home is critical to migrants and immigrants for whom border crossings may signify losses, exile, and displacement while also evoking potential "gains," including transnational coalitions and geopolitical forms of solidarity and resistance. Also, her discussion reminds us of the fact that migration is not simply abstract but deeply material, grounded in real people's experiences of home, community, and nation, always gendered and racialized, always shaped by power relations.[3]

This chapter addresses some of the gendered, racialized dimensions of migration. Meg Wilkes Karraker, in the first chapter of this collection, makes the point that 49 percent of migrants today are women, leading to a "feminization of international migration." While there has been increased attention to the relationship between gender and migration in recent years, there remain

* Address correspondence to Patti Duncan, PhD, Women's Studies Program, School of Language, Culture, and Society, Oregon State University, 266 Waldo Hall, Corvallis, OR 97331–6208. Email: patti.duncan@oregonstate.edu.

multiple exclusions that continue to shape the production of knowledge and discourse about migration. I ask, in what ways is migration gendered and what impact does this have on our understanding of the processes of migration? By gendered, I do not simply imply a focus on women's experiences of migration, although of course this is a necessary and central part of the discussion. Rather, I suggest a consideration of the ways in which ideas and constructions of masculinity and femininity shape and are shaped by migration patterns, processes, and experiences. To highlight ways in which gendered, racialized practices and processes may shape our understanding of migration, I discuss three conceptualizations of migration in which racialized gender figures prominently: women's labor migration, particularly for domestic work; politics of transnational adoption; and discourse surrounding the global sex industry and sex trafficking. My intention is not a comprehensive review of these areas or a complete theoretical analysis of their gendered, racialized dimensions. Rather, I suggest that these three forms of migration have something to teach us about the ways in which migration may (must) be understood as gendered.

Recent feminist scholarship on women and migration includes research by Pierrette Hondagneu-Sotelo, Lourdes Arizpe, and Rhacel Salazar Parrenas, who examine ways in which gendered practices, kinship and social networks, and economic transitions shape migration processes. And as M. Bianet Castellanos points out, recent scholarship also accounts for greater understanding of the subjective and embodied experiences of migration, particularly gendered and racialized experiences.[4] The *World Survey on the Role of Women and International Migration 2004* focused on women and international migration, stating that gender is "central in any discussion of the causes of international migration—the decision-making involved and the mechanisms associated with enacting migrating decisions—as well as the consequences of migration."[5] As Jindy Pettman suggests, the entire process associated with migration is always already gendered in terms of the different household and familial roles associated with men and women, masculinity and femininity, and also in terms of the kinds of work available locally and through migration, as well as the ways in which mobility and border crossings may be experienced. In addition, "forms of exploitation, violence or discrimination facing migrants in the new state are also gendered, and mediated through other body differences, including race, class, and nationality."[6]

I focus on gender in recent migration patterns in an attempt to draw out the significant meanings of racialized gender within these contexts, highlighting the ways in which gender constructions organize social, political, and economic experiences of migration. I explore these themes within a transnational framework in order to address the ways in which migration implies not only a crossing of national (and other) borders but also the relationship between and among nation-states, in which the politics of the "local" affect processes of the "global" and vice versa, within an era of globalization, increased feminization of labor, neoliberalism, and religious fundamentalism. In this context a focus on transnational feminist perspectives of gendered, racialized migration enables and emphasizes possibilities for cross-cultural, international politics of solidarity. Also, as Inderpal Grewal and Caren Kaplan suggest, the term transnational "does a particular kind of work in the U.S. academy . . . circulat[ing] widely as a more useful term to describe migration at the present time."[7]

Women Migrants, Reproductive Labor, and Transnational Motherhood

Within the global economy, it is crucial to consider the international (gendered, racialized) division of labor as "central to the establishment, consolidation, and maintenance of the current world order."[8] As Cynthia Enloe and others suggest, global assembly lines are not simply driven by economics—they also participate in the production of people, in this case certain groups of people as expendable, "cheap" labor and others as citizen-consumers within a global marketplace. Citizens of the global South often migrate, as Grace Chang notes, as a result of First World imperialism, economic and military interventions, and/or following the extraction of their nations' resources by First World nations.[9] Chang argues that migrant women workers are actually "imported into the United States from the Third World and subsequently channeled into the service sector, specifically in care work or paid reproductive labor."[10] For this reason, migration may be viewed as a labor issue, in addition to, as Pettman highlights, "a foreign policy issue, a security issue, and a national political issue touching in identity politics, citizenship, . . . and human rights."[11]

Ideas about labor and workers are central to an analysis of the sexual politics of global capitalism. Globally, women's identities as mothers, wives, and family members often supersede their identities as workers, and hence their labor is often regarded as simply a "'natural extension' of their familial duties."[12] In particular, the boundaries between home/family and work, historically, have consistently been violated for poor and working-class women. In the current political economy, this enables new forms of exploitation and a process of (re)colonization of women of the global South, at home and as migrant workers. The very concept of work/labor draws upon notions of masculinity, femininity, and sexuality, as well as the naturalization of heteronormativity within racialized capitalist patriarchies.[13] So-called women's work naturalizes women as housewives, always already in relation to men and heterosexual marriage and often renders women's labor invisible, as "ideologies of domesticity, femininity, and race form the basis of the construction of 'women's work' for Third World women in the contemporary economy."[14] Third world women migrant workers, depicted as cheap—or "cheapened"[15]—labor, migrate as domestic workers, nannies, nurses and in-home caregivers, sex workers, and mail-order brides, work that is often done in the "home," resulting in the systematic invisibility of such labor. Also, this work, characterized by intimate household services, referred to as "labor intimacy" by Kimberly A. Chang and L. H. M. Ling, is explicitly sexualized, racialized, and class based.[16] "What allows this work to be so fundamentally exploitative as to be invisible as a form of work are ideologies of domesticity, dependency, and (hetero)sexuality, which designate women—in this case, Third World women—as primarily housewives/mothers and men as economic supporters/breadwinners."[17] Such a pattern sometimes results in the creation of binaries between male migrant "workers" who make the choice to migrate for work and women as "victims" of male violence who are trafficked across national borders against their will, a point to which I will return later in this chapter.

Neoliberalism, resulting in cuts to government expenditures on social programs, the privatization of state programs and enterprises, decreased wages, the devaluing of local currency, and the opening of local markets to foreign investment, among other things, has extremely deleterious effects on women and families of the global South. Structural adjustment programs contribute to increased poverty and negatively impact working conditions, health, housing, nutrition, and access to resources including education, health services, and childcare. Such policies contribute to the feminization of the global labor force, pushing women into the low-paid service sector and the informal economy.[18] When women are unable to find ways to support their families in their home countries, they may have no other option than to leave their families to migrate for work. Asian women organizers at the Fourth World Conference on Women and the NGO forum in China in 1995 highlighted the "massive migration from their countries as a result of SAP-driven poverty."[19] Millions of women have migrated from all over Asia to work in the service and sex industries of the United States, Canada, Europe, Japan, and the Middle East, often employed in informal sectors performing work that is "feminized" and conditional. For example, it is estimated that more than 4 percent of the Philippines' total population consists of overseas contract workers, and in the early 1990s, women "constituted a larger proportion of the country's overseas workforce (41 percent) than its domestic workforce (36 percent)."[20]

The majority of Filipina overseas contract workers—approximately 70 percent—are employed as domestic workers and nannies, the "quintessential service workers of globalization."[21] They work in middle- and upper-middle-class households throughout North America, Europe, Japan, and the Middle East. The fact that they overwhelmingly perform reproductive labor illustrates that "gender is a controlling factor of the outflow of labor in globalization and show[s] another dimension by which gender shapes the economic divisions of labor in migration."[22] Also, because reproductive labor is considered a commodity available to class- and race-privileged women and families, the experiences of Filipina domestic workers also suggest a racial and class-based division of reproductive labor.[23] These migrant women workers are extremely vulnerable, working in private homes and under immigration policies like those of the United States, in which temporary workers are not eligible for protections granted to citizens. In fact, Mohanty suggests that "homework is one of the most significant, and repressive, forms of 'women's work' in contemporary global capitalism."[24] Performing various forms of care work, these women migrants illustrate the increasingly globalized, transnational division of reproductive labor, in which women of poorer nations perform "international sex and service" work for families in the global North.[25] As Pettman suggests, "Women moving internationally for care work are, like women everywhere, caught between the public and the private, and between productive and reproductive work, where the latter is seen as women's work, or as not really work at all. This makes for a triple burden of vulnerability, as women, as migrants, and in forms and places of work that are largely unregulated or hard to monitor, or organise [sic]."[26] Transnational care work, as she suggests, is always gendered, racialized, and "culturalised [sic]."[27] Host countries save money by offering extremely low wages and denying public benefits to temporary workers. At the same time, their home countries come to depend on their remittances. In the case of the Philippines, for example, Chang reports that approximately 30–50 percent of the population relies on migrant workers' remittances, which sustain not only the families of migrant women workers but also the entire local economy.[28]

The case of Filipina migrant workers illustrates the centrality of social reproductive labor in women's lives, embedded within the processes of global capitalism. According to Charlene Tung, a growing demand for home care workers in the United States, as well as United States–Philippine neocolonial relations, results in increasing numbers of Filipina migrants to the United States, where they must negotiate the demands of caring for their employers' families while sending remittances home to support the children left behind in the Philippines.[29] Tung explores how Filipina women's experiences of transnational marriage and motherhood in effect redefine both institutions, demonstrating their shifting meanings within an increasingly globalized transnational context. Similarly, Pierrette Hondagneu-Sotelo and Ernestine Avila examine the construction of transnational motherhood for Latina transnational mothers working as domestic workers and nannies in the United States, who must leave their own children behind. As such, the authors argue, they create alternative constructions of motherhood that contradict dominant US white, middle-class models and Latina models of motherhood, often involving taking care of their employers' children while demonstrating their love for their own children through phone calls, letters, and sending money home.[30]

When women migrant workers experience violence in their host countries, there is very little their own governments can do. Chang cites numerous cases of violence against Filipina migrant women workers, including that of 15-year-old Sarah Balabagan, who was raped at knifepoint by her employer in the United Arab Emirates. She killed her rapist in self-defense and was sentenced to death. Other women reported physical and psychological abuse, sexual assault, and a range of other forms of abuse and exploitation including being denied wages, time off, food, and a place to sleep.[31] Transnational feminist responses to such widespread abuses include the mobilization of migrant workers worldwide as well as local organizing for rights and greater awareness. Gabriela Network, a Filipina organization, staged numerous protests regarding Balabagan's case in order to put pressure on the governments of both the United Arab Emirates and the Philippines. INTERCEDE, based in Toronto, Canada, advocates for Filipina and Caribbean migrant domestic workers. Kalayaan is a UK-based organization working for overseas domestic workers' rights. And Campaign for Migrant Domestic Worker Rights is a US-based coalition working to monitor and end abuses of migrant workers employed in the homes of US officials and others employed by international agencies.[32] Other networks including NGOs and grassroots local movements also indicate an increase in transnational feminist solidarity, posing a significant challenge to neoliberal policies worldwide.[33]

The recognition of women migrant workers' commonalities of experiences and histories form a basis for political unity and solidarity, as well as transnational feminist organizing. However, these solidarities are not without conflict. As Naples, Desai, and others document, international networks and NGOs are often dominated by women from the North and more elite, educated, and middle-class women from the South. Also, such organizations often rely on funding from northern donors, who may exert control over the work the organizations do.[34] An analysis of the gendered, racialized dynamics of migration, in this case labor migration, must include recognition of such challenges in transnational feminist organizing for solidarity.

Politics of Transnational Adoption

In "Transnational Adoption and Queer Diasporas," David Eng writes that a notable challenge to traditional orderings of family and kinship has emerged in the form of Asian transnational movements in terms of both labor and capital. The late twentieth century, he suggests, has witnessed an increase in cheap, flexible Asian immigrant labor as well as the expansion of Asian immigration into spheres of transnational capitalism. "'Mail-order brides' and 'domestic servants' are two of the more significant terms in a global age associated with the exploitation of Third World women in an ever increasing international gendered division of labor supporting First World middle-class family households."[35] Into this realm, Eng suggests, we might also consider the transnational adoptee—another gendered, racialized migrant, representing capital or labor or some combination of the two.[36] The politics of transnational adoption are complex, not only demonstrating the ways in which global migration patterns are deeply gendered, racialized, and structured by political economies and structures associated with economic globalization, but also suggesting certain implications and ideas about (gendered, racialized) citizenship and national belonging.

In *Babies without Borders: Adoption and Migration across the Americas*, Dubinsky suggests that children are central to the histories of nations, often functioning as metaphors for fractured nations. From 1961 to 1962, for example, more than 14,000 Cuban children were taken to Miami, a process dubbed Operation Peter Pan. Parents sent their children out of the country because of rumors circulated by anti-Castro forces that the children would be taken to the Soviet Union for indoctrination. Many of these parents never saw their children again.[37] Immediately following the war in Vietnam, a similar practice occurred, referred to as Operation Babylift, a 1975 US government program that resulted in the evacuation of more than 4,000 children to be placed for adoption with families in the United States, Australia, Canada, and France. According to multiple reports, many of these children were not actually orphans; their mothers had sent them out of the country because of rumors that they would be stigmatized and victimized because of the mothers' presumed relationships with US servicemen. Mixed race children in Vietnam and Korea, following wars in both countries, were often seen as being saved through transnational adoption. As such they came to embody the losses experienced by the nations at large, and for these reasons, transnational adoption in Korea, Vietnam, and elsewhere is often perceived as a source of national shame and suffering.

Transnational adoption, as I have argued elsewhere, has a complex history in relation to wars and Western empire building. It highlights power differences between nations as well as a global militarized economy that enables the flow of children from disempowered occupied nations to wealthy, dominant Western nations. US representations of transnational adoption often focus on rescuing "innocent" children from poverty and neglect, and as Laura Briggs suggests, such processes are "invested with colonial legacies and can be allied with U.S. state power and other kinds of violence."[38] For example, in Latin America, transnational adoption is often characterized as an extension of US military and economic power and hence US foreign policy.[39]

The gendered dimensions of transnational adoption suggest a more explicit relationship to gendered migration, according to Eng. He writes, "Scholarship in postcolonial and transnational feminism links the historical emergence of war brides and mail-order brides to foundations of military prostitution and the commodification of Third World female bodies for First World male consumption and pleasure. From this perspective, we might say that the historical phenomena of war brides and mail-order brides make explicit what is often only implicit or absent in traditional analyses of transnational adoption (the majority of adoptees being baby girls)."[40] Returning to an earlier question regarding the type of gendered, racialized "labor" performed by the transnational adoptee—a form of gendered commodification shaped by an international gendered division of labor—Eng concludes that what is performed for the (adoptive) family and the (US) nation is actually *ideological* labor: "the shoring up of an idealized notion of kinship, the making good of the white heterosexual nuclear family."[41] Within the United States, Asian immigration is characterized by a long history of anti-Asian exclusion, bars to naturalization and citizenship, and the deliberate fracturing of families, all of which were deeply embedded in ideas about gender and race. In this regard, Eng suggests, considering the intersections of both domestic and transnational histories of race and racial formation, "the privileged migration of Chinese baby girls in our contemporary moment marks not only a striking gendered reversion of this history of racialized exclusion but also an emergent form of Asian American subjectivity of considerable consequence to Asian American politics, history, and community."[42]

Sex Trafficking and the Global Sex Industry

It would be impossible to discuss gendered migrations without taking into account the issues of sex trafficking and the global sex industry. Sex trafficking, the forced migration and labor of individuals into the sex industry, emerged as a major international feminist and human rights issue in the 1990s, often linked to a broader discourse surrounding male violence against women, which included concerns about rape, domestic violence, pornography, and prostitution.[43] Rooted in a histories of a social purity movement, idealized femininity, and "racialized social panic" about gendered international migration patterns in the early twentieth century, dominated by fear of "white slavery," where European women might be abducted and transported against their will to be forced into prostitution, the antitrafficking movement originated with particular constructions of race and gender.[44] A radical feminist formulation of trafficking, rooted in the movement for the abolition of all forms of prostitution, understood trafficking as "sexual slavery"—"taken to be epitomize the very worst of patriarchal oppression and the greatest injury to women."[45]

While individuals of any gender may be trafficked into prostitution, much of the discourse surrounding trafficking and the antitrafficking movement has focused on women and girls. Also, as Karraker notes, individuals may be trafficked into many different industries, including agricultural and domestic work; however, the focus has revolved around prostitution and sex industries. These are the primary areas of concern represented in the media, as well as for law and policymakers, activists, and researchers. In the midst of these discussions, however, another feminist perspective also emerged, grounded in grassroots organizing primarily in and with women of the global South, which links women in the sex industry with other migrant women and has attempted to separate the problem of trafficking from prostitution.[46] From this transnational feminist perspective, the global sex trade is considered one—but not the only—site where trafficking may occur. And as Barbara Sullivan notes, "While anti-trafficking campaigns have clearly led to the rescue of some women trapped in dire circumstances, they can also have a serious and negative impact on the human rights of migrant women workers and women who engage in sex work."[47] Current antitrafficking discourse implies a division of migrants into "criminals" or "victims."[48] For example, Elizabeth Bernstein suggests that grouping all commercial sex acts together under the rubric "trafficking" often results in arrests and deportations of migrant women. It may also lead to the criminalization of some women—those who do not fit the ideal image of "innocent victims." As Bernstein writes, "Only a small minority conform to the images of 'sexual slavery' that have been endlessly recycled by abolitionist feminist groups and the press. For the overwhelming majority of female migrants, it is not brute force, pure deceit, or random abduction that propels them to engage in sexual labor, but rather the desire for economic, social, and geographic mobility; the potentially pleasurable aspects of being an object of affection and desire; and the allure of flexible schedules and instant cash."[49] Hence the conflation of sex trafficking with migration obscures migrant women's agency and leads to overly simplistic solutions within the mainstream antitrafficking movement.[50] Also, antitrafficking campaigns may limit women's mobility as immigration controls tighten and lead to greater surveillance of migrant women workers.[51] In particular, Chandre Gould suggests that international concern about human trafficking leads to increased securitization, linked to the "War on Terror," securing of national borders, and ideas about "illegal" immigration.[52]

To consider the issue of trafficking alongside patterns of international migration and labor allows us to understand the ways in which poor women and women of the global South bear the brunt of the sex and service work discussed earlier in this chapter. Also, sex trafficking demonstrates how, globally, women of color seeking economic security through migration experience particular forms of exploitation and sexualization but also express agency as they negotiate these processes. Kamala Kempadoo, in her discussion of the global interplay of race, gender, sexuality, nationality, and the economy, highlights three features that contribute to the overrepresentation of women of color in the global sex trade: militarized prostitution or the sex industries surrounding military bases in nonwestern countries, particularly in Asia and the Pacific, in which sex with local women often become integral to constructions of heterosexual militarized masculinity; sex tourism in "exotic" (i.e., "third world") countries, where racist, sexualized stereotypes of local women intermingle with governments' need for foreign exchange (a result of global economic restructuring); and discourses of trafficking, in which young women and girls of the global South are seen as the most frequent "victims," a representation that fails to capture the complex histories, forms of oppression, and experiences of women of color, particularly in relation to legacies of racism, colonialism, imperialism, and globalization.[53] For many women in postcolonial societies, Kempadoo suggests, sex work has become deeply embedded in social and economic relations. "Within the international gendered division of labor and the demands of the globalization of capitalism, it presents one of the few income-generating alternatives for Asian, African, Caribbean, and Latin American women."[54]

Human trafficking is an important issue in today's global economy, and it is undeniable that some women and girls experience violence and forced prostitution. However, it is important to consider the issue of trafficking within a larger framework that is attentive to multiple forms of migration, situated within the current global political economy. Doing so allows us to understand the issues associated with trafficking and the sex industry in relation to gendered and racialized forms of migration within the current international division of labor. Also contextualizing the issue of trafficking within the global economy, with attention to the ways in which trafficking and migration intersect and overlap enables greater understanding of human rights abuses experienced by migrant workers, as well as the ways in which law-enforcement responses to trafficking often fail to actually improve the working or living conditions of migrant women workers and their families.

Conclusion

In each of the three dynamics discussed in this chapter, experiences of migration are deeply gendered and racialized. Patterns of migration are shaped by constructions of racialized femininity and masculinity as well as heteronormativity, producing notions of "ideal" (im)migrants, domestic workers, sex workers, and families. The dynamics discussed earlier represent not only examples of gendered, racialized migrations but also sites of contestation, in which normative discourses are constituted by and with state policies and practices and challenged and reconceptualized by transnational feminist activists and scholars and those identifying themselves as migrants and immigrants in today's world order. In particular, Palmary discusses challenges to the "assumed distinction between economic and political migration alongside exploring consequences of the gendered division between the body and the nation."[55]

Gender is a central factor of women's labor migration. In the case of Filipina migrant workers, the experience is gendered in multiple ways. "The process of migration for women involves escaping their gender roles in the Philippines, easing the gender constraints of women who employ them in industrialized countries, and finally relegating their gender roles to women left in the Philippines."[56] The gendering of migration is demonstrated in terms of the international gendered, racialized division of labor, in which reproductive labor (or "care work") is most commonly associated with women of the global South—the "ideal" nannies and domestic workers. It is also demonstrated through the prevalence of gendered forms of violence experienced by these migrant women workers. And we see the gendering of migration through the history and politics of split-family households and transnational motherhood, in which women migrant workers are often expected to perform care work for the families of their employers while mothering their own children from afar.

The politics of transnational adoption highlight questions of childhood, family structure and kinship, citizenship, and belonging. The fact that transnational adoption is gendered and racialized, as well as structured through relations between nation-states, suggests a reconsideration and broadening of our conceptualizations of migration. Current US concern with "anchor babies"—a pejorative term for the young children of undocumented immigrants, who qualify for US citizenship and may later sponsor their parents and/or family members—has increased since 9/11. Curiously, mainstream media coverage of transnational adoptees, particularly when framed with the discourse of salvation or rescue, diverges sharply from some of the vitriolic responses that occur when children migrate to the United States *with* their (in some cases undocumented) parents. While there exists a fantasy of the contemporary immigrant's newfound freedoms in America, the policing of national borders actually results in the institutionalization of racialization, marking certain migrants as always already "Other." As Pettman suggests, "Migration produces difference. The visible presence of 'others' can trigger debates about who 'we' are, who belongs here, and who cannot belong. That strange word 'naturalisation,' meaning to acquire citizenship, hints that there is something alien about the stranger, the guest worker, the migrant."[57]

Some of the discourse surrounding trafficking and the antitrafficking movement have tended to conflate trafficking with prostitution while assuming a separation between trafficking and migration. To consider the relationship between trafficking and migration allows us to understand the "often benevolent discourse of state protection that functions to obscure its violence against migrants."[58] In particular, Palmary and others note the preoccupation with migrant women's sexuality and sexual transgressions, in which "sexuality and racialized gender norms are disciplined by social institutions, assumptions and practices that normalize (racialized) heterosexuality and subject different migrants to different kinds of gendered stereotypes."[59] Such practices, they note, are often about protecting "women and children," while legitimating practices of racism and exclusion and relying on patriarchal and heteronormative discourses and processes. Also, state protection of migrant women is often rooted in assumption that they must be protected *from* migrant men, effectively obscuring ways in which such state "protections" actually render migrants more vulnerable—for example, through detention periods, deportations, and increased surveillance. "In this way, the history of racism, sexism and colonialism of Western societies is erased at the same time as, and by virtue of, migrants being positioned as those who are bringing intolerance to host societies."[60]

An example of such (gendered, racialized) state protection is offered by Jasmin Zine, in her discussion of a Citizen's Code in Herouxville, Quebec, designed to delineate boundaries between "us" and "them"—or "good" and "bad" immigrants—through the outlawing of face veils, the banning of *hijab* in girls' soccer, and the framing of an "honor killing" of a Pakistani Canadian teen. In the cases she discusses, Zine makes the point that, within this post-9/11 context, "Orientalist fears and fantasies of the violent and pathological Muslim are codified and reproduced in the apparatuses of the state and through the relations of ruling."[61] In particular, Muslims are cast as "anti-citizens," or as perpetual foreigners who can never fully assimilate. As dangerous interlopers, Muslims represent the threat of terrorism, and Muslim women—particularly veiled Muslim women—are seen both as threats to national security and as oppressed victims in need of liberation from Muslim men. "As a result of the 'war on terror,' citizenship regimes and security regimes are becoming increasingly interconnected in Western contexts."[62] A recent move that Zine discusses is the government's plan to require new immigrants to sign a declaration of their respect for "Quebec's common values," values based on xenophobic and Islamophobic gendered assumptions.[63] As such, we may consider some of the ways in which migration and its attendant themes of home, citizenship, and belonging is continually shaped and discursively constituted through constructions of gender, race, nation, and culture.

Notes

1. Chandra Talpade Mohanty, *Feminism without Borders: Decolonizing Theory, Practicing Solidarity* (Durham, NC: Duke University Press, 2003), 126.

2. Mohanty, *Feminism without Borders,* 128.

3. Also, Ingrid Palmary suggests that home, in the literature about migration, is complex, often simultaneously associated with safety and stability and violence and mobility and structured by race, class, and gender. Ingrid Palmary, "Sex, Choice and Exploitation: Reflections on the Anti-Trafficking Discourse," in *Gender and Migration: Feminist Interventions,* ed. Ingrid Palmary et al. (London: Zed Books, 2010).

4. M. Bianet Castellanos, "Becoming Chingon/a: A Gendered and Racialized Critique of the Global Economy," in *Strange Affinities: The Gender and Sexual Politics of Comparative Racialization,* ed. Grace Kyungwon Hong and Roderick A. Ferguson (Durham, NC: Duke University Press, 2011). Castellanos describes Maya migrants' subjectivity and resistance in their experiences of migration.

5. UN Department of Economics and Social Affairs (UNDESA), *World Survey on the Role of Women and International Migration 2004* (New York: United Nations, 2006), 11.

6. Jindy Pettman, "Migration," in *Gender Matters in Global Politics: A Feminist Introduction to International Relations,* ed. Laura J. Shepherd (London: Routledge, 2010), 255.

7. Inderpal Grewal and Caren Kaplan, "Global Identities: Theorizing Transnational Studies of Sexuality," in *GLQ* 7, no. 4 (2001).

8. Mohanty, *Feminism without Borders,* 141.

9. Grace Chang, *Disposable Domestics: Immigrant Women Workers in the Global Economy* (Cambridge, MA: South End Press, 2000), 3.

10. Ibid., 12.

11. Pettman, "Migration," 252.

12. Mohanty, *Feminism without Borders,* 158.

13. Ibid., 148.

14. Ibid., 158.

15. Cynthia Enloe, "Daughters and Generals in the Politics of the Globalized Sneaker," in *Beyond Borders: Thinking Critically about Global Issues,* ed. Paula S. Rothenberg (New York: Worth Publishers, 2006).

16. Kimberly A. Chang and L. H. M. Ling, "Globalization and Its Intimate Other: Filipina Domestic Workers in Hong Kong," in *Gender and Global Restructuring: Sightings, Sites and Resistances*, ed. Marianne H. Marchand and Anne Sisson Runyan (London: Routledge, 2000).

17. Mohanty, *Feminism without Borders,* 159.

18. Manisha Desai, "Transnational Solidarity: Women's Agency, Structural Adjustment, and Globalization," in *Women's Activism and Globalization: Linking Local Struggles and Transnational Politics,* ed. Nancy A. Naples and Manisha Desai (New York: Routledge, 2002).

19. Chang, *Disposable Domestics,* 124.

20. Ibid., 129.

21. Rhacel Salazar Parrenas, *Servants of Globalization: Women, Migration, and Domestic Work* (Stanford, CA: Stanford University Press, 2001), 1.
22. Ibid., 61.
23. Evelyn Nakano Glenn, "From Servitude to Service Work: The Historical Continuities of Women's Paid and Unpaid Reproductive Labor," *Signs* 18, no. 1 (1992); Parrenas, *Servants of Globalization.*
24. Mohanty, *Feminism without Borders,* 167.
25. Pettman, "Migration," 258.
26. Ibid.
27. Ibid.
28. Chang, *Disposable Domestics,* 130.
29. Charlene Tung, "Caring across Borders: Motherhood, Marriage, and Filipina Domestic Workers in California," in *Asian/Pacific Islander American Women: A Historical Anthology,* ed. Shirley Hune and Gail M. Nomura (New York: New York University Press, 2003).
30. Pierrette Hondagneu-Sotelo and Ernestine Avila, "'I'm Here, but I'm There': The Meanings of Latina Transnational Motherhood," in *Women and Migration in the U.S.-Mexico Borderlands: A Reader,* ed. Denise Segura and Patricia Zavella (Durham, NC: Duke University Press, 2007).
31. Chang, *Disposable Domestics,* 138.
32. Ibid., 137–46.
33. Desai, "Transnational Solidarity."
34. Ibid.; Nancy Naples, "The Challenges and Possibilities of Transnational Feminism Praxis," in *Women's Activism and Globalization: Linking Local Struggles and Transnational Politics,* ed. Nancy A. Naples and Manisha Desai (New York: Routledge, 2002).
35. David Eng, "Transnational Adoption and Queer Diasporas," *Social Text* 76, no. 21.3 (2003): 5.
36. Ibid., 5.
37. Karen Dubinsky, *Babies without Borders: Adoption and Migration across the Americas* (New York: New York University Press, 2010).
38. Laura Briggs, "Making 'American' Families: Transnational Adoption and U.S. Latin American Policy," in *Haunted by Empire: Geographies of Intimacy in North American History,* ed. Ann Laura Stoler (Durham, NC: Duke University Press, 2006), 344–65; 348.
39. Dubinsky, *Babies Without Borders.*
40. Eng, "Transnational Adoption," 10.
41. Ibid., 11.
42. Ibid.
43. Kamala Kempadoo, "Women of Color and the Global Sex Trade: Transnational Feminist Perspectives," *Meridians: Feminisms, Race, Transnationalism* 1, no. 2 (2001); Barbara Sullivan, "Trafficking in Human Beings," in *Gender Matters in Global Politics: A Feminist Introduction to International Politics,* ed. Laura J. Shepherd (London: Routledge, 2010).

44. Kamala Kempadoo, "From Moral Panic to Global Justice: Changing Perspectives on Trafficking," in *Trafficking and Prostitution Reconsidered: New Perspectives on Migration, Sex Work, and Human Rights,* ed. Kamala Kempadoo with Jyoti Sanghera and Bandana Pattanaikv (Boulder, CO: Paradigm Publishers, 2005), x; Chandre Gould, "The Problem of Trafficking," in *Gender and Migration: Feminist Interventions,* ed. Ingrid Palmary et al. (London: Zed Books, 2010).
45. Kempadoo, "From Moral Panic," xi.
46. Ibid.
47. Sullivan, "Trafficking," 89–90.
48. Wendy Chapkis, "Soft Glove, Punishing Fist: The Trafficking Victims Protection Act of 2000," in *Regulating Sex: The Politics of Intimacy and Identity,* ed. Elizabeth Bernstein and Laurie Schaffner (New York: Routledge, 2005), 51–67; 52.
49. Elizabeth Bernstein, *Temporarily Yours: Intimacy, Authenticity, and the Commerce of Sex* (Chicago: University of Chicago Press, 2007), 184.
50. Jyoti Sanghera, "Unpacking the Trafficking Discourse," in *Trafficking and Prostitution Reconsidered: New Perspectives on Migration, Sex Work, and Human Rights,* ed. Kamala Kempadoo with Jyoti Sanghera and Bandana Pattanaikv (Boulder, CO: Paradigm Publishers, 2005).
51. Sullivan, "Trafficking"; Sanghera, "Unpacking the Trafficking Discourse."
52. Gould, "The Problem of Trafficking."
53. Kempadoo, "Women of Color."
54. Ibid., 34.
55. Ingrid Palmary et al., "Gender and Migration: Feminist Interventions," in *Gender and Migration: Feminist Interventions,* ed. Ingrid Palmary et al. (London: Zed Books, 2010), 1–11; 5.
56. Parrenas, *Servants of Globalization,* 73.
57. Ibid., 260.
58. Palmary et al., "Gender and Migration," 3.
59. Ibid., 6.
60. Ibid.
61. Jasmin Zine, "Unsettling the Nation: Gender, Race, and Muslim Cultural Politics in Canada," *Studies in Ethnicity and Nationalism* 9, no. 1 (2009): 148.
62. Ibid., 158.
63. For example, Zine cites the preamble to the town charter, which upholds women's rights to drive a car, "decide for herself," have a job, and so on, and explicitly states, "We consider that killing women in public beatings, or burning them alive are not part of our standards of life" (158).

Bibliography

Bernstein, Elizabeth. *Temporarily Yours: Intimacy, Authenticity, and the Commerce of Sex.* Chicago: University of Chicago Press, 2007.

Briggs, Laura. "Making 'American' Families: Transnational Adoption and U.S. Latin American Policy." In *Haunted by Empire: Geographies of Intimacy in North American*

History, edited by Ann Laura Stoler, 344–65. Durham, NC: Duke University Press, 2006.

Castellanos, M. Bianet. "Becoming Chingon/a: A Gendered and Racialized Critique of the Global Economy." In *Strange Affinities: The Gender and Sexual Politics of Comparative Racialization,* edited by Grace Kyungwon Hong and Roderick A. Ferguson, 270–92. Durham, NC: Duke University Press, 2011.

Chang, Grace. *Disposable Domestics: Immigrant Women Workers in the Global Economy.* Cambridge, MA: South End Press, 2000.

Chang, Kimberly A., and L. H. M. Ling. "Globalization and Its Intimate Other: Filipina Domestic Workers in Hong Kong." In *Gender and Global Restructuring: Sightings, Sites and Resistances,* edited by Marianne H. Marchand and Anne Sisson Runyan, 30–47. London: Routledge, 2000.

Chapkis, Wendy. "Soft Glove, Punishing Fist: The Trafficking Victims Protection Act of 2000." In *Regulating Sex: The Politics of Intimacy and Identity*, edited by Elizabeth Bernstein and Laurie Schaffner, 51–67. New York: Routledge, 2005.

Dubinsky, Karen. *Babies without Borders: Adoption and Migration across the Americas.* New York: New York University Press, 2010.

Eng, David. "Transnational Adoption and Queer Diasporas." *Social Text* 76, volume 21, no. 3 (2003): 1–37.

Enloe, Cynthia. "Daughters and Generals in the Politics of the Globalized Sneaker." In *Beyond Borders: Thinking Critically about Global Issues,* edited by Paula S. Rothenberg, 271–77. New York: Worth Publishers, 2006.

Gould, Chandre. "The Problem of Trafficking." In *Gender and Migration: Feminist Interventions*, edited by Ingrid Palmary, Erica Burman, Khatidja Chantler, and Peace Kiguwa, 31–49. London: Zed Books, 2010.

Grewal, Inderpal, and Caren Kaplan. "Global Identities: Theorizing Transnational Studies of Sexuality." *GLQ: A Journal of Lesbian and Gay Studies* 7, no. 4 (2001): 663–79.

Hondagneu-Sotelo, Pierrette, and Ernestine Avila. "'I'm Here, but I'm There': The Meanings of Latina Transnational Motherhood." In *Women and Migration in the U.S.-Mexico Borderlands: A Reader,* edited by Denise Segura and Patricia Zavella, 388–412. Durham, NC: Duke University Press, 2007.

Kempadoo, Kamala. "From Moral Panic to Global Justice: Changing Perspectives on Trafficking." In *Trafficking and Prostitution Reconsidered: New Perspectives on Migration, Sex Work, and Human Rights,* edited by Kamala Kempadoo with Jyoti Sanghera and Bandana Pattanaikv, vii–xxxiv. Boulder, CO: Paradigm Publishers, 2005.

———. "Women of Color and the Global Sex Trade: Transnational Feminist Perspectives." *Meridians: Feminism, Race, Transnationalism* 1, no. 2 (2001): 28–51.

Mohanty, Chandra Talpade. *Feminism without Borders: Decolonizing Theory, Practicing Solidarity.* Durham, NC: Duke University Press, 2003.

Nakano Glenn, Evelyn. "From Servitude to Service Work: The Historical Continuities of Women's Paid and Unpaid Reproductive Labor." *Signs* 18, no. 1 (1992): 1–44.

Palmary, Ingrid. "Sex, Choice and Exploitation: Reflections on the Anti-Trafficking Discourse." In *Gender and Migration: Feminist Interventions,* edited by Ingrid Palmary,

Erica Burman, Khatidja Chantler, and Peace Kiguwa, 50–63. London: Zed Books, 2010.

Palmary, Ingrid, Erica Burman, Khatidja Chantler, and Peace Kiguwa. "Gender and Migration: Feminist Interventions." In *Gender and Migration: Feminist Interventions,* edited by Ingrid Palmary, Erica Burman, Khatidja Chantler, and Peace Kiguwa, 1–11. London: Zed Books, 2010.

Parrenas, Rhacel Salazar. *Servants of Globalization: Women, Migration, and Domestic Work.* Stanford, CA: Stanford University Press, 2001.

Pettman, Jindy. "Migration." In *Gender Matters in Global Politics: A Feminist Introduction to International Relations,* edited by Laura J. Shepherd, 251–64. London: Routledge, 2010.

Sanghera, Jyoti. "Unpacking the Trafficking Discourse." In *Trafficking and Prostitution Reconsidered: New Perspectives on Migration, Sex Work, and Human Rights,* edited by Kamala Kempadoo with Jyoti Sanghera and Bandana Pattanaikv, 3–24. Boulder, CO: Paradigm Publishers, 2005.

Sullivan, Barbara. "Trafficking in Human Beings." In *Gender Matters in Global Politics: A Feminist Introduction to International Politics,* edited by Laura J. Shepherd, 89–101. London: Routledge, 2010.

Tung, Charlene. "Caring across Borders: Motherhood, Marriage, and Filipina Domestic Workers in California." In *Asian/Pacific Islander American Women: A Historical Anthology,* edited by Shirley Hune and Gail M. Nomura, 301–15. New York: New York University Press, 2003.

Zine, Jasmin. "Unsettling the Nation: Gender, Race, and Muslim Cultural Politics in Canada." *Studies in Ethnicity and Nationalism* 9, no. 1 (2009): 146–63.

CHAPTER 4

Human Trafficking, Migration, and Gender
An Interdisciplinary Approach

*Jennifer K. Blank**

The US government estimates that between 600,000 and 800,000 people are trafficked across international borders annually.[1] At any given time the United Nations Office on Drugs and Crime estimates that 2.5 million people are being trafficked around the world; approximately 80 percent of trafficked individuals are women and girls, and 50 percent are minors.[2] The revenue from human trafficking is large with an annual estimated average of US $13,000 per trafficked victim, totaling US $32 billion per year.[3] Kevin Bales, co-founder of Free the Slaves, believes that international human trafficking has become a modern euphemism for international slavery.[4] Bales estimates that there are 27 million people enslaved around the world at any given time.[5] Even though slavery has been outlawed in almost all countries worldwide, trafficking in persons continues to be one of the fastest growing criminal enterprises, ranking second only to the drug trade, recently outpacing the illegal arms trade.[6] Despite the fact this global crisis is receiving international cooperation from policymakers and researchers alike; there is still little change in the conditions that are conducive to trafficking. In fact, the statistics we receive are, in fact, just estimates. No one really knows the extent of this phenomenon and many scholars have stated that we are only seeing the tip of the iceberg.

* Address correspondence to Jennifer K. Blank, 712 5th Ave SE, Minneapolis, MN 55414. Email: JennyK24@aol.com.

There are several reasons for this lack of understanding: definitional issues, lack of gender in research, understanding labor migration/trafficking patterns, and misconstrued laws and policies. While trafficking is relatable to migration patterns, women and children are more prone to gross violations of their human rights because of traditional gender roles and heightened vulnerabilities. The direction of this chapter will address these issues by beginning with the differences between human trafficking and smuggling and how they intersect with migration and gender. These sections will be followed by reports from interviews with three human traffickers I collected in London, England in 2003. This research is one of the first studies to interview human traffickers in a non-incarcerated setting through snowball sampling. I will be using direct quotes from the traffickers and their names will be changed to protect their identities. These traffickers' thoughts and experiences will only further support why trafficking continues to grow at an exponential rate.

This research will articulate that migration, trafficking, and gender create a separate category within "the Other." This population of women migrants has become "the Other within the Other" because of their further experiences of oppression. In addition, the networks that are used in migration are the same paths used in trafficking. This overlap has produced a thoroughfare for all sorts of illegal activity, and the criminal justice system has not been able to stop this pattern. In fact, in some cases, criminal justice systems are complicit with these trafficking rings. Lastly, I will examine migration and globalization and suggest policy directions for combating trafficking on a transnational, global scale. The overarching goals of this chapter are to provide insight into the trafficking world from the trafficker's perspectives and attempt to explain the stagnant movement in research.

Human Trafficking and Smuggling

The word *trafficking* comes from the word *traffic*, which means transportation. Human trafficking is a gross human rights violation that includes the infringement of rights to life, liberty, personal security, privacy, mental and physical integrity, freedom from slavery, and freedom from torture and other forms of inhumane or degrading treatment.[7] Between 1895 and 1949 there were seven successive international agreements on the issue of trafficking with their own definitions.[8] The definitions varied around themes of prostitution, recruitment into prostitution, the issue of coercion and validity of consent, and movements across frontiers.[9] Today, trafficking in women may be understood in the context of "subordination of women, globalization, a gendered international labor market, and the worldwide feminization of labor migration."[10] The Global Alliance against Traffic in Women (GAATW) has added that trafficking also involves "all acts involved in the recruitment and/or transportation of a woman within and across national borders for work or services by means of violence or threat of violence, abuse of authority or dominant position, debt bondage, deception, or other forms of coercion."[11] While all these definitions are relevant to this issue, there is no single definition of human trafficking that encompasses all forms of modern-day slavery.[12] The United States' Trafficking Victims Protection Act (TVPA) of 2000 defined severe forms of trafficking as the following:

1. Sex trafficking in which a commercial sex act is induced by force, fraud, or coercion, or in which the person induced to perform such an act has not attained 18 years of age; or
2. The recruitment, harboring, transportation, provision, or obtaining of a person for labor or services, through the use of force, fraud, or coercion for the purpose of subjection to involuntary servitude, peonage, debt bondage, or slavery.

The UN Convention against Transnational Organized Crime (UNTOC) and the UN Protocol to Prevent, Suppress and Punish Trafficking in Persons, Especially Women and Children define trafficking as follows:

1. The recruitment, transportation, transfer, harboring or receipt of persons, by means of threat or use of force or other forms of coercion, of abduction, of fraud, of deception, of the abuse of power or of a position of vulnerability of giving or receiving payments or benefits to achieve the consent of a person having control over another person, for the purpose of exploitation.
2. Exploitation shall include, at a minimum, the exploitation of prostitution or other forms of sexual exploitation, forced labor or services, slavery or practices similar to slavery, servitude or the removal or organs.

These trafficking protocols are the only international definition of "trafficking in persons," but there are several issues that lead to its universal demise. GAATW states that the protocol intentionally does not define the phrase "exploitation of prostitution of others or other forms of sexual exploitation" because "government delegates to the negotiations could not agree upon a common meaning"[13] nor does it specify what is meant by "other forms of coercion" or "abuse of power or of a position of vulnerability."[14] The absence of clarity in this definition leaves ample room for convenient interpretations to suit one's social, political, or criminal agenda. The protocol's failure to explicitly define terms such as "exploitation," "coercion," and "vulnerability" leads to highly problematic interpretations for those who are trafficked. Overall, these definitional problems are made "particularly intractable by the fact that 'trafficking in persons' is used as an umbrella term to cover a range of actions and outcomes, rather than a single, unitary act leading to one specific outcome."[15] Trafficking is viewed as a process, involving recruitment, transportation between countries or within one country, and control in the place of destination. It then becomes almost impossible to configure the term "trafficking" into one solitary definition because of the multiple people and events involved.

While human trafficking is based on the supply and demand for labor, smuggling is based on the supply and demand for illegal migration services.[16] The Human Smuggling and Trafficking Center identifies a smuggled person as one who willingly works with smugglers to cross an international border. The UNTOC advocates that each member state should adopt all necessary measures to make trafficking in human beings a crime in their national criminal laws. Article 3 of the Protocol against the Smuggling of Migrants by Land, Sea and Air defines it as the following: "'Smuggling of migrants' shall mean the procurement . . . of the illegal entry of a person into a State Party of which the person is not a national or permanent resident." Article 3 (1[b]) of the Protocol on Smuggling of Migrants states, "Illegal Entry shall mean crossing borders without complying with the necessary requirements for legal entry into the receiving State."

Smuggling of migrants is viewed as illegal entry, but the difference is that smuggled humans have the ability to move and change jobs as desired and are not considered victims. While smuggling is not on the same playing field as trafficking, the two intersect, because, in some cases, smuggling plays a crucial role for the commission of trafficking in human beings when borders are crossed. Smuggling may only occur when a person crosses a border, whereas trafficking does not require national or international border crossings. The key difference between the two is that trafficking concentrates on the "purpose of exploitation." Some trafficking victims may start off as smuggled persons, but they become trafficking victims when they are not allowed to move about freely when brought to the destination country.

Migration and Gender

One reason migration occurs is that the host country is not able to provide a standard of living that is acceptable to its citizens. Some other reasons for migration include civil war and lack of access to education and income-producing work. All migrants encounter hurdles when leaving their home countries to look for better opportunities, yet some are better placed economically in their home countries and are able to maintain comparable levels of comfort versus those who migrate illegally or are in tough economic situations and are forced to migrate.[17] Chew explains that "in the neoliberal world of transnational capitalism and imperialism, migration can undermine and compromise class position and identity; it becomes fluid and volatile."[18]

As the global economy continues on a downslide, so too do the lines between "developed" and "less developed" or "first world" and "third world."[19] A prime example of this change is the former Soviet Bloc. The reversion to capitalism in that area has led to an overwhelming pressure to compete on a global scale for resources. Plus, the globalization of capital and the New International Division of Labor (NIDL) allows these conditions to thrive because production is displaced to third world countries, thus providing for the feminization of poverty. This strategy of globalization of capital and feminization of labor took place in the formal, informal, agricultural, and service sectors of the economy. Plus, while these women are suffering the effects of globalization, "transnational business masculinity" has kept these women subordinate in the dominating patriarchal structure of global capital.[20] These actions allow a growing tendency to commodify relations with women, especially the prostitution business because they cater to international businessmen.

Migration cannot be seen as a universal option for most populations because not all people have the same access to migration. Pessar and Maher conclude that gender, race, ethnicity, nationality, class and sexuality shape and discipline people's thoughts toward migration.[21] With this evidence, we may determine that research on migrants should be woman focused, but "the invisibility of women in international migration scholarship does not correspond to the reality of international migration. Women migrate across international borders at approximately the same rate as men."[22] Yet until about twenty years ago, there was no evidence of women in migration research. With the feminist boom in the 1970s and 1980s there was a new dedication to women-centric research that documented the predominance of women in migration patterns.[23] As this idea continued to grow, so too did the disappearance of men in migration research. In fact, men almost disappeared to the same degree that women had in previous research, which was extremely problematic.

Both angles are objectionable because they "both miss the more important theoretical innovation of treating gender less as a variable and more as a central concept for studying migration."[24] While these studies made women visible, they also drew attention to some "exclusionary dichotomies whereby women are perceived as being (passive) victims of trafficking by the general public, the media and policy-makers, while men are seen as (active) economic migrants."[25] Furthermore, there are arguments that the absence of men in trafficking data has prevented the development of a gender-awareness in trafficking research.[26]

Gender is typically interpreted as "women," and human trafficking is inextricably linked to the "sex trade." Merging these categories together minimizes their complexities. Gender should be understood "simultaneously as a *structure*, that is, a latticework to institutionalized social relationships that, by creating and manipulating the categories of gender, organize and signify power at levels above the individual."[27] Moreover, "major areas if life—including sexuality, family, education, economy, and the state—are organized according to gender principles and short through with conflicting interests and hierarchies of power and privilege."[28] Several scholars have noted the problematic aspects of grouping migration and trafficking. Kapur believes the increase in criminal laws and policing borders, the discussion on security, and the war on terror around the world to be contributing factors to the criminalization of the movement of people, a demonizing of the Other and a victimizing of the victim.[29] From the gender perspective, it infantilizes women and reinforces patriarchal hierarchies that women are in need of protection.

Women's work has traditionally been in the home providing for their family—cooking, cleaning, and raising children. Even when women migrate for work in the private spheres, this work is often ignored in labor migration and trafficking statistics.[30] The demand for domestic work by women is a reflection of the employment of larger numbers of women who work outside the home in industrialized, Western countries and also in parts of Asia. Typically, women from these sending countries are more likely to have traditional and social divisions of labor. From here, we may gather that it is not men who cannot do this work, but it is more profitable for women to do this work and there is a strong cultural justification for it.[31] Chew states that "traditional gender constructions of masculinity make it harder for men to take on what are seen as female roles. So even though a migrant woman might be the breadwinner, she is still the wife and subordinate."[32] This gender ideology affects the way policymakers view migration because of women's assigned domestic responsibilities. There is a federal perception among policymakers that, should women leave their homes, social and moral disintegration would follow.[33]

Human Trafficking from the Trafficker's Perspective: Exploitation of Women

The justified exploitation and denigration of migrant women is a significant part of the worldview of the trafficker. I gained access into that world through a bouncer at several London clubs. I asked him about the business, and he casually said, "Oh, I know people who do that," and the interviews began. He accompanied my research partner and me to every interview. He told me he would perform "favors" for the traffickers in return for their interviews. I never asked what those favors were, because I did not want to be involved, nor did I want to have any connection to his favors. I conducted the face-to-face interviews in public settings, such as coffee shops and a movie theater, with our "gatekeeper" for protection, while my research partner manually recorded their responses. I did not record their voices, nor did I ask their real names, so as to ensure their confidentiality. I also did not want to have anything to link me to these men for fear of retaliation or police involvement. I did, however, ask the traffickers' home countries. Ahmet said he was from Albania; Cyril said he was from England but of Persian descent; and Demitri said he was from Bulgaria and had a master's degree in economics. These traffickers were very candid in their interviews and offered a unique glimpse into the business of trafficking from the perspective of the trafficker.

One of the main themes in this research was the large demand for foreign prostitutes. According to the traffickers, the majority of the men who use prostitutes ask for someone different than themselves. Ahmet said, "A lot of people like to shag foreign girls because they do a bit more. They are more into it." He also said that men "want something different. It's like eating the same food everyday. You want something different." What was interesting is that when I asked Cyril if clients request foreign or local women, he used the same type of food analogy. He asked me, "Can you imagine just having bacon for the rest of your life? Some want to try a kebab." When I asked him what most of the clients ask for, Ahmet told me that they want "Eastern European or Asian women" because they are "exotic." On the same note, Demitri told me that men look for something "exotic, something different, [and] younger women will do." The word "exotic" and "young" have played a big part in the prostitution business because it gives men "something different." Ahmet and Cyril told me that all types of men go to prostitutes, but whoever the client is, he always asks for someone of a different race or nationality. Ahmet said that the clients are "white, black, anyone. We even had a priest come in and ask for a Russian girl. A lot of military guys come in. The American soldiers ask for foreign women. They like Chinese, specifically. They ask for the Asians, but the biggest demand is the Chinese. I've heard friends say police officers, but I've never seen it." Even though he has not seen police officers go to prostitutes, Ahmet said, "Police do drugs and use whore houses as well. I have a friend . . . he's a copper and he sniffs a lot of charlie [cocaine] and he tells me this." On the same note, Cyril told me that police officers have gone to prostitutes. When I asked him if he sees repeat customers and what kind of clients he had, he said, "Yeah, you get regulars [because] they offer good services. Judges, lawyers, police, guys off the street, [a] young guy who wants to break his virginity, any walk of life really. Married men, mostly." What this suggests is that there are no barriers for who the clients are. The people who are supposed to be enforcing the laws against prostitution and trafficking are breaking them in order to satisfy their sexual cravings or to put money in their pockets. Ahmet said, "The demand is quite big. [There are] a lot of businessmen around and they pay. [There are] a lot of desperate, old men, ugly men [that] use them a lot and their wives are in a different country, but the American businessmen were the most consistent clients." The demand keeps growing despite the new measures that are being taken against trafficking because, as Ahmet says, "there is a lot of money to be made [and] they create the market, don't they? The recruiters and traffickers are following the demand from clients' requests.

Plus, a lot of the time a client has more control over foreign prostitutes. Ahmet said, "Foreign girls can't go to the police because they'll get deported back [to their country of origin]. They need the money more. The pimps tell them to satisfy the customer because they want them coming back." This technique works very well because, as Ahmet said, "when you buy [a foreign woman] you know her family, where she comes from. You can force 'em. They don't know any better about the world. They grow up beaten and bossed around. They don't know any better." He continues, "Pimps can't stress the English girls a lot. They have more chances of getting nicked" by the police. Foreign women are the easiest to control and because there is a big demand. Ahmet told me, "Three years ago [in 2000] the price for a good-looking Russian woman was about 1,500 [British pounds] plus the couple grand getting her over here [England]." Even though it cost around 4,000 British Pounds to buy a good-looking Russian girl, Ahmet rationalized his position by saying that the "prostitutes make about a thousand *dollars* a month" (emphasis added). This statement confused me because this prostitution took place in the United Kingdom, and you would think they would be paid in British pounds. However, he said, "The girls can use the dollars. The pounds can't really be used. Sometimes the pimps will just send the American money to her family." At the time of this research, the globalization of the American dollar had caused a "McDonaldization" of American money in the fact that it was everywhere, especially in the illegal sex industry. American capitalism had forced its way into every dominant, money-producing industry. With changes in the global economy, the American dollar is still sought after for migrant populations because its value, in most cases, remains superior to their own.

When I asked the traffickers why they entered the business Ahmet and Cyril both entered the business at a very young age but had different responses on why they entered the human trafficking trade. Ahmet defended himself by saying that it is

> not a good thing, but some people have to do it. It is a way of life. Some of us are not accepted in this society so we are basically forced to do other things. Some are fucked up in their brains though and do it just for the money. Most people just see it as a taxi and extra cash. You don't get involved; you're just like a taxi. I've done it and as far as I am concerned that's a way of life and it's over and I don't feel any regrets. I had to do it. I had to help out my dad for a better life for

myself. Sometimes you have no choice but to do the wrong thing and God knows I've done a lot of wrong things, but you can't have regrets otherwise you might as well go shoot yourself.

Ahmet rationalized his position by blaming his background and lifestyle for his behavior. When I asked Cyril to justify his position he said that there was no reason because it's my opinion against his; he said, "Everyone's got their own opinion." There was nothing I could say at that point because he was right; he did not need to justify himself to me. He told me that trafficking to him was "just work. The excitement, the money, [and] the fun" was what lured him into it; "it was the money." They all claim that they are trying to make a living just like the next person, but in this particular scenario, the man is the one with the upper hand because of what patriarchy produces for women in the male-dominated capitalistic market.

Networks: Is the Criminal Justice System Complicit with Traffickers?

The criminal justice system has not deterred human trafficking. It continues to be a much lower risk to traffic in women than it is to traffic in drugs or guns. Ahmet told me "Drugs and guns will get you 25 years [in prison]. Women, five to ten. So yeah, its better that way . . . and the women don't talk because they'll likely be killed." When companies use trafficked labor there is little threat of prosecution for employers. Penalties (including prison time and fines) for trafficking in human beings are steep, but they are only effective if the traffickers can be caught and convicted.[34]

For example, it has been noted in the Minnesota Human Trafficking Reports (September 2005, 2008) by the Office of Justice Programs (OJP) that because of the interaction between vulnerable populations, a demanding labor market, and the use of women and girls in commercial sexual exploitation, sex and labor trafficking flourish in Minnesota. One of the vulnerable populations mentioned by many respondents (service providers, nurses and law enforcement) in the 2005 study was the "newly immigrated or illegal worker." Many of these workers are easily exploited through fraud, force and/or coercion because they lack language skills and other skills that are easily exploited by those who use them for cheap labor and sexual exploitation.[35]

On September 30, 2005, the US Department of Homeland Security concluded that more reported immigrants arrived in Minnesota that year than any of the previous 25 years. In 2005, two in every five immigrants in Minnesota came from Africa, and Asia was second with 28 percent of all immigrants. Minnesota is now ranked second after California in the number of refugee arrivals, outpacing Florida and Washington, which ranked higher than Minnesota in 2004. And with all those numbers being reported and the high propensity for trafficking victims, in 2011 Minnesota only reported seven convictions under Minnesota Statute 609.322 (solicitation inducement and promotion of prostitution; sex trafficking); 24 convictions under Minnesota Statute 609.352 (Solicitation of a child); 5 convictions under Minnesota Statute 617.245 and 617.246 (Use of a Minor in a Sexual Performance); and 7 convictions under Statute 609.27 (Coercion). These convictions are insignificant when compared to the previous numbers reported in migrants, refugees, and asylum seekers and the estimated numbers of trafficking victims in Minnesota and the United States.

Nevertheless, the most considerable flows of migrants and trafficked persons are from poorer to richer destinations within and between countries. These examples are just the beginning of the complex trade routes used to ensure the stability of illegal trafficking. When we look at female migration and trafficking, most victims are from the Balkans and other Central European countries. Women are also trafficked from South America, West Africa (particularly Nigeria), and Southeast Asia (Thailand and Vietnam). When I asked the traffickers I interviewed where the majority of women came from, Cyril told me that women are trafficked from "Russia, Romania, Bulgaria, Germany, France, Holland . . . wherever." Ahmet told me that to the best of his knowledge, they are from "Albania, Russia, Poland, Czech Republic, Yugoslavia, and Africa." Ahmet transported women from Albania to Italy and then Italy to France. He went on to explain, "The base is Albania. The Eastern Europeans go to Albania and they are sold from there. They line them all up and you just go there and take your pick. The pimp is the main guy. The customer, if you will, no—let's say you are the pimp and go on the Internet and it's here tomorrow, that's like the business. I would be the middle guy who brings the stuff, what you ordered. They always have a middleman. I don't have anything to do with it after that." Ahmet indicated that there is a "middleman" that no one outside of the business necessarily knows or even hears about. In the business, "you are called the middleman because you know everyone and have the connections. You are the only one talking to both guys [the pimp and recruiter], so you are kind of the main man, I guess." These middlemen are also involved in other illegal trafficking businesses, such as drugs and weapons, because "they know everyone and everything." Ahmet also indicated that he has been involved in other trafficking businesses such as transporting refugees, drugs, and guns, which is not surprising since all these businesses follow the same transportation patterns. To them, whether it is people, drugs, or guns, they're all going to the same destinations and are all seen as a profitable commodity.

Discussion

If there were stable, reliable economic opportunities for women, would prostitution still be an appealing option? It is essential that we see gender and migration as an integrated piece of the puzzle; however, it should not be implied that all migration is gendered or that gendered migration only happens through trafficking. What should be evident is that this intersection is a growing aspect of international labor migration.[36] In more recent years, the United Kingdom proposed a "points-based" migration system where points will be allocated on the basis of skills, qualification, education, capital, and age. The person with the highest score on the first four topics and lowest score on the last topic (age) will be given the most points.[37] The higher the points one earns, the more likely he/she will be able to immigrate to a new country. While this system may seem harmless, it actually discriminates against women in developing countries because they are more likely to have less skills, education, and capital based upon what the global economy is searching for. In addition, when combined with a preference for younger migrant workers, this system further discriminates against women because of their tendency to take time off work or school to care for their children.[38] These restrictions are most likely linked to fact that government restrictions on migration are aimed at low-skilled migrants, namely women.[39] Plus, as legal immigration is made more difficult, the profit for traffickers rises proportionately.[40] Post 9/11 policies have made immigration guidelines more restrictive, making it more difficult for foreign workers, especially women, to migrate legally and find work. If they are not able to migrate legally, it forces them to seek out illegal ways to enter the country by being smuggled or even trafficked. Human traffickers connect the supply side of labor in the source countries to the demand side of labor in the destination countries. When there is no one to stop them (i.e.: government officials, police, etc) the business continues to grow.

Wheaton and her colleagues believe that "economic models are useful for the modeling of labor markets, and thus the market for human trafficking created by the supply and demand of exploitable labor."[41] A main theme in human trafficking research is the role traffickers' play in connecting employers (the source of "labor demand") to vulnerable migrants seeking employment.[42] As long as we have vulnerable, migrant populations searching for work in or outside of their country, we will continue to have trafficking in persons. Chuang refers to human trafficking as "'an opportunistic response' to the tensions between the economic necessity to migrate, on the one hand, and the politically motivated restrictions on migration, on the other."[43] Wheaton and her colleagues conclude that at very low quantities, traffickers can charge high prices for to those employers who demand trafficked workers.[44] Mass emigration lowers this recruitment cost for traffickers and those departing from high-emigration regions may share characteristics that make them more prone to being trafficked.[45]

In the United States, the George W. Bush campaign against trafficking put countries on a tier system, and depending on where they were placed, the United States would impose sanctions on them if they were not complying with US standards. The interesting fact here is that countries that oppose US imperialism—the majority having Muslim populations—or are labeled "rogue states" do not fare well.[46] Kempadoo details how the United States backed out of international plans to crack down on trafficking to avoid imposing sanctions on "friends" of the United States, including Israel, Russia, South Korea and Greece, while announcing its intentions to impose sanctions on Myanmar, Cuba, and North Korea.[47]

Bales gives a list of antitrafficking policies: ending world poverty, terminating corruption, slowing the population explosion, halting environmental destruction and armed conflict, canceling international debts, and getting governments to keep the promises they make every time they pass a law.[48] While this list seems out of reach in the immediate future, it does pinpoint the root causes of this growing global, social problem and gives us insight to the next steps. For one, it calls for a system of international cooperation to decrease the benefits that employers receive for using trafficked labor.[49] Wheaton and her colleagues believe that with the constant and growing supply of vulnerable populations, international border issues, and crime prevention obstacles, decreasing the supply of human trafficking is economically less efficient, although vitally necessary.[50]

Plus, the fact we still do not have a concise, all-encompassing, international definition of human trafficking is alarming. How are we supposed to stop something when we cannot agree on what it is? Because of this, the statistics that are being reported are meager attempts when compared to what they really should be. In Minnesota law, the conviction rate is embarrassing when compared to the projected number of trafficked persons in the state. The US TVPA leads the world in its definition of human trafficking, but as it has been expressed by several bodies of research, there are several words used in the definition that lack common ground on their subdefinitions. It can be implied here that if a felony lacks a definition, it cannot be controlled, nor can it be counted, measured, or controlled.[51] Only with precise definitions can we begin to gather data and apply conclusive analyses. At this point, human trafficking literature is almost entirely subjective.

Another action we must adopt is ending restrictive migratory practices, particularly against women. It has been documented throughout this chapter that gender is an imperative piece of migration. Restrictive migration policies make it more difficult for foreign workers to migrate and find work legally because they feel more insecure and vulnerable. Historically and economically, prohibition has not been a deterrent to stopping the illegal trade of goods and services. Bales suggests that a better solution would be to increase workers' ability to emigrate legally.[52] Having restrictions on migration further pushes it underground as restrictions have done for sex trafficking, in particular. He adds, "Making something illegal doesn't make it cease to exist; making it illegal only causes it to vanish from view."[53]

With dedicated attention to awareness campaigns and resources, this new-found awareness may allow populations to become educated on human trafficking—the warning signs and what to do when one suspects a person is being trafficked. The United Kingdom's plan of action against human trafficking calls for raising awareness of men who frequent establishments where sex trafficking is known to be used in its operation. The point here is to deter the demand for forced labor. While it is important to educate the general population, it is also imperative that we train the authorities including, but not limited to, the police, medical professionals (including first responders), homeless shelters, social workers, and street outreach organizations. The United Nations Office of Drugs and Crimes states, "Successful convictions depend on the police and others making the right decisions. This can only happen if they have the knowledge and capacity to respond to human trafficking."[54]

Furthermore, we must address how law enforcement and judicial systems treat trafficking victims as criminals. With the rapid increase in anti-immigration policies in first world countries post-9/11, laws and law enforcement agencies tend to identify *anyone* who enters the country illegally as a criminal.[55] Immigration and refugee policies post-9/11 narrowed the concepts of "safe third country," "secure borders," "safe haven," "fortress America," and others, but that did not stop the flow of people seeking to migrate for a better life; rather, migrants were more willing to take greater risks, often putting their lives or their families' lives on the line.[56] The United Nations Office on Drugs and Crime states, "Police and criminal justice staff need standard working procedures to guarantee the physical safety of victims, protect their privacy, and make it safe for them to testify against their abusers."[57] Until these root causes are addressed, trafficked humans will continue to be sold over and over again. If we continue on this path, it will not be long before human trafficking surpasses drugs as the most lucrative, illegal trade in the world.

Notes

1. US Government Accountability Office. "Better Data, Strategy, and Reporting Needed to Enhance U.S. Anti-trafficking Efforts Abroad." (2006), accessed September 26, 2012, http://www.gao.gov/products/GAO-06-825.

2. Under Secretary for Democracy and Global Affairs. "Trafficking in Persons Report: June 2007 (Trafficking Victims Protection Act of 2000)," US Department of State, Washington, DC (2007).

3. Patrick Belser. "Forced Labour and human trafficking: estimating the profits", Working paper no. 42, InFocus trafficking on Promoting the Declaration of Fundamental Principles and Rights at Work, *International Labour Organization*, Geneva. (2005).

4. Kevin Bales. *Disposable People: New Slavery in the Global Economy*, rev. ed. Berkeley: University of California Press (2004).

5. Ibid.

6. Minnesota Office of Justice Program: Minnesota Statistical Analysis Center. "Human Trafficking in Minnesota: A Report to the Minnesota Legislature" (2012).

7. Pranati Datta. "Female Trafficking and illegal migration from Bangladesh to India." *Pakistan Journal of Women's Studies: Alam-e-Niswan* 18, no.1 (2011): 47–62.

8. Ibid.

9. Jo Bindman. *Redefining Prostitution as Sex Work on the International Agenda*. London: Anti-Slavery International (1997).

10. Kathryn McMahon and Jennifer Stanger. *Speaking Out: Three Narratives of Women Trafficked to the United States*. Los Angeles: Coalition to Abolish Slavery and Trafficking (2002: i).

11. Bindman, *Redefining Prostitution as Sex Work on the International Agenda*, 3.

12. Minnesota Office of Justice Program, "Human Trafficking in Minnesota: A Report to the Minnesota Legislature."

13. Global Alliance Against Traffic in Women (GAATW). *Human Rights and Trafficking in Persons: A Handbook*. Bangkok: Indochina Publishing (2001:31).

14. Ibid., 32.

15. Bridget Anderson and Julia O'Connell Davidson. *Trafficking—a demand led problem?* Stockholm: Save the Children (2002:5).

16. Elizabeth M. Wheaton, Edward J. Schauer, and Thomas V. Galli. "Economics of Human Trafficking," *International Migration* 48, no. 4 (2010): 115–41.

17. Dolores Chew, "Gender, Migration and Trafficking—an Introduction." *Labour Capital and Society* 39, no.2 (2006): 1–18.

18. Ibid., 4.

19. Patricia R. Pessar and Sarah J. Mahler. "Transnational Migration: Bringing Gender In." *International Migration Review* 37, no.3 (2003): 812–46.

20. Ibid., 814.

21. Ibid.

22. Tania Bastia, "Stolen Lives or Lack of Rights? Gender, Migration and Trafficking," *Labour Capital and Society* 39, no.2. Retrieved from http://search.proquest.com/docview/235098427?accountid=14756.

23. Pessar and Mahler, "Transnational Migration."

24. Chew, "Gender, Migration and Trafficking."

25. Raewynn Connell, "Masculinities and Globalization," *Men and Masculinities* 1 (1998): 3–23.

26. Bastia, "Stolen Lives or Lack of Rights?" 20–47.

27. Connell, "Masculinities and Globalization."

28. Bastia, "Stolen Lives or Lack of Rights?"

29. Pessar and Mahler, "Transnational Migration."

30. Chew, "Gender, Migration and Trafficking."

31. Ibid.
32. Ibid., 11.
33. Bastia, "Stolen Lives or Lack of Rights?"
34. Pessar and Mahler, "Transnational Migration," 814.
35. Evelyn Nakano Glenn, "The Social Construction and Institutionalization of Gender and Race: An Integrative Framework," in *Revisioning Gender*, ed. M. M. Feree, J. Lorber, and B. B. Hess (Thousand Oaks, CA: Sage, 1999), 3–43.
36. Ratna Kapur, "Cross Border Movements and the Law," in *Trafficking and Prostitution Reconsidered—New Perspectives on Migration, Sex Work, and Human Rights*, ed. Kamala Kempadoo (Boulder, CO: Paradigm, 2005), 25–41.
37. US Department of Justice, "Assessment of U.S. Activities to Combat Trafficking in Persons," Washington, DC (2003).
38. Minnesota Office of Justice Programs, "Human Trafficking in Minnesota: A Report to the Minnesota Legislature" (September 2005).
39. Chew, "Gender, Migration and Trafficking."
40. Bastia, "Stolen Lives or Lack of Rights?"
41. Wheaton, Schauer, and Galli, "Economics of Human Trafficking," 116.
42. Wheaton, Schauer, and Galli, "Economics of Human Trafficking."
43. Janie Chuang, "Beyond a Snapshot: Preventing Human Trafficking in the Global Economy," *Indiana Journal of Global Legal Studies* 13, no.1 (2006): 137–63; Kevin Bales, *Ending Slavery: How We Free Today's Slaves* (Berkeley: University of California Press, 2007).
44. Wheaton, Schauer, and Galli, "Economics of Human Trafficking."
45. Ibid.
46. Kamala Kempandoo, ed. *Trafficking and Prostitution Reconsidered—New Perspectives on Migration, Sex Work and Human Rights* (Boulder, CO: Paradigm, 2005).
47. Kempandoo, *Trafficking and Prostitution Reconsidered*.
48. Kevin Bales, *Ending Slavery: How We Free Today's Slaves* (Berkeley: University of California Press, Berkeley (2007).
49. Wheaton, Schauer, and Galli, "Economics of Human Trafficking."
50. Ibid.
51. Toman O. Mahmoud and Christoph Trebesh, "The Economics of Human Trafficking and Labour Migration: Micro-evidence from Eastern Europe," *Journal of Comparative Economics*, 38 (2010): 173–88.
52. Kevin Bales, *Understanding Global Slavery* (Berkeley: University of California Press, 2005).
53. Bales, "Ending Slavery," 135.
54. UN Office of Drugs and Crime (2009), http://www.unodc.org.
55. Wheaton, Schauer, and Galli, "Economics of Human Trafficking."
56. Chew, "Gender, Migration and Trafficking."
57. UN Office of Drugs and Crime (2009), http://www.unodc.org/unodc/en/human-trafficking/protection.html.

Bibliography

Anderson, Bridget and Julia O'Connell Davidson. "Trafficking—a demand led problem?" Stockholm: Save the Children (2002).

Askola, Heli. "Violence against Women, Trafficking, and Migration in the European Union." *European Law Journal* 13, no.2 (2007): 204–17.

Bales, Kevin. *Disposable People: New Slavery in the Global Economy*, rev. ed. Berkeley: University of California Press (2004).

———. *Ending Slavery: How We Free Today's Slaves.* Berkeley: University of California Press, 2007.

———. *Understanding Global Slavery.* University of California Press, Berkeley (2005).

Bastia, Tanja. "Stolen Lives or Lack of Rights? Gender, Migration and Trafficking." *Labour Capital and Society* 39, no.2. (2006): 20–47. Retrieved from http://search .proquest.com/docview/235098427?accountid=14756.

Belser, Patrick. "Forced Labour and Human Trafficking: Estimating the Profits," Working paper no. 42, InFocus Programme on Promoting the Declaration of Fundamental Principles and Rights at Work, International Labour Organization, Geneva. (2005).

Bindman, Jo. *Redefining Prostitution as Sex Work on the International Agenda.* London: Anti-Slavery International (1997).

Blank, Jennifer K. "Sex Trafficking: An Exploratory Study." Unpublished master's thesis. Middlesex University. London, England (2003).

———. "Sex Trafficking—A 'Family Business.'" In Chapter 4, "International Violence and Oppression: Family Legacies of Colonization and Wars" In *Global Families*, rev. ed., edited by M. W. Karraker. Thousand Oaks: Sage. (2012).

Bridger, Sue, Rebecca Kay, and Kathryn Pinnick. *No More Heroines? Russia, Women and the Market.* London: Routledge (1996).

Chew, Dolores. "Gender, Migration and Trafficking-An Introduction." *Labour, Capital and Society* 39, no.2 (2006).

Chuang, Janie. "Beyond a Snapshot: Preventing Human Trafficking in the Global Economy." *Indiana Journal of Global Legal Studies.* Vol. 13, no.1 (2006): 137–63.

Connell, Raewyn. "Masculinities and Globalization" in *Men and Masculinities.* Vol. 1. (1998): 3–23.

Datta, Pranati. "Female Trafficking and Illegal Migration from Bangladesh to India." *Pakistan Journal of Women's Studies: Alam-e-Niswan* 18, no.1 (2011): 47–62.

Glenn, Evelyn Nakano. "The Social Construction and Institutionalization of Gender and Race: An Integrative Framework." In *Revisioning Gender.* Ed. M.M. Feree, J. Lorber, and B.B. Hess Thousand Oaks, CA: Sage. (1999): 3–43.

Global Alliance against Traffic in Women (GAATW). *Human Rights and Trafficking in Persons: A Handbook.* Bangkok: Indochina Publishing (2001).

Kapur, Ratna. "Cross Border Movements and the Law," in Kamala Kempadoo (ed), *Trafficking and Prostitution Reconsidered—New Perspectives on Migration, Sex Work, and Human Rights.* Boulder, CO: Paradigm (2005): 25–41.

Kempandoo, Kamala. *Trafficking and Prostitution Reconsidered- New Perspectives on Migration, Sex Work and Human Rights*. Boulder & London: Paradigm (2005).

Mahmoud, Toman O., and Christoph Trebesh. "The Economics of Human Trafficking and Labour Migration: Micro-evidence from Eastern Europe." *Journal of Comparative Economics* 38 (2010): 173–88.

McCreight, Matilde Ventrella. "Smuggling of Migrants, Trafficking in Human Beings and Irregular Migration on a Comparative Perspective." *European Law Journal* 12, no.1 (2006): 106–29.

McMahon, Kathryn, and Jennifer Stanger. "Speaking Out: Three Narratives of Women Trafficked to the United States." Los Angeles: Coalition to Abolish Slavery and Trafficking (2002).

Minnesota Office of Justice Program. "Human Trafficking in Minnesota: A Report to the Minnesota Legislature." Minnesota Statistical Analysis Center. September 2005. Accessed October 12, 2012. http://archive.leg.state.mn.us/docs/2010/mandated/100923.pdf.

Pessar, Patricia R., and Sarah J. Mahler. "Transnational Migration: Bringing Gender in." *International Migration Review* 37, no. 3 (2003): 812–45.

Ross-Sheriff, Fariyal. "Global Migration and Gender." *Affilia: Journal of Women and Social Work* 26, no. 3 (2011): 233–38.

Troshynski, Emily I., and Jennifer K. Blank. "Sex Trafficking: An Exploratory Study Interviewing Traffickers." *Trends in Organized Crime* 11, no.1 (2008): 30–41.

United Nations. "Protocol against the Smuggling of Migrants by Land, Sea and Air, Supplementing the United Nations Convention against Transnational Organized Crime (2000)." Accessed October 6, 2012, http://www.uncjin.org/Documents/Conventions/dcatoc/final_documents_2/convention_smug_eng.pdf.

———. "Protocol to Prevent, Suppress and Punish Trafficking in Persons, Especially Women and Children, Supplementing the United Nations Convention against Transnational Organized Crime (2000)." Accessed October 6, 2012, http://www.uncjin.org/Documents/Conventions/dcatoc/final_documents_2/convention_traff_eng.pdf.

United Nations, International Migration and Development. "International Migration Facts and Figures." Accessed September 19, 2012. http://www.ciett.org/fileadmin/templates/ciett/docs/Un>Migration_-_factsheet.pdf.

UN Office of Drugs and Crime. (2009). "Protecting Victims of Human Trafficking." Accessed September 26, 2012. http://www.unodc.org/unodc/en/human-trafficking/protection.html

Under Secretary for Democracy and Global Affairs. "Trafficking in Persons Report: June 2007 (Trafficking Victims Protection Act of 2000)." US Department of State, Washington, DC (2007).

US Department of Justice. "Assessment of U.S Activities to Combat Trafficking in Persons." Washington DC (2003).

US Department of State, "Human Smuggling and Trafficking Center." Accessed October 9, 2012. http://www.state.gov/m/ds/hstcenter/.

_____. "Trafficking in Persons Protection Act of 2000." Accessed September 26, 2012. http://www.state.gov/j/tip/rls/tiprpt/2007/86205.htm.

US Government Accountability Office. "Better Data, Strategy, and Reporting Needed to Enhance U.S. Anti-trafficking Efforts Abroad." (2006). Accessed September 26, 2012. http://www.gao.gov/products/GAO-06-825.

Warren, Kay B. "Troubling the Victim/Trafficker Dichotomy in Efforts to Combat Human Trafficking: The Unintended Consequences of Moralizing Labor Migration." *Indiana Journal of Global Legal Studies* 19, no. 1 (2012): 105–20.

Wheaton, Elizabeth M., Edward J. Schauer, and Thomas V. Galli. "Economics of Human Trafficking." *International Migration* 48, no. 4 (2010): 115–41.

CHAPTER 5

The Ripple Effects of Deportation Policies on Mexican Women and Their Children

*Joanna Dreby**

Since 2009, the US government has deported a record high of 1.06 million people, nearly 400,000 each year.[1] This represents more than twice the 189,000 who were deported in 2001.[2] Now at an all-time high, deportation and removal is one of the primary features of immigration enforcement efforts at the start of the twenty-first century.

Much of the public support for deportation policies rests on the assumption that deportees are criminals and undesirable members of US society. Yet research shows that deportees typically are not criminal offenders.[3] Many live in families with spouses and children; more than 100,000 of those deported between 1998 and 2007 were parents of US-born citizens.[4] In the first six months of 2011, the Department of Homeland Security deported more than 46,000 parents of US citizen children.[5]

Deportations disproportionally affect men. While the Department of Homeland Security has not released data on the gender composition of deportees, research suggests that in most cases, men are the ones who are arrested, detained, and deported.[6] For example, a recent report on Secure Communities found that men constituted 93 percent of detainees, even though only 57 percent of the unauthorized population is male.[7] Women and children must manage the aftermath of their fathers', husbands', and sons' removals.

* Address correspondence to Joanna Dreby, PhD, Department of Sociology, University at Albany, State University of New York, Arts and Sciences 327, 1400 Washington Avenue, Albany, NY 12222. Email: jdreby@albany.edu.

Deportations also disproportionally affect Mexicans. Mexicans make up approximately 30 percent of the foreign-born and 58 percent of the unauthorized population in this country.[8] In 2010, 83 percent of the detained, 73 percent of those forcibly removed, and 77 percent of voluntary departures were Mexican.[9] In the United States, more than seven million children in 2009 lived with parents from Mexico.[10]

Deportation policies differentially affect Mexicans because few legalization opportunities exist for undocumented Mexicans. Parents cannot apply for legal status through their minor children. Family-based petitions through resident or citizen siblings or parents take years due to a lengthy waiting list and backlogs in applications from Mexico. Even those who marry US citizens find the pathway to legalization blocked. Under current law, those who entered the United States without inspection—in other words, across the border—face bars to readmission via a spousal petition: three or ten years (depending on the length of unlawful presence) or a permanent bar for repeat offenders (those who have illegally crossed more than once). Visas from Mexico are hard to obtain; thus many Mexicans enter without inspection. They are ineligible to legalize through a US citizen spouse or an employer without returning to Mexico first, in the best case scenario. These family members of US citizens and permanent residents can be deported at any time.

Women and children in Mexican immigrant households increasingly face what De Genova terms the "threat of deportability."[11] Regardless of whether or not a family member is actually deported, attentive to the significant increase in deportations, Mexican family members begin to fear and prepare for this potential outcome. The threat of deportation devastates immigrant communities and carries a huge burden for children and their families.[12]

This chapter tells the story of how under existing US immigration policy, deportations have had a rippling effect, shaping the daily lives of women and children in Mexican families who have *never* experienced a detention or deportation. Between 2009 and 2012, I interviewed 110 children and 91 parents in two sites, one in central New Jersey and one in northeast Ohio. The sites in Ohio and New Jersey differ strategically: the Mexican community in Ohio is small and disperse while the community in New Jersey is densely concentrated and highly visible. Despite these and other differences across the two communities, members of the more than eighty families I met in both sites described the similar effects (il)legality[13] has had on their lives. Under a system in which legalization is not an option and the possibility of deportation looms large, the impact of (il)legality on family members' everyday experiences intensifies.

In this chapter, I showcase the accounts of three families, two in Ohio and one in New Jersey. Each family member's experiences are unique but illustrate patterns evident in my larger sample. The story of Isabel in Ohio exemplifies the ways that (il)legality uniquely shapes women's lives, whether due to the way it complicates domestic disputes or more simply makes everyday survival a challenge. The stories of 11-year-old Carmen in Ohio and 12-year-old Edward in New Jersey show how (il)legality affects children. Carmen is undocumented, unlike her parents and siblings; her legal status stymies her future prospects. Edward, in contrast, is a US citizen. Yet (il)legality also shapes his fears about potential separations and the stigma he associates with immigration.[14]

Taken together these stories point to the ways that current public policy compromises the health and well-being of women and children in the United States as well as their prospects for integration. The threat of deportation affects families' interpersonal relationships, as all three accounts attest. The complications of (il)legality—and especially mixed legal statuses within families—also make daily life extremely difficult, producing a culture of fear, socially segregating those without status, and heightening inequalities within families.

Abused and Illegal

Thirty-nine-year-old Isabel—dressed in a matching eggplant-colored sweat suit—prepared a varied breakfast of eggs, quesadillas, sausages, and French toast in her newly renovated kitchen. I sat on a tall stool at the in kitchen table: a black marbled countertop jutting out from the wall. Not sure how to help, I listened. Isabel, a good head shorter than me, her hair dyed blond and face heavily made up for 11 o'clock on a Sunday morning, took her time with the breakfast, slowly grating cheese and breaking eggs, enjoying the ritual while explaining her predicament. More than an hour later, when my two children and her three, ages seven, five, and three, came in to eat, they barely dented the mounds of food she had made.

Isabel had moved in only a few weeks ago but seemed settled. The kitchen opened into an equally small dining room, where a glass-top table stood, and then into another room, cramped by a white faux-leather sectional, glass coffee table, and large-screen television. For a woman recently separated from a husband who had turned violent and mean, I was impressed.

Isabel may have had her physical needs met, but emotionally she was on edge. Later in the afternoon, after pulling out a photo of her ex—a tall, blond all-American—she told me, "But I love this man still. If this man said, 'Come back with me,' I would go back. For my children, because I love him. It's that he is my güero [my white boy]."

During the breakfast prep, Isabel described her struggles to provide for her children with the $320 she earned a week cleaning the house of her wealthy employer. "My husband has never given me even a dollar. Not when we were married, and now even less. He used to say that he wouldn't ever give money to any women." Isabel switched to English to mimic him, "He would say, 'I'm not giving money to any woman. I don't care who she is.'" Then she said in Spanish, "Y yo le decía, 'Pero yo soy tu esposa' [I'd say but I am your wife]. [He'd answer] I don't care."

Isabel fell in love with her American-born husband five years earlier, in 2005, at her job on the line at a factory where he worked in quality control. They dated for three months and then, Isabel pregnant, they married. They traveled to Mexico for the wedding. "We made all the arrangements from here, so that all I did was go back to get married there. I wanted to be with my family. It was the first time I ever got married."

I am not sure how Isabel managed that trip. Isabel did not have legal permission to reenter the United States because she had first crossed the border in 2000 and was an undocumented immigrant. Originally, Isabel aspired to migrate legally; from Mexico she applied for a visa three times. Repeatedly denied, she took a visa for Canada instead and crossed into Seattle, Washington, to live with her mother's cousins. In Mexico, Isabel had been an aerobics instructor. All her classmates studied abroad. Her cousins lived here. She wanted to come too.

In Seattle, Isabel got pregnant with a boyfriend who then left her. Family members on her father's side encouraged her to move closer to them in Ohio, where the cost of living was lower so they could help with the baby. She agreed. But in Ohio working and providing for her daughter proved difficult, so she sent the baby to live with a sister in Mexico. During that period, Isabel met her husband, "el güero." They lived together for four years, raising their own two children alongside Isabel's daughter, who they brought back from Mexico.

This was before the relationship turned sour, apparently due to el güero's sudden lack of interest and his abuse. Isabel explained, "You cannot beg for love. You cannot beg someone who is telling you, 'I don't love you. I don't feel anything for you. Everything about you bothers me.'"

Isabel had not yet divorced. But she continued to be undocumented. Laws prevented her application for legal residency through her marriage to el güero or her three US-born citizen children. Even if she were eligible, I doubt he would have complied.

I never met el güero, but I spoke with him at length over the phone. This was months later when I'd hoped to observe Isabel's seven-year-old at school. Although el güero was not the girl's biological father, he was unemployed and so he watched all three children after school until Isabel got home from work. She felt she needed his consent. So I called. After a forty-minute conversation that felt more like an argument, he assented. Given the trouble he gave me over the phone for something that did not involve him, I could not imagine his cooperation for a family-based petition that requires a written affidavit of financial support.

What's more, when Isabel and el güero fought, he was violent and repeatedly threatened to report her undocumented status to the authorities. Once, for example, instead of hitting her, he kicked the television, breaking it to pieces. Although no longer together, the fighting continued. "At any moment he arrives, he grabs the yellow pages and he says, 'I am going to call immigration right now, the police.' I say 'Call them. What are they going to do to me? Absolutely nothing.' So he doesn't call. But it is always the same. [She switches to English.] 'I'll call immigration. Then I'll get my kids. And you'll go like this' [snapping her fingers]."

If not for Isabel's employer, she would not have been in this house serving breakfast. Shortly after meeting el güero, Isabel left the factory and began working for an older Jewish couple. At first, she lived in their home. After she had her son and brought her daughter from Mexico, she moved into a house el güero purchased. But he lost his job and stopped paying the mortgage. The house went into foreclosure; then he moved out. Eventually, Isabel had to leave. "My boss bought this house for me when he saw all these problems that I was having." At the time, Isabel had not told him about her legal situation, only her personal dilemmas. When he agreed to help and requested some paperwork, she realized she had to tell.

> I gathered my courage and I said, "Sir, I need to speak with you about something very important. You know what? I am illegal. What you are asking me for [paperwork for the purchase of the home] I cannot give you." He asked me to explain. I explained. "Whatever you decide, I accept. If you want to dismiss me, I will still thank you with all of my heart." "What are you talking about? My wife adores you." He made me laugh. "My wife loves you more than me." Thank God I told him the truth. I told him absolutely everything.

Isabel's employer's support was unwavering. "He said, 'Don't worry, we will get you the best lawyer.' But the best lawyer wouldn't take the case. He said we wouldn't win."

Isabel also depended on her in-laws. El güero's sister was angry with her brother for his abuse and for his sudden change of heart. She agreed to put all Isabel's bills for the house in her name, since Isabel would not have been able to set up the utilities without a social security number. She insured Isabel's car, which Isabel drove without a license out of necessity.

Isabel managed to piece together a living arrangement that worked, for the time being. But it was a fragile support system in which she depended heavily on her employer's benevolence, the goodwill of her in-laws, and the cooperation of her ex, despite his abuse.

One version of the American dream is to come to this country, fall in love, and make a new life here. Isabel did all that, but it turned into a nightmare. The man she fell in love with stopped working, let their house fall into foreclosure, refused to support her economically, and—when he decided he didn't love her anymore—left and became angry and abusive.

Isabel's (il)legality frames this American dream-turned-nightmare. The US embassy denied her visa applications repeatedly. She came anyway. Then Isabel married a US citizen, but she was ineligible for residency due to her undocumented status. She fell in love, regardless. When the love turned sour and her ex turned abusive, she faced the threat of deportation every time they argued. Isabel persevered with the help of others. But her lack of a legal status deeply affected her personal relationships, from the one with her employers marked by dependency to the one with her ex, who used the legal status issue as a tool for his abuse.

Isabel's (il)legality also added difficulties to her parenting. Single motherhood involved economic challenges, but Isabel also worried about her ability to retain custody of her children. I visited Isabel eight months after our first interview. She recounted the extent to which she continued in a legal limbo, what Cecilia Menjivar has described in other circumstances as a state of "liminal legality."[15]

> Last week I was over there because the kids wanted to play in his backyard. So I went to pick them up and was sitting on the step. And he started to get abusive. So I called the police. The police asked for my ID—my license—because my car was there in the driveway. And el güero said, "Oh, she doesn't have a license," just to get me in trouble. The police officer was nice and just said that I had better get a license before I start driving the car all around. But he keeps trying to get me in trouble. He wants custody of the kids. He is saying that since I have no papers he should get custody of the kids so they won't be abandoned if I ever get deported.

Undocumented and Unequal

"Her biggest worry is this [her legal status]. She evades people so they will not ask her questions because she is afraid that they will ask her for a social security number . . . she started biting her nails out of worry."

This was Anita describing her 12-year-old daughter, Carmen, when I first interviewed the family in 2009. I had asked Anita how their move to the United States had affected each of her five daughters. According to Anita, it had been hardest on Carmen, who was nine when they arrived in Ohio.

Although Carmen could be shy, she never was around me. Whenever we met in the church basement during the Saturday youth program, Carmen pointedly came over to say hi, smiling brightly and squeezing my son Dylan's hand or patting his hair, exclaiming, "He is soooo cute." Often she wore her shoulder-length light brown hair back in a tight ponytail, revealing a perfectly clear complexion. Carmen stood as tall as her 14-year-old sister but had not yet developed a teenager's curves. While her older sister attended soccer practice and her mother worked, Carmen usually took charge of her younger siblings, ages 10, 6, and 5.

The siblings had all been born in Mexico. Anita migrated to Ohio three years ago with a visa. But four of her children had not, making their story fairly unique. In most mixed-status families, the parents are undocumented and the children are US citizens.[16] It is also typical for the older children to be undocumented and the younger siblings to be citizens. Here the situation flipped. Anita, her husband, and their oldest daughter were legal permanent residents. Eventually, they applied for citizenship. But the younger four children were undocumented and ineligible for legalization.

Anita's husband first migrated in 1992 to California as a seasonal laborer. "My husband had been living in the United States for nine years, I didn't see him . . . I mean, he would come and go for temporary work. He would be here for seven to eight months and then he would go back to Mexico. Every year." After California he moved to Tennessee and then to Ohio, which he liked best. "He was able to put in an immigration application in 1995. Ten years of waiting and then it went through in 2006."

When Anita's husband originally applied for a visa, the couple only had one daughter, so she they only included her on the application. "Since we didn't know all the rules, we didn't put in for the other ones." At the time, Anita lived in a small rancho, an agricultural community, in the state of Guadalajara. Neither she nor her husband had studied past the third grade, and Anita never worked outside of the home in Mexico. Dependent on the money her husband sent from his work abroad, she hired someone to help her with the domestic chores involved with raising five children on her own and looking after the family's land.

Anita clearly recalled the day of her immigration appointment on March 22, 2006. The trip to the consulate for the appointment exhausted her emotionally and mentally, as did figuring out where the family would live over the next few months. "I came [to Ohio] after a month, the 21st of May, with my oldest daughter. I went back for the other four in June." Anita and her husband planned for their eldest to live in Ohio; she would study while her father worked and looked after her. But Anita's husband found he couldn't watch his daughter and keep his job. So Anita came back, this time with her other children, who she could not bear to live without. "I came back. I entered legally.

My four daughters didn't . . . A woman put them under a blanket and thank God we all arrived well."

The move deeply affected Anita and her family. "I thought that life in the US was very different. That it was nice clothes. That is was a life without pressure. But it isn't like that. If I don't work, I don't have. Here life is very hurried; one doesn't enjoy life, nor the kids."

Above all, the mixed legal status of Anita and her children presented a major hurdle and a source of tension in the family. "For me coming to this country when we don't all have documents has been mentally exhausting. The children have the attitude that they cannot—for example, that they cannot have medical insurance. This affects them a lot." Aside from access to doctors and the dentist, Anita said her children worried about college, even at the young age of ten. They aspired to do well at school, but then "they don't know how they will go on to college, as illegals. They ask questions that are sometimes so difficult to answer."

The ability to travel also differentiated the siblings. The oldest had been back to Mexico periodically with her parents. After Anita and her oldest returned to Mexico for two weeks for an aunt's graduation, for example, "the others complain[ed], 'How come you don't take us?'"

Carmen still remembered Mexico but did not want to talk much about it in our interview. When I pressed she struggled to articulate feelings of constraint.

> CARMEN: Um . . . if I could describe it, it's—I don't know—it's very different than here.
> JOANNA: Okay. How is it different?
> CARMEN: In some ways, it's like a tad bit . . . [pause] like . . . the ability to talk to different people . . . like you meet somebody, and you're not as concerned as here. You, like you have to be careful everywhere, but it's just different in Mexico.

In interviews the children regularly complained that they experienced more physical freedom in Mexico. But Carmen described not only constraint but also the need to be *careful*. Taken together with Anita's comments about Carmen's fears and tendency to evade others and her otherwise exuberant personality, Carmen's comment suggests that she felt her (il)legality marked her and had to be carefully managed.

Carmen—like many others—avoided directly talking about how (il)legality affected her life. She denied feeling jealous of her older sister, for example. But when I visited and asked about school, Carmen alluded to the scholarship her sister received as an opportunity she herself would not be able to take advantage of despite her better grades. And while her older sister studied extra to meet the heavy requirements of the program, Carmen's responsibilities at home augmented.

Carmen also admitted that she felt afraid, at times, due to her legal status, though she did not want to talk about it. I asked, "Does it ever make you scared that you're an immigrant?"

> **CARMEN:** Yea, sometimes.
> **JOANNA:** Why?
> **CARMEN:** 'Cause.
> **JOANNA:** Just 'cause?
> **CARMEN:** Yea.
> **JOANNA:** Are you ever afraid you'll be sent back?
> **CARMEN:** Yea.

Research suggests that the negative impact of an undocumented status on youth becomes more pronounced as children age.[17] The normalizing routines of elementary and middle school protect students like Carmen from the negative impacts of (il)legality. But once youth move outside of school settings, begin to look for a job, get ready to drive a car, or seek admission to college, their lack of status stands out as compared to their peers with status, effectively excluding them from US society.[18] My interviews show that in an era of increased deportation, undocumented children at younger ages know that legal status makes them different from their peers, requiring them to "be careful."

Undocumented youth differ not only from their peers but also from members of their families, especially US citizen siblings who are able to apply for college scholarships, access health insurance, travel to Mexico, and eventually get driver's licenses. With the high prevalence of mixed-status families nationwide, (il)legality diminishes opportunities outside the home. It also exacerbates and intensifies existing inequalities within families. This is true for siblings like Carmen whose lack of opportunities contrasted to those of her sister. It also is true for parents and children, as the next story illustrates.

The Stigma of Immigration

Eleven-year-old Edward had never been to Mexico. I perched on the edge of a secondhand sofa covered by a white sheet in the second-floor apartment where he lived with his parents, an eight-year-old brother, and a three-year-old sister. Olive-skinned Edward had the same thick, wavy black hair, round race, and earnest look of his father, Mauro. I first met Mauro years ago when he registered for ESL classes. At the time Mauro had been in New Jersey for two years: he left his school on the coast of Oaxaca at the age of 16 to come work in the United States.

Young and bright, Mauro placed in the higher-level class. He dreamed of college. Now having spent half of his life in the United States, Mauro aspired only for his children. "I wanted to be someone in life. To be a professional. I could not do it. So I would like my children to be someone."

As a US citizen, Edward's future prospects differed from those of his father and mother, who were both undocumented. Edward and his brother and sister had health insurance through Medicaid; his parents tried not to get sick. Edward could potentially go on to college, something his father was never able to do. He could also travel back to Mexico. Neither Mauro nor his wife had been able to go back to Mexico since they had migrated as teenagers, although each continued to call and send monthly remittances back to their parents.

Despite these differences between Edward's and Mauro's outlook, some of the disadvantages of (il)legality passed down from father to son.[19] For one, Edward lived in a low-income family; both his parents earned little in jobs that did not require proper documentation and had no room for advancement. They could not afford to move out of the two-bedroom apartment where they had lived for the past ten years in an area of the city where youth gangs dominate. Mauro kept a tight rein on Edward and his siblings; he encouraged Edward's interest in soccer, taking him to practice and games three to four days a week. But Mauro could not prevent Edward from hanging out with the neighborhood kids. "There are some friends who are out until nine at night, hanging out down there. I say, 'No, I don't want that. You can play for a little while then you come back up here' . . . I tell them, 'I love you very much. I don't want to see you in jail or in the hospital.'"

Second, like his parents, Edward had never traveled. His parents could not take him on vacation due to their hectic work schedules, nor did they have enough resources to send him on his own to Mexico. Edward said he doesn't know anything about Mexico. "What do you think it's like?" I asked. "They say to come visit. They say it's nice. That it never snows there. You could be playing, playing every day, running around, going to a beach."

"That sounds kind of fun, would you like to go to Mexico?" I added. He shook his head no. "No? How come? You make it sound so nice. Why don't you want to go?"

"I don't know," said Edward, coming up with an excuse. "I'm afraid of heights."

His parents' (il)legality shaped Edward's life in contradictory ways. Citizenship afforded Edward opportunities unavailable to his parents, yet the disadvantages of his parents' (il)legality curtailed these opportunities. Edward was not undocumented, as were his parents. But like Carmen he too was socially different from his peers who had citizen parents.

Mexico loomed large for both Edward and his parents but had different meanings for each, introducing a chasm between parent and child. Mauro and his wife wanted to stay in New Jersey "for the children." But they had begun plans to build a home on land they purchased in the event that they must return. "If they send us, we will go and work there," Mauro explained.

Edward, in contrast, proudly plastered photos of the Mexican national soccer team on his bedroom walls but simultaneously distanced himself from his Mexican heritage. Edward preferred that the other kids at school not know that his parents were immigrants from Mexico, because, he said, "then everybody gets everything spread around the whole school. Then they start making rumors." For Edward, the fact that his parents are Mexican immigrants was a private affair: "'Cause I don't really like to tell what happened, like what has happened in, like in our life." Other children mirrored Edward's reaction. Of those interviewed, nearly a third (n = 32) said they preferred that their peers not know their parents are Mexican (if they did not already know), and approximately half (n = 51) preferred that others not know their parents are immigrants.

Ironically, Edward lived in a community with a high concentration of Mexican immigrants. Most of the parents of the other kids at his school were born in Mexico. Why did Edward associate a stigma with being the child of a Mexican immigrant when so many others were just like him?

It is not so much Mexico but the meaning children like Edward ascribed to immigration. I asked Edward (and all the children I interviewed) if he knew what an immigrant was and what it was like to be an immigrant. "Weird," he told me.

"In what way is it weird?" I asked.

"That, um, people think . . . like the people that are not from here that, um, they're not supposed to be here." Other children also equated immigrant with illegal, like the ten-year-old who told me, "Yeah, [an immigrant] is when someone is illegal in this country and police-ICE [Immigration Control and Enforcement] come to look for them to send them back to their country." As a US citizen, Edward knew he was different from an immigrant and thus dissociated from his parents' immigrant past in peer group interactions. Like others, he had begun to link a stigma with immigration, confounding immigration with (il)legality.[20]

ICE had never picked up Edward's mother and father, but he knew this was a possibility. Once, when Edward was three, the police stopped Mauro while he was driving with a "bad" license. Mauro explained, "I thought that the license and insurance were valid. But they were fakes. When the police stopped me, right there they arrested me and they made [my wife] and Edward and [brother] get out to the car." He added, "They were crying, there on the side of the road." Mauro received a fine, but at that time local police did not report him to ICE, something that has since become a much more common.

I asked Edward, "Do you ever feel proud that you have family of immigrants?" He said no. "No? Do you ever feel scared that your family members are immigrants?"

EDWARD: A little.
JOANNA: Can you tell me about that? Why do you feel scared?
EDWARD: Um, 'cause they take, they take parents away from little kids. They take them back to their country.

Edward went on to say he did not know anyone this had happened to except on the news. Later that evening, my thighs stuck to the white plastic seat covers sitting at Mauro's metal kitchen table while I picked at the chicken slow-cooked in red chile sauce Mauro's wife served me with homemade tortillas. We laughed at my inability to eat too much chile, and then our conversation turned back to immigration. I asked if the kids ever seemed scared. Mauro and his wife explained that earlier in the year the father of Edward's friend at school was deported.

MAURO: There was a time that he came home very worried.
WIFE: There was a time when there was a bunch of immigration raids. Here.
MAURO: So they said.
WIFE: I think he was scared because of [what happened] to the father of one of the kids, his classmate . . . he would come home crying . . . he didn't want them to get us. I told him, "Papi, we won't go out. If they say [ICE] is by French Street, I wouldn't go near French Street for the life of me. And here in the apartment, they cannot come get me." That calmed him down some.

The potential deportation of his parents clearly haunted Edward's imagination.

Edward did not fully comprehend the nuances of immigration, equating illegality and immigration. But he recognized the implications immigration policy had for his family. He worried his parents would be deported, so he avoided talking about immigration with his friends and to some extent with me, deciding it was a private affair. He also identified a stigma with immigration and distanced himself from it. Edward knew that as a US-born citizen, he was different from his parents. This scared him. Yet this difference ultimately put both he and his parents at risk, making his prospects growing up in the United States different from those with legal status. Edward left this parting message when I asked him what he would like to tell President Obama if he could: "To get a better economy and to not have them to take our parents away and take them back to their country."

Conclusion

In this chapter I told the stories of just three of the eighty families I interviewed to illustrate the rippling effects (il)legality has had on women and children living in the United States. Deportation policies tear apart families when a member is deported.[21] But the reach of such policies goes beyond families who are directly impacted by a deportation act. Taken together the stories highlight three themes in the ways deportation policies shape the lives of women and children who have never experienced a deportation.

First, the threat of deportation creates a culture of fear in immigrant communities and families.[22] Women and children fear their own potential deportation; they act in ways to hide aspects of their experiences from others or to be "careful" in their interactions so as not to get asked too many questions that might reveal their status. Edward did not tell his peers about his parent's background. Carmen avoided interactions with others so they would not ask her too many questions. Isabel hid her status from her employers until she could no longer do so and grew nervous every time her husband threatened to call ICE. This underlying state of fear compromises women and children's sense of well-being.

Second, under the threat of deportation, (il)legality makes aspects of daily life difficult, disadvantaging women and children as compared to their peers with legal status. Isabel struggled to survive as a single mother, mobilizing various people to help her with utility bills, car insurance, and ultimately her home. Although impressive, Isabel remained highly dependent on these social networks for daily survival. (Il)legality increased her dependency. Carmen's own undocumented status presented challenges to her schooling; while her sister attended a college prep program, Carmen went on to the poor-performing neighborhood high school, curtailing her mobility and integration post-migration. For Edward, it was his parents' (il)legality that prevented him from enjoying all the rights of his own citizenship. The disadvantages of (il)legality get passed down from parent to child, making Edwards prospects distinctly different from other children whose parents do not face such legal barriers.[23]

Third, the stories show that (il)legality complicates existing inequalities between spouses, siblings and parents, and children in families. For Isabel, the lack of status shaped all her interactions with her abusive ex, who threatened with reporting her so that he could gain custody of the couple's children. Carmen's (il)legality differentiated her the most from her older sister, who gained a prestigious school scholarship, traveled frequently to Mexico, and would soon apply for a driver's license, all things that Carmen would be unable to do. Instead she spent much of her time caring for her siblings. And for Edward, (il)legality shaped his identity formation, differentiating him from his immigrant parents. Associating a stigma with his parents' immigration story, Edward did not feel proud that they had worked so hard to provide him with a better life. Edward hid his family's experiences from his peers even though many, ironically, were in a similar situation.

Public policy quite often impacts microlevel relationships between family members. However, the direct link between policy and family life is usually not nearly so apparent. In this case, we see how deportation policies create a culture of fear, socially differentiate those with status irregularities from their peers, and intensify inequalities between family members. As long as the US government continues to use deportation tactics as the primary means for immigration enforcement, (il)legality and the threat of deportability will continue to negatively affect the lives of women and children.

Notes

1. US Department of Homeland Security, "FY 2011: ICE Announces Year-End Removal Numbers, Highlights Focus on Key Priorities Including Threats to Public Safety and National Security," accessed July 20, 2012, http://www.ice.gov/news/releases/1110/111018washingtondc.html.

2. US Department of Homeland Security, Office of Immigration Statistics, "Immigration Enforcement Actions: 2010," accessed July 20, 2012, http://www.dhs.gov/xlibrary/assets/statistics/publications/enforcement-ar-2010.pdf.

3. Tanya Golash-Boza, *Immigration Nation: Raids, Detentions, and Deportations in Post–9/11 America* (Boulder, CO: Paradigm, 2011).

4. US Department of Homeland Security, Office of the Inspector General, "Removals of Illegal Alien Parents of United States Citizen Children," Report No. OIG-09-15, 2009, accessed July 20, 2012, http://www.dhs.gov/xoig/assets/mgmtrpts/OIG_09 -15_Jan09.pdf.

5. Seth Wessler, "U.S. Deports 46K Parents with Citizen Kids in Just Six Months," *Colorlines* (2011), accessed July 20, 2012, http://colorlines.com/archives/2011/11/shocking_data_on_parents_deported_with_citizen_children.html.

6. David Brotherton and Luis Barrios, *Banished to the Homeland: Dominican Deportees and Their Stories of Exile* (New York: Columbia University Press, 2011); Joanna Dreby, "The Burden of Deportation on Children in Mexican Immigrant Families," *Journal of Marriage and Family* 74 (2012): 829–45; Golash-Boza, *Immigration Nation*; Pierette Hondagneu-Sotelo and Tanya Golash-Boza, "Latino Immigrant Men and the Deportation Crisis: A Gendered Racial Removal Program?," unpublished manuscript.

7. Anarti Kohli, Peter Markowitz, and Lisa Chavez, *Secure Communities by the Numbers: An Analysis of Demographics and Due Process* (Berkeley: University of California, Berkeley Law School, 2011), accessed July 20, 2012, http://www.law.berkeley.edu/files/Secure_Communities_by_the_Numbers.pdf.

8. Jeffrey Passel and D'Vera Cohn, *Unauthorized Immigrant Population: National and State Trends 2010* (Pew Hispanic Center, 2011), accessed July 20, 2012, http://pewhispanic.org/files/reports/133.pdf.

9. US Department of Homeland Security, "Immigration Enforcement Actions: 2010."

10. Urban Institute, data from the Integrated Public Use Microdata Series datasets drawn from the 2005–2009 American Community Survey, accessed July 20, 2012, http://datatool.urban.org/charts/datatool/pages.cfm.

11. Nicolas De Genova, "Migrant 'Illegality' and Deportability in Everyday Life," *Annual Review of Anthropology* 31 (2002): 419–47.

12. Dreby, "The Burden of Deportation on Children in Mexican Immigrant Families"; Jaqueline Hagan, Briana Castro, and Nestor Rodriguez, "The Effects of U.S. Deportation Policies on Immigrant Families and Communities: Cross-border Perspectives," *North Carolina Law Review* 88 (2010): 1799–1824; Cecilia Menjivar, "The Power of the Law: Central America's Legality and Everyday Life in Phoenix, Arizona," *Latino Studies* 9 (2011): 377–95.

13. I use the term *(il)legality* to emphasize the fluidity of legal statuses that shape family members' lives. This encompasses both those who are undocumented or illegal as well as those who have legal status but may have family members who are illegal.

14. I use pseudonyms throughout this chapter and have changed minor details in the family accounts to protect the identities of the participants.

15. Cecilia Menjivar, "Liminal Legality: Salvadoran and Guatemalan Immigrants' Lives in the United States," *American Journal of Sociology* 111 (2006): 999–1037.

16. Passel and Cohn, *Unauthorized Immigrant Population: National and State Trends 2010*.

17. Leisy Abrego, "'I Can't Go to College Because I Don't Have Papers': Incorporation Patterns of Latino Undocumented Youth," *Latino Studies* 4 (2006): 212–31; Roberto Gonzales, " Learning to be Illegal," *American Sociological Review* 76 (2011): 602–19.

18. Abrego, "'I Can't Go to College Because I Don't Have Papers'"; Gonzales, "Learning to be Illegal."

19. Kalina Brabeck and Qingwen Xu, "The Impact of Detention and Deportation on Latino Immigrant Children and Families: A Quantitative Exploration," *Hispanic Journal of Behavioral Sciences* 32 (2010): 341–61; Hiro Yoshikawa, *Immigrants Raising Citizens: Undocumented Parents Raising Children* (New York: Russell Sage Foundation, 2011).

20. Leisy Abrego, "Legal Consciousness of Undocumented Latinos: Fear and Stigma as Barriers to Claims-making for First and 1.5 Generation Immigrants," *Law & Society Review* 45 (2011): 337–69; Dreby, "The Burden of Deportation on Children in Mexican Immigrant Families."

21. Applied Research Council, "Shattered Families" (2011), accessed July 20, 2012, http://arc.org/shatteredfamilies; Randy Capps et. al., *Paying the Price: The Impact of Immigration Raids on America's Children* (Urban Institute for the National Council of La Raza, 2007), accessed July 20, 2012, http://www.urban.org/Uploaded-PDF/411566_immigration_raids.pdf; Ajay Chaudry et al., *Facing Our Future: Children in the Aftermath of Immigration Enforcement* (Urban Institute, 2010), accessed July 20, 2012, http://carnegie.org/fileadmin/Media/Publications/facing_our_future.pdf.

22. Hagan, Castro, and Rodriguez, "The Effects of U.S. Deportation Policies on Immigrant Families and Communities"; Menjivar, "The Power of the Law."

23. Brabeck and Xu, "The Impact of Detention and Deportation on Latino Immigrant Children and Families."

Bibliography

Abrego, Leisy. "'I Can't Go to College Because I Don't Have Papers': Incorporation Patterns of Latino Undocumented Youth." *Latino Studies* 4 (2006): 212–31.

———. "Legal Consciousness of Undocumented Latinos: Fear and Stigma as Barriers to Claims-Making for First and 1.5 Generation Immigrants." *Law & Society Review* 45 (2011): 337–69.

Applied Research Council. "Shattered Families." 2011. Accessed July 20, 2012. http://arc.org/shatteredfamilies.

Brabeck, Kalina, and Qingwen Xu. "The Impact of Detention and Deportation on Latino Immigrant Children and Families: A Quantitative Exploration." *Hispanic Journal of Behavioral Sciences* 32 (2010): 341–61.

Brotherton, David, and Luis Barrios. *Banished to the Homeland: Dominican Deportees and Their Stories of Exile.* New York: Columbia University Press, 2011.

Capps, Randy, Rosa Castañeda, Ajay Chaudry, and Robert Santos. *Paying the Price: The Impact of Immigration Raids on America's Children.* Urban Institute for the National Council of La Raza, Washington DC, 2007. Accessed July 20, 2012, http://www.urban.org/UploadedPDF/411566_immigration_raids.pdf.

Chaudry, Ajay, Randy Capps, Juan Pedroza, Rose Castañeda, Robert Santos, and Molly Scott. *Facing Our Future: Children in the Aftermath of Immigration Enforcement.* Urban Institute, Washington DC 2010. Accessed July 20, 2012, http://carnegie.org/fileadmin/Media/Publications/facing_our_future.pdf.

De Genova, Nicolas. "Migrant 'Illegality' and Deportability in Everyday Life." *Annual Review of Anthropology* 31 (2002): 419–47.

Dreby, Joanna. "The Burden of Deportation on Children in Mexican Immigrant Families." *Journal of Marriage and Family* 74 (2012): 829–45.

Golash-Boza, Tanya. *Immigration Nation: Raids, Detentions, and Deportations in Post–9/11 America.* Boulder, CO: Paradigm, 2011.

Gonzales, Roberto. "Learning to be Illegal." *American Sociological Review* 76 (2011): 602–19.

Hagan, Jaqueline, Briana Castro, and Nestor Rodriguez. "The Effects of U.S. Deportation Policies on Immigrant Families and Communities: Cross-Border Perspectives." *North Carolina Law Review* 88 (2010): 1799–1824.

Hondagneu-Sotelo, Pierette, and Tanya Golash-Boza. "Latino Immigrant Men and the Deportation Crisis: A Gendered Racial Removal Program?" Unpublished manuscript.

Kohli, Aarti, Peter Markowitz, and Lisa Chavez. *Secure Communities by the Numbers: An Analysis of Demographics and Due Process.* Berkeley: University of California, Berkeley Law School, 2011. Accessed July 20, 2012, http://www.law.berkeley.edu/files/Secure_Communities_by_the_Numbers.pdf.

Menjívar, Cecilia. "Liminal Legality: Salvadoran and Guatemalan Immigrants' Lives in the United States." *American Journal of Sociology* 111 (2006): 999–1037.

———. "The Power of the Law: Central America's Legality and Everyday Life in Phoenix, Arizona." *Latino Studies* 9 (2011): 377–95.

Passel, Jeffrey, and D'Vera Cohn. *Unauthorized Immigrant Population: National and State Trends 2010.* Pew Hispanic Center, Washington, DC 2011. Accessed July 20, 2012, http://pewhispanic.org/files/reports/133.pdf.

Urban Institute. Data from the Integrated Public Use Microdata Series datasets drawn from the 2005–2009 American Community Survey, 2011. Accessed July 20, 2012, http://datatool.urban.org/charts/datatool/pages.cfm.

US Department of Homeland Security. "FY 2011: ICE Announces Year-End Removal Numbers, Highlights Focus on Key Priorities Including Threats to Public Safety and National Security." 2011. Accessed July 20, 2012, http://www.ice.gov/news/releases/1110/111018washingtondc.html.

US Department of Homeland Security, Office of Immigration Statistics. "Immigration Enforcement Actions: 2010." 2010. Accessed July 20, 2012, http://www.dhs.gov/xlibrary/assets/statistics/publications/enforcement-ar-2010.pdf.

US Department of Homeland Security, Office of the Inspector General. "Removals of Illegal Alien Parents of United States Citizen Children." Report No. OIG-09-15. 2009. Accessed July 20, 2012, http://www.dhs.gov/xoig/assets/mgmtrpts/OIG_09 -15_Jan09.pdf.

Wessler, Seth. "U.S. Deports 46K Parents with Citizen Kids in Just Six Months." *Colorlines* (2011). Accessed July 20, 2012, http://colorlines.com/archives/2011/11/shocking_data_on_parents_deported_with_citizen_children.html.

Yoshikawa, Hiro. *Immigrants Raising Citizens: Undocumented Parents Raising Children.* New York: Russell Sage Foundation, 2011.

CHAPTER 6

Parent-Child Relationships in Hmong Immigrant Families in the United States

Zha Blong Xiong, * *Veronica Deenanath, and Dung Mao*

The story of migration is a familiar one in our nation of immigrants. Every year millions of immigrants[1] arrive at our shores looking forward to the start of a new life in America.[2] Yet what many immigrant parents do not realize is that they will find themselves in unfamiliar environments where what they know about parent-child relationships and what the host culture expects are often at odds. For example, research shows that as acculturation takes place in immigrant families, the relationship between parents and children tends to shift,[3] partly due to the accelerated acculturation of the children[4] and partly due to the dependency of parents to their children because of the children's English-speaking skills.[5] Dinh and Nguyen[6] studied Vietnamese families and found that "the more children perceived their parents as 'too traditional' or believed their parents perceived them as 'too Americanized' the more likely they were to report a poorer quality of parent-child relationship."

The story of Hmong families adjusting to life in the United States also fits into this larger trend of the acculturation process. Studies show that Hmong families undergo significant acculturative stress[7] and experience intense and frequent conflicts between parents and children.[8] What is unique about the Hmong, however, is the degree of change they have to endure during the adjustment process because of their immigration history and lack of exposure to the Western culture[9] prior to their resettlement in America. The purpose of this chapter is to highlight the Hmong immigration situation, their traditional

* Address correspondence to Zha Blong Xiong, Department of Family Social Science, University of Minnesota, 290 McNeal Hall, 1985 Buford Avenue, St. Paul, Minnesota 55108. Email: xiong008@umn.edu.

parent-child relationships, factors that influence changes in their parent-child relationships in America, and the effect parent-child relationships have on adolescent children's behavior.

The Hmong Immigration Situation

The Hmong are a people without a physical country. Thus immigration has always been part of their story. Historical record shows that the Hmong first migrated from China to Southeast Asia in the first part of the nineteenth century due to war and taxation.[10] In Southeast Asia, most Hmong resided in mountainous regions of the country where contact to the outside world was minimal in order to avoid conflict and oppression.[11] However, during the Indo-Chinese War in Laos, the Hmong were recruited by the US Central Intelligence Agency (CIA) to serve as secret armies in a covert "special force" to gather intelligence about North Vietnamese movements in Laos and assist the US military to block military supplies on the Ho Chi Minh trail.[12] However, after the United States withdrew from Laos and the communist regime took over Laos in 1975, Hmong were being hunted down and forced to escape their own villages to hide in the jungle. They endured years of widespread revenge attacks launched by the new government prior to escaping to the refugee camps in Thailand.[13] Once in the camps, they were less likely to be resettled right away since most host countries preferred the more educated Vietnamese and Lao over the Hmong.[14] Indeed, they were held back in the refugee camps the longest (i.e., an average of three years) compared to any other Southeast Asian group, and their mental health status was much worse compared to other refugee populations.[15] Their resettlement to the United States spread over 19 years, from 1975 to 1994, with close to 80,000 individuals admitted.[16]

Today, there are about 260,073 Hmong persons living in the United States. The majority of them tend to concentrate in California (91,224), Minnesota (66,181), and Wisconsin (49,240). They are among the fastest-growing Asian immigrant populations and are one of the youngest Asian groups in the United States, with 62 percent of its population under the age of 24, compared to 34.2 percent of the US population.[17] Hmong are more likely to be concentrated in poor neighborhoods and their poverty rate is among the highest compared to other ethnic groups. For instance, 12.3 percent of Hmong households reported of receiving public assistance income compared to only 2.6 percent of the US households and 2.4 percent Asian American households. The Hmong per capita income was about $11,012, one of the lowest in the nation, compared to other Asian Americans' per capita income of $28,159.[18]

Traditional Hmong Parent-Child Relationships

The Hmong are based on a collectivist culture built on the foundation of the clan structure where various members of the community share a common ancestral line or last name called *xeng (xeem)*.[19] As Barney[20] states, "The clan name refers to descent from a mythical ancestor, and common membership in a clan serves as a bond of kinship and friendship between people who would otherwise be strangers." Those who share the same last name are considered family members and treated with deeper respect.[21] Because of the importance of clan, endogamous marriage is taboo and exogamous marriage is enforced.[22] Indeed, exogamous marriage is the formula to sustain the culture, a culture that is essentially based on a complex kinship system that includes two kin categories, the *kue tee* (kwv tij) and *neng cha* (neej tsa). *Kue tee* literally means "brothers," and it refers to individuals with the same ascribed last name. People with the same last name are considered to be in the same family despite geographical and generational distance. *Neng cha,* on the other hand, literally means "in-laws," and it refers to individuals outside of the kue tee but are related by marriage.[23] For example, Nengher Yang is part of the Yang kue tee but his wife, Xue Xiong, is from the Xiong kue tee. Because of their marriage, the Yang and Xiong kue tees are related as neng cha. As such, people in the Hmong community theoretically are related to one another by kue tee and/or neng cha.

Within the clan structure is the family. Family consists of three types: the nuclear family household, the extended family household, and the lineage family. First, the nuclear family household is the smallest unit that typically consists of two married adults or multiple marital partners for polygamous marriages, their biological or adopted children (married and/or single), and occasionally the aging parents (in the case of the youngest son). This unit usually shares the same household space, unless the unit involves multiple marital partners. Second, the extended family unit includes the aging parents, adult male siblings who are related by blood or adoption, the siblings' wives, and their children (married and single)/nieces and nephews. They do not live in the same physical household space but usually stay in the same geographical location or neighborhood. Third, the lineage family consists of all members of the family who share the same ancestral line, practice the same spiritual ritual (or *koom dab qhuas*), and worship the same ancestors. Like the extended family, members of the same lineage do not share the same household space, but they usually try to maintain family closeness and offer love and support for one another.[24] Therefore, it is not uncommon to find clusters of lineage families in various cities and states across America.[25] For example, within the first author's lineage family, his lineage family members have been dispersed into four major states in America: Minnesota, California, Wisconsin, and Washington.

To maintain order and proper relationships, the structure of the Hmong nuclear family household is arranged hierarchically where the elderly male (i.e., father or grandfather) of the family has the most authority, followed by the married son and the grandmother or the mother in the case where there is a missing grandmother. Children are born not just to a nuclear family but to the clan, especially in the case of sons. Sons, theoretically, will remain in the clan that they were born into even in the case of divorce and the mother has custody over them. Sons are expected to contribute to the clan and carry the clan name into the future. Therefore, in the family sons are preferred and given greater privileges but have fewer restrictions and responsibilities compared to daughters. Daughters, on the other hand, are considered "guests" to the clan, including their family of origin, because when they get married they belong to their husbands' clans; their biological family and ascribed clan become their *neej tsa* or relatives. Thus daughters are given less privileges, are subjected to greater control, and are supervised closely by the mother.[26]

Because of the clan system and patrilocal practice, the parent-child relationship is extremely important as it helps to build the foundation for the family, lineage, and clan. For example, since daughters are expected to get married and leave the family, parents, especially the mothers, play a major role in the training and upbringing of the daughter to get her to be marriageable. To be considered marriageable, daughters are trained to be obedient, patient, and responsible early in life, especially by the mother. For example, daughters are expected to know how to cook and clean, as well as how to take care of their family and younger siblings, since these traits and skills are necessary to fulfill the role of a wife and daughter-in-law.[27] On the other hand, traits such as independence, ambition, and assertiveness are not sought after because they counter what constitutes a good daughter-in-law or wife.[28] Sons, on the other hand, are expected to practice the spiritual ceremonies (soul calling or *hu plig*) and perform spiritual duties (*ua nyuj dab*), including worshipping the ancestors (*laig dab*), caring for the parents in old age, and taking care of the parents' funeral (*pam niam thiab txiv*). Therefore, they are expected to be independent, capable, hardworking, and civically engaged, especially related to social and spiritual duties. Like daughters, sons are also expected to be filial and never to talk back to, argue with, or disobey their parents or the elderly.[29]

These clearly defined roles and responsibilities between parents and children, coupled with the early transition to adulthood—namely, early marriage—tended to help ease the parent-child relationship in Hmong immigrant families in the past. Children were expected to get married as soon as they reached puberty because of the labor-intensive lifestyle in an agrarian society. In such a society, the sooner the marriage, the sooner the family gains additional help from the daughter-in-law and eventually the grandchildren.[30] Studies show that the average age of first marriage for Hmong ranged between 12 and 23, with a mean age of 16.[31] Therefore, by the time children entered into adolescence, many of them had started their own families through marriage. As a result, the parent-child "storm and stress" relationship[32] tended to be kept at a minimum prior to coming to the United States.

Factors That Influence Hmong Immigrant Parent-Child Relationships in America

When the Hmong came to the United States, the nature and dynamics of parent-child relationships changed dramatically as illustrated by the following case published by the Sacramento Bee on August 8, 2008:[33]

> Ka Thao Vang, a Hmong refugee who came from Laos in the 1970s to the United States, shot his 16-year-old son Phong Vang and then killed himself. According to family members of the Vang family, Ka and Phong had a turbulent relationship and often clashed over many issues relating to school, peers, and family obligations over the years. As conflicts became intensified and solutions to the daily nagging and arguments seemed impossible, Ka Thao became more and more frustrated and angry. A daughter said, "As soon as my dad starts yelling, he just doesn't stop. He doesn't understand [Phong's] a teenager." On the day of the shooting, "My brother was sitting on this sofa with his two friends, and the last thing my mom heard was my dad told Phong's two friends very loudly to go home" before he took out his .45-caliber handgun to shoot Phong.

Although not every Hmong immigrant parent would do what Mr. Ka Thao Vang did to his son, this tragic case is an example of the frustration that many Hmong immigrant parents and their adolescent children experience in America.[34] Based on our research and studies conducted by others with Hmong immigrant families in particular and immigrant families in general, three factors seem to influence Hmong immigrant parent-child relationships in the United States.

First, immigration and acculturation play a major role in the changes of Hmong immigrant parent-child relationships, especially refugee parents who had little time to prepare for the country of resettlement. Studies show that immigrant parents in general and Hmong parents in particular tend to be ill-prepared to deal with their adolescent children in the new culture, especially a culture that emphasizes autonomy, values reasoning, and promotes freedom of expression.[35] At the same time, immigrant children tend to adapt to the language and values of the mainstream society at a much faster rate compared to their parents, which results in role reversal, power struggles, and conflicts between the two generations.[36] For example, some scholars who studied immigrant families suggest that as children acculturate, they are more likely to be asked to serve as the family spokesperson, and serving in this capacity some-times leads to a role reversal in the relationship and makes the child feel embar-rassed of the parents, two conditions that have been found to predict more conflicts for immigrant parents, especially Hmong parents.[37] One longitudinal study on immigrant children found that Hmong children who scored high on the embarrassment scale also reported significant higher scores on the parent-adolescent conflict indicator compared to more than a dozen other immigrant groups.[38]

Second, the culture of adolescence[39] in the United States also plays a major role in the changing parent-adolescent relationships in Hmong immigrant fam-ilies. In the past, Hmong children tended to transition quickly from childhood to adulthood through early marriage,[40] and the parent's roles and responsibilities to children were clearly defined to help children make that transition. However, when parents came to the United States, some of the roles and responsibilities shifted due to acculturation,[41] along with the prolonged years of adolescence.[42] As a result, many Hmong parents lacked an in-depth understanding of what adolescence means[43] and the associated expected parenting repertoires to raise "Americanized" children to become bicultural adults.

To illustrate this, Xiong[44] conducted an interactional study with 18 Hmong immigrant families. He found that parents are furious about their adolescent children's fashions—baggy clothes, long hair on boys, dark lipstick, and heavy necklaces—because they lack an understanding of what it means to be an ado-lescent in America, especially in urban America. Parents want their adolescent children to dress and behave in a particular way because they expect them to conform to their family standard (e.g., dress in moderation) and community norm (e.g., dress in white shirt and dress pants or skirts). One parent said, "Wearing clothes like that [referring to the baggy pants in the video scenario] will make you look beautiful and handsome!? You have to wear good, good clothes [white shirt and dress pants] to make others respect you, so when they see you they'll say, 'Oh, that person also wears clothes like the rest of the soci-ety too.'" Another parent stated, "If you [the adolescent] don't listen to us, then other people will say, 'Oh, your son becomes a gangster. Why don't you say anything to him?' So we will lose face." To the adolescents, on the other hand, fashions are mechanisms to help them express their individuality and personal taste, as well as allowing them to fit into certain peer groups in their neighborhood and school. One adolescent told her parents, "Every kid in the United States already wears like that [baggy pants] nowadays, so why can't we?" Another adolescent argued, "It's a fashion . . . [and] we don't like old styles . . . we like those [clothes that] are in fashion now, you know!"

Third, the children's friends and their newly adopted behaviors have been found to influence parent-adolescent relationships in Hmong immigrant families.[45] In the past, Hmong children usually lived in remote villages or captive refugee camps with an enclosed Hmong community without the influences of the outside world, including the media and peers from other cultures.[46] However, in the United States the majority of Hmong immigrants live in urban areas, especially in poor neighborhoods,[47] where children have been bombarded by the media with different messages about being an adolescent, have been pressured to act in certain ways by their peer groups, and interact with other troubled adolescents who live in the same neighborhood.[48] Zhou and Bankston[49] studied more than one hundred Vietnamese immigrant families in the St. Louis area and found that many of the parent-adolescent conflicts were related to the adolescents' problem behaviors such as truancy, delinquency, and affiliation with delinquent peers. Barber[50] and Laursen and colleagues[51] studied different ethnic groups in the United States and found that parent-adolescent conflicts were significantly related to the adolescents' histories of problem behaviors. Shek and Ma[52] conducted a longitudinal study with 150 Chinese students in Hong Kong when the students were in 7th and 9th grades and found that antisocial behavior such as truancy and telling lies to teachers when the students were in 7th grade was significantly related to father-adolescent conflict when the students were in 9th grade. Xiong et al.[53] recently conducted a study with Hmong adolescents in an upper midwestern state and found problem behaviors and school difficulties were significantly related to parent-adolescent conflict. Specifically, they found "problem behavior and school difficulty variables explain 26 percent of the variance in father-adolescent conflicts and 21 percent of the variance in mother-adolescent conflicts."

Effect of Parent-Child Relationships on Adolescents' Problem Behavior

Why is it important to understand parent-child relationships in Hmong immigrant families? We argue that it is extremely important to understand this family dynamic since it serves as a foundation for healthy child development. Studies show that children who are coming from strained family relationships tend to perform poorly in school,[54] be more likely to engage in early marriage,[55] and carry higher risks of getting involved in delinquent acts.[56] In 2005, Roosa and colleagues[57] conducted a comparative study examining inner-city, low-income Anglo and Mexican American families and found significant relationships between parent-adolescent conflicts and youth delinquency and other externalizing behaviors. Similarly, Sivan and colleagues[58] studied delinquent adolescents in immigrant families and concluded that the absence of bonds with parents due to conflicted family relationships served as a reason for adolescents to depend on gangs as a replacement for the family.

Recently, Xiong conducted a study with 206 Hmong youths (115 males and 91 females), ranging in age from 11 to 25 years old (mean = 15.90; standard deviation = 2.11), where the majority were either born in the United States (53.4 percent) or born in the refugee camps in Thailand (35.9 percent), to examine the role of parent-child relationships as measured by parent-child conflict and attachment and parent's monitoring on Hmong youth's problem behaviors. Using structural equation models,[59] Xiong ran two separate structural equation models for the fathers' and mothers' data testing two hypothesized models positing that school performance, affiliation with deviant peers, and participation in organized activities served as the pathways between parent-child relationships and the youth's problem behavior.

The results on both models showed that parent-child relationships have a significant effect on the youth's problem behavior, especially through the youth's school performance, affiliation with deviant peers, and participation in organized activities for the fathers' model. For example, the results showed that youth who reported experiencing a higher degree of parent-child conflict also reported a higher score on the affiliation with deviant peers and a lower score on their grade point averages (GPAs) and in turn reported a higher score on the problem behavior scale. Similarly, youth who reported a higher score on the monitoring scale were also more likely to report a higher score on school commitment, GPA, and participation in organized activities. Conversely, these youth's monitoring score was inversely related to the score of the affiliation with deviant peers scale. More important, youth who reported better school performance (or higher GPA) and participating in organized activities were less likely to engage in problem behavior, while youth who reported more affiliation with deviant peers were more likely to engage in problem behavior. In sum, the data suggest that Hmong youth's problem behavior is substantially influenced by the nature and dynamic of parent-child relationships, especially when the youth are involved with peers who are delinquent, lack of the chance to get involved in organized or extracurricular activities, and perform poorly in school.

Conclusion

The story of Hmong families adjusting to life in the United States is a unique case because of their legacy of immigration, limited exposure to the West and formal education, and abrupt resettlement. Once in the country of resettlement, their prior work experience in their native country was not transferable, especially in the United States.[60] As a result, many Hmong families ended up living in poor neighborhoods where there are high crime rates.[61] Coupled with this lack of preparation and employable skills, the Hmong collectivistic culture, which is oriented toward clan, lineage, and familism, also made it difficult for parents and children to adjust to life in America, especially for the second-generation children—who were either brought to the United Sates during childhood or born in the United States[62]—and their immigrant parents. As a result, studies have consistently found Hmong parents and their adolescent children to have the most difficult time adjusting.

Lack of attachment between parents and children during adolescence is critical since this is a time when children are making the transition to adulthood. Without the relationship, trust, and support in the parent-child dyad, adolescent children tend to put themselves at risk to deal with pressures growing up as Hmong Americans: the pressure to do well in school, to fit in with a peer (including delinquent peer) group, to be civically engaged in the community, and, most important of all, to get married quickly and be part of the adult circle. Thus it is imperative that community programs working with immigrant families in general and Hmong immigrants in particular continue to find ways to engage immigrant families in strengthening the parent-child relationships before and after the resettlement in order to minimize conflicts and maximize the parent-child attachment; strengthen parent's parenting skills, especially how to set, monitor, and enforce limits; and, at the same time, provide additional resources to assist children's academic work, build children's skills to resist peer influence, and get children involved in age-appropriate extracurricular activities.[63]

Notes

1. Nancy Foner, Ruben G. Rumbaut, and Steven Gold, "Immigration and Immigration Research in the United States," in *Immigration Research for a New Century: Multidisciplinary Perspectives*, ed. Nancy Foner, Ruben G. Rumbaut, and Steven J. Gold (New York: Russell Sage Foundation, 2000).

2. Alejandro Portes and Rubén G. Rumbaut, *Legacies: The Story of the Immigrant Second Generation* (New York: Russell Sage Foundation, 2001).

3. Rosenthal Doreen, Ranieri Nadia, and Klimidis Steven, "Vietnamese Adolescents in Australia: Relationships between Perceptions of Self and Parental Values, Intergenerational Conflict, and Gender Dissatisfaction," *International Journal of Psychology* 31 (1996).

4. Nga A. Nguyen and Harold L. Williams, "Transition from East to West: Vietnamese Adolescents and Their Parents," *American Academy of Child and Adolescent Psychiatry* 28 (1989).

5. Karen Pyke, "Immigrant Families in the US," in *American Families: A Multicultural Reader*, ed. Stephanie Coontz, Maya Parson, and Gabrielle Raley (New York: Routledge, 2008).

6. Khanh T. Dinh and Huogn H. Nguyen, "The Effects of Acculturative Variables on Asian American Parent-Child Relationships," *Journal of Social and Personal Relationships* 23 (2006): 420.

7. Quang DuongTran, Serge C. Lee, and Sokley Khoi, "Ethnic and Gender Differences in Parental Expectations and Life Stress," *Child and Adolescent Social Work Journal* 13 (1996).

8. Zha B. Xiong, Kathryn D. Rittig, and Arunya Tuicomepee, "Parent-Adolescent Conflicts and Adolescent Adjustment in Hmong Immigrant Families in the United States," in *Parent-Child Relations,* ed. Dorothy M. Devore (New York: NOVA Publishers, 2006); Zha B. Xiong, Daniel F. Detzner, and Kathryn D. Rettig, "Southeast Asian Immigrant Parenting Practices and Perceptions of Parent-Adolescent Conflicts," *Journal of Teaching in Marriage & Family* 1 (2001).

9. Timothy Dunnigan et al., "Hmong," in *Refugees in America in the 1990s: A Reference Handbook,* ed. David W. Haines (Westport, CT: Greenwood Press, 1996).

10. Wu Dekun, "A Brief Introduction to the Hmong of China," *Hmong Forum* 2 (1991).

11. Yang Dao, *Hmong at the Turning Point* (Minneapolis: Worldbridge Associates, 1993).

12. Jane Hamilton-Merritt, *Tragic Mountains: The Hmong, the Americans, and the Secret Wars for Laos, 1942–1992* (Bloomington: Indiana University Press, 1999).

13. Ibid.

14. Dao Yang, "The Hmong Odyssey from Laos to America" (paper presented at the Tenth Hmong National Development Conference, Fresno, California, 2005).

15. Rubén. G. Rumbaut, "Portraits, Patterns, and Predictors of the Refugee Adaptation Process: Results and Reflections from the IHARP Panel Study," in *Refugees as Immigrants: Cambodians, Laotians, and Vietnamese in America,* ed. David. W. Haines (Totowa, NJ: Rowman & Littlefield Publishers, 1989).

16. Detzner, Xiong, and Eliason, *Helping Youth Succeed.*

17. US Census Bureau, "2010 American Community Survey 5-Year Estimates," accessed August 15, 2012, http://factfinder2.census.gov.

18. Ibid.

19. Serge C. Lee, Zha B. Xiong, and Francis K. Yuen, "Explaining Early Marriage in Hmong Immigrant Community," in *Teen Pregnancy and Parenthood: Global Perspectives, Issues, and Interventions,* ed. Helen S. Holgate, Roy Evans, and Francis K. O. Yuen (London: Taylor & Francis, 2009).

20. Linwood G. Barney, "The Miao of Xiengkhouang Province, Laos," in *Southeast Asian Tribes, Minorities, and Nation,* ed. Peter Kunstadter (Princeton: Princeton University Press, 1967), 275.

21. Nancy D. Donnelly, *Changing Lives of Refugee Hmong Women* (Seattle: University of Washington Press, 1994).

22. Somporn Phanjaruniti, *Traditional Child Rearing Practices among Different Ethnic Groups in Houaphan Province, Lao People's Democratic Republic* (Vientiane, Laos: UNICEF, 1994).

23. Detzner, Xiong, and Eliason, *Helping Youth Succeed.*

24. Zha B. Xiong, Arunya Tuicomepee, Laura LaBlanc, and Julie Rainey, "Hmong Immigrants' Perceptions of Family Secrets and Recipients of Disclosure," *Families in Society: The Journal of Contemporary Social Services* 87 (2006).

25. Mark E. Pfeifer, John Sullivan, Kou Yang and Wayne Yang, "Hmong Population and Demographic Trends in the 2010 Census and 2010 American Community Survey," Hmong Studies Journal 13(2) (2012).

26. Lillian Faderman and Ghai Xiong, *The Hmong and the American Immigrant Experience: I Begin My Life All Over* (Boston: Beacon Press, 1998); Kou Yang, "Hmong Men's Adaption to,Life in the United States," *Hmong Studies Journal* 1 (1997).

27. Lee, Xiong, and Yuen, "Explaining Early Marriage."

28. William R. Geddes, *Migrants of the Mountain: The Cultural Ecology of the Blue Miao of Thailand* (Oxford: Clarendon Press, 1976); Rini Savitridina, "Determinants and Consequences of Early Marriage in Java, Indonesia," *Asia-Pacific Population Journal* 12 (1997).

29. Xiong, Rittig, and Tuicomepee, "Parent-Adolescent Conflicts."

30. Lee, Xiong, and Yuen, "Explaining Early Marriage."

31. Detzner, Xiong, and Eliason, *Helping Youth Succeed*; Lee, Xiong, and Yuen, "Explaining Early Marriage"; Miles McNall, Timothy Dunnigan, and Jeylan T. Mortimer, "The Educational Achievement of the St. Paul Hmong," *Anthropology & Education Quarterly* 25 (1994).

32. Arnett J. Jeffery, "Adolescent Storm and Stress, Reconsidered," *American Psychologist* 54 (1999).

33. Stephen Magagnini, "Hmong Man Shot Son and Then Committed Suicide," *Sacramento Bee*, August 8, 2008, accessed July 30, 2012, https://groups.google.com/forum/#!msg/soc.culture.laos/cDgh89o3LCg/0GfKsP0fWJAJ

34. Anthony T. Vang, "Hmong-American Students: Challenges and Opportunities," in *Asian-American Education: Prospects and Challenges*, ed. Clara C. Park and Marilyn M. Chi (Westport, CT: Bergin and Garvey, 1999); Detzner, Xiong, and Eliason, *Helping Youth Succeed*.

35. Zha B. Xiong, Daniel F. Detzner, and Kathryn K. Rettig, "Southeast Asian Immigrant Parenting Practices and Perceptions of Parent-Adolescent Conflicts," *Journal of Teaching Marriage and Family: Innovations in Family Science Education* 1 (2001).

36. Portes and Rumbaut, *Legacies*.

37. Andrew J. Fuligni, "Authority, Autonomy, and Parent-Adolescent Conflict and Cohesion: A Study of Adolescents from Mexican, Chinese, Filipino, and European Backgrounds," *Developmental Psychology* 34 (1998); Paul J. Handal, Nicole Le-Stiebel, and Margret Dicarlo, "Perceived Family Environment and Adjustment in American-Born and Immigrant Asian Adolescents," *Psychological Reports* 85 (1999); Portes and Rumbaut, *Legacies*.

38. Portes and Rumbaut, *Legacies*.

39. Brett Laursen, Katherine C. Coy, and Andrew W. Collins, "Reconsidering Changes in Parent-Child Conflict across Adolescence: A Meta-Analysis," *Child Development* 69 (1998).

40. Lee, Xiong, and Yuen, "Explaining Early Marriage," 30.

41. Kathryn Rick and John Forward, "Acculturation and Perceived Intergenerational Differences among Hmong Youth," *Journal of Cross-Cultural Psychology* 23 (1992).

42. Glen R. Elliot and Shirley Faldeman, "Capturing the Adolescence Experience," in *At the Threshold: The Developing Adolescent*, ed. Glen R. Elliot and Shirley Faldeman (Cambridge, MA: Harvard University Press, 1990); Judith G. Smetana, "Adolescents' and Parents' Reasoning about Actual Family Conflict," *Child Development* 60 (1989).

43. Andrew W. Collins, "Parent-Child Relationships in the Transition to Adolescence: Continuity and Change in Interaction, Affect, and Cognition," in *Advances in Adolescent Development. Vol. 2: From Childhood to Adolescence: A Transitional Period?*, ed. Gerald R. Adams, Raymond Montemayor, Thomas P. Gullotta, and Gerald R. Adams (Newbury Park, CA.: Sage, 1990).

44. Zha B. Xiong, "Hmong American Parent-Adolescent Problem-Solving Interactions: An Analytic Induction Analysis" (PhD diss., University of Minnesota, 2000).
45. Zha B. Xiong, Arunya Tuicomepee, and Kathryn D. Rettig, "Adolescents' Problem Behaviors and Parent-Adolescent Conflicts in Hmong Immigrant Families," *Hmong Studies Journal* 9 (2008).
46. Lee, Xiong, and Yuen, "Explaining Early Marriage."
47. Zha B. Xiong, Kao K. Yang, and Jesse K. Lee, *What Helps and Hinders Hmong Pre-Kindergartens' School Readiness: Learning from and about the Hmong in Saint Paul, Minnesota* (St. Paul: Ready4K, 2008).
48. Zha B. Xiong, Patricia A. Eliason, Daniel F. Detzner, and Michael J. Cleveland, "Southeast Asian Immigrants' Perception of Good Adolescents and Good Parents," *Journal of Psychology* 31 (2005).
49. Min Zhou and Carl L. Bankston, *Growing Up American: How Vietnamese Children Adapt to Life in the United States* (New York: Russell Sage Foundation, 1998).
50. Brian K. Barber, "Cultural, Family, and Personal Contexts of Parent-Adolescent Conflict," *Journal of Marriage and the Family* 56 (1994).
51. Laursen, Coy, and Collins, "Reconsidering Changes."
52. Daniel T. L. Shek and Hing K. Ma, "Parent-Adolescent Conflict and Adolescent Antisocial and Prosocial Behavior: A Longitudinal Study in a Chinese Context," *Adolescence* 36 (2001).
53. Zha B. Xiong and Ju-Ping Huang, "Predicting Hmong Adolescent Boys' and Girls' Delinquent Behaviors: An Exploratory Study," *Hmong Study Journal* 12 (2011): 10.
54. Rubén G. Rumbaut, "The Crucible Within: Ethnic Identity, Self-Esteem, and Segmented Assimilation among Children of Immigrants," *International Migration Review* 28 (1994); Abigail B. Sivan, Lisa Koch, Claudia Baier, and Mala Adiga, "Refugee Youth at Risk: A Quest for Rational Policy," *Children's Services: Social Policy, Research, and Practice* 2 (1999).
55. Bic Ngo, "Contesting 'Culture': The Perspectives of Hmong American Female Students on Early Marriage," *Anthropology and Education Quarterly* 33 (2002).
56. Craig A. Manson, Ana M. Cauce, Nancy Gonzales, and Yumi Hiraga, "Neither Too Sweet nor Too Sour: Problem Peers, Maternal Control, and Problem Behavior in African American Adolescents," *Child Development* 67 (1996).
57. Mark W. Roosa et al., "Family and Child Characteristics Linking Neighborhood Context and Child Externalizing Behavior," *Journal of Marriage and Family* 67 (2005).
58. Sivan, Koch, Claudia, and Adiga, "Refugee Youth at Risk."
59. Karl G. Jöreskog and Dag Sörbom, *LISREL 7: A Guide to the Program and Applications* (Chicago, IL: SPSS Inc., 1988).
60. Detzner, Xiong, and Eliason, *Helping Youth Succeed*; Xiong, Detzner, and Rettig, "Southeast Asian Immigrant Parenting Practices"; Lee, Xiong, and Yuen, "Explaining Early Marriage"; McNall, Dunnigan, and Mortimer, "The Educational Achievement."
61. Arthur Sakamoto and Hyeyoung Woo, "The Socioeconomic Attainments of Second-Generation Cambodian, Hmong, Laotian, and Vietnamese Americans," *Sociological Inquiry* 77 (2007); Xiong, Yang, and Lee, *What Helps and Hinders Hmong Pre-Kindergartens' School Readiness.*

62. Portes and Rumbaut, *Legacies: The Story of the Immigrant Second Generation* (2001).
63. See the Helping Youth Succeed Program, which was designed for Southeast Asian parents, including Hmong immigrant parents. For more information about the program, please contact Asian Media Access at http://amamedia.org.

Bibliography

Arnett, Jeffery J. "Adolescent Storm and Stress, Reconsidered." *American Psychologist* 54 (1999): 17–326.

Barber, Brian K. "Cultural, Family, and Personal Contexts of Parent-Adolescent Conflict." *Journal of Marriage and the Family* 56 (1994): 375–86.

Barney, Linwood G. "The Miao of Xiengkhouang Province, Laos." In *Southeast Asian Tribes, Minorities, and Nation*, edited by Peter Kunstadter, 271–94. Princeton: Princeton University Press, 1967.

Collins, Andrew W. "Parent-Child Relationships in the Transition to Adolescence: Continuity and Change in Interaction, Affect, and Cognition." In *Advances in Adolescent Development. Vol. 2: From Childhood to Adolescence: A Transitional Period*, edited by Gerald R. Adams, Raymond Montemayor, Thomas P. Gullotta, and Gerald R. Adams, 85–106. Newbury Park, CA: Sage, 1990.

Dekun, Wu. "A Brief Introduction to the Hmong of China." *Hmong Forum* 2 (1991): 1–15.

Detzner, Daniel F., and Kathryn D. Rettig. "Southeast Asian Immigrant Parenting Practices and Perceptions of Parent-Adolescent Conflicts." *Journal of Teaching in Marriage & Family* 1 (2001): 27–48.

Detzner, Daniel F., Zha B. Xiong, and Patricia A. Eliason. *Helping Youth Succeed: Bicultural Parenting for Southeast Asian Families*. St. Paul, MN: Regents of the University of Minnesota, 1999.

Dinh, Khanh T., and Nguyen H. Huogn. "The Effects of Acculturative Variables on Asian American Parent-Child Relationships." *Journal of Social and Personal Relationships* 23 (2006): 407–26.

Donnelly, Nancy D. *Changing Lives of Refugee Hmong Women*. Seattle: University of Washington Press, 1994.

Dunnigan, Timothy, Douglas P. Olney, Miles A. McNall, and Marline A. Spring. "Hmong." In *Refugees in America in the 1990s: A Reference Handbook*, edited by David W. Haines, 191–212. Westport, CT: Greenwood Press, 1996.

DuongTran, Quang, Serge Lee, and Sokley Khoi. "Ethnic and Gender Differences in Parental Expectations and Life Stress." *Child and Adolescent Social Work Journal* 13 (1996): 515–26.

Elliot, Glen R., and Shirley Faldeman. "Capturing the Adolescence Experience." In *At the Threshold: The Developing Adolescent*, edited by Glen R. Elliot and Shirley Faldeman, 1–14. Cambridge, MA: Harvard University Press, 1990.

Faderman, Lillian, and Ghai Xiong. *The Hmong and the American Immigrant Experience: I Begin My Life All Over*. Boston: Beacon Press, 1998.

Foner, Nancy, Ruben G. Rumbaut, and Steven Gold. "Immigration and Immigration Research in the United States." In *Immigration Research for a New Century:*

Multidisciplinary Perspectives, edited by Nancy Foner, Ruben G. Rumbaut, and Steven J. Gold, 1–19. New York: Russell Sage Foundation, 2000.

Fuligni, Andrew J. "Authority, Autonomy, and Parent-Adolescent Conflict and Cohesion: A Study of Adolescents from Mexican, Chinese, Filipino, and European Backgrounds." *Developmental Psychology* 34 (1998): 782–92.

Hamilton-Merritt, Jane. *Tragic Mountains: The Hmong, the Americans, and the Secret Wars for Laos, 1942–1992*. Bloomington: Indiana University Press, 1999.

Handal, Paul J., Nicole Le-Stiebel, and Margret Dicarlo. "Perceived Family Environment and Adjustment in American-Born and Immigrant Asian Adolescents." *Psychological Reports* 85 (1999): 1244–49.

Karl G. Jöreskog and Dag Sörbom, *LISREL 7: A Guide to the Program and Applications* (Chicago, IL: SPSS Inc., 1988).

Laursen, Brett, Katherine C. Coy, and Andrew W. Collins. "Reconsidering Changes in Parent-Child Conflict across Adolescence: A Meta-Analysis." *Child Development* 69 (1998): 817–32.

Lee, Serge C., Zha B. Xiong, and Francis K. O. Yuen. "Explaining Early Marriage in Hmong Immigrant Community." In *Teen Pregnancy and Parenthood: Global Perspectives, Issues, and Interventions,* edited by Helen S. Holgate, Roy Evans, and Francis K. O. Yuen, 25–37. London: Taylor & Francis, 2009.

Magagnini, Stephen, "Hmong Man Shot Son and Then Committed Suicide." *Sacramento Bee*, August 8, 2008. Accessed July 30, 2012, https://groups.google.com/forum/#!msg/soc.culture.laos/cDgh89o3LCg/0GfKsP0fWJAJ.

Manson, Craig A., Ana M. Cauce, Nancy Gonzales, and Yumi Hiraga. "Neither Too Sweet nor Too Sour: Problem Peers, Maternal Control, and Problem Behavior in African American Adolescents." *Child Development* 67 (1996): 2115–30.

McNall, Miles, Timothy Dunnigan, and Jeylan T. Mortimer. "The Educational Achievement of the St. Paul Hmong." *Anthropology & Education Quarterly* 25 (1994): 44–65.

Ngo, Bic. "Contesting 'Culture': The Perspectives of Hmong American Female Students on Early Marriage." *Anthropology and Education Quarterly* 33 (2002): 163–88.

Nguyen, Nga A., and Harold L. Williams. "Transition from East to West: Vietnamese Adolescents and Their Parents." *American Academy of Child and Adolescent Psychiatry* 28 (1989): 505–15.

Phanjaruniti, Somporn. *Traditional Child Rearing Practices among Different Ethnic Groups in Houaphan Province, Lao People's Democratic Republic*. Vientiane, Laos: UNICEF, 1994.

Pfeifer, Mark E., John Sullivan , Kou Yang, and Wayne Yang, "Hmong Population and Demographic Trends in the 2010 Census and 2010 American Community Survey," Hmong Studies Journal 13(2) (2012).

Portes, Alejandro, and Rubén G. Rumbaut. *Legacies: The Story of the Immigrant Second Generation*. New York: Russell Sage Foundation, 2001.

Pyke, Karen. "Immigrant Families in the US." In *American Families: A Multicultural Reader*, vol. 2, edited by Stephanie Coontz, Maya Parson, and Gabrielle Raley, 210–21. New York: Routledge, 2008.

Rick, Kathryn, and John Forward. "Acculturation and Perceived Intergenerational Differences among Hmong Youth." *Journal of Cross-Cultural Psychology* 23 (1992): 85–94.

Roosa, Mark W., Shiying Deng, Ehri Ryu, Ginger L. Burrell, Jenn-Yun Tein, Sarah Jones, Vera Lopez, and Sakina Crowder. "Family and Child Characteristics Linking Neighborhood Context and Child Externalizing Behavior." *Journal of Marriage and Family* 67 (2005): 515–29.

Rosenthal, Doreen, Nadia Ranieri, and Steven Klimidis. "Vietnamese Adolescents in Australia: Relationships between Perceptions of Self and Parental Values, Intergenerational Conflict, and Gender Dissatisfaction." *International Journal of Psychology* 31 (1996): 81–91.

Rumbaut, Rubén G. "The Crucible Within: Ethnic Identity, Self-Esteem, and Segmented Assimilation among Children of Immigrants." *International Migration Review* 28 (1996): 748–94.

———. "Portraits, Patterns, and Predictors of the Refugee Adaptation Process: Results and Reflections from the IHARP Panel Study." In *Refugees as Immigrants: Cambodians, Laotians, and Vietnamese in America*, edited by D. W. Haines. Totowa, NJ: Rowman & Littlefield Publishers, 1989.

———. "Vietnamese, Laotian, and Cambodian Americans." In *Asian Americans: Contemporary Trends and Issues*, edited by Pyong G. Min, 232–77. Thousand Oaks, CA: Sage, 1995.

Sakamoto, Arthur, and Hyeyoung Woo. "The Socioeconomic Attainments of Second-Generation Cambodian, Hmong, Laotian, and Vietnamese Americans." *Sociological Inquiry* 77 (2007): 44–75.

Savitridina, Rini. "Determinants and Consequences of Early Marriage in Java, Indonesia." *Asia-Pacific Population Journal* 12 (1997): 3–25.

Shek, Daniel T. L., and Hing K. Ma. "Parent-Adolescent Conflict and Adolescent Antisocial and Prosocial Behavior: A Longitudinal Study in a Chinese Context." *Adolescence* 36 (2001): 545–55.

Sivan, Abigail B., Lisa Koch, Claudia Baier, and Mala Adiga. "Refugee Youth at Risk: A Quest for Rational Policy." *Children's Services: Social Policy, Research, and Practice* 2 (1999): 139–58.

Smetana, Judith G. "Adolescents' and Parents' Reasoning about Actual Family Conflict." *Child Development* 60 (1989): 1052–67.

Sodowsky, Gargi R., Edward W. Lai, and Barbara S. Plake. "Moderating Effects of Sociocultural Variables on Acculturation Attitudes of Hispanic and Asian Americans." *Journal of Counseling & Development* 70 (1991): 194–204.

US Census Bureau. "2010 American Community Survey 5-Year Estimates." Accessed August 15, 2012, http://factfinder2.census.gov.

Vang, Anthony T. "Hmong-American Students: Challenges and Opportunities." In *Asian-American Education: Prospects and Challenges*, edited by Clara C. Park and Marilyn M. Y. Chi, 219–36. Westport, CT: Bergin and Garvey, 1999.

Xiong, Zha B. "Hmong American Parent-Adolescent Problem-Solving Interactions: An Analytic Induction Analysis." PhD diss., University of Minnesota, 2000.

Xiong, Zha B., Daniel F. Detzner, and Kathryn D. Rettig. "Southeast Asian Immigrant Parenting Practices and Perceptions of Parent-Adolescent Conflicts." *Journal of Teaching Marriage and Family: Innovations in Family Science Education* 1 (2001): 27–48.

Xiong, Zha B., Patricia A. Eliason, Daniel F. Detzner, and Cleveland J. Micheal. "Southeast Asian Immigrants' Perception of Good Adolescents and Good Parents." *Journal of Psychology* 39 (2005): 159–75.

Xiong, Zha B., and Ju-Ping Huang. "Predicting Hmong Adolescent Boys' and Girls' Delinquent Behaviors: An Exploratory Study." *Hmong Study Journal* 12 (2011): 1–34.

Xiong, Zha B., Kathryn D. Rittig, and Arunya Tuicomepee. "Parent-Adolescent Conflicts and Adolescent Adjustment in Hmong Immigrant Families in the United States." In *Parent-Child Relations,* edited by Dorothy M. Devore, 65–82. New York: NOVA Publishers, 2006.

Xiong, Zha B., Arunya Tuicomepee, Laura LaBlanc, and Julie Rainey. "Hmong Immigrants' Perceptions of Family Secrets and Recipients of Disclosure." *Families in Society: The Journal of Contemporary Social Services* 87 (2006): 231–39.

Xiong, Zha B., Arunya Tuicomepee, and Kathryn D. Rettig. "Adolescents' Problem Behaviors and Parent-Adolescent Conflicts in Hmong Immigrant Families." *Hmong Studies Journal* 9 (2008): 1–21.

Xiong, Zha B., Kao K. Yang, and Jesse K. Lee. *What Helps and Hinders Hmong Pre-Kindergartens' School Readiness: Learning from and about the Hmong in Saint Paul.* Saint Paul, MN: Ready4K, 2008.

Yang, Dao. *Hmong at the Turning Point.* Minneapolis: Worldbridge Associates, 1993.

———. "The Hmong Odyssey from Laos to America." Paper presented at the 10th Hmong National Development Conference, Fresno, California, 2005.

Yang, Kou. "Hmong Mens' Adaption to Life in the United States." *Hmong Studies Journal* 1 (1997): 1–22.

Zhou, Min, and Carl L. Bankston. *Growing Up American: How Vietnamese Children Adapt to Life in the United States.* New York: Russell Sage Foundation, 1998.

CHAPTER 7

From Model Minority to Second-Gen Stereotypes

Korean Canadian and Korean American Accounts

*Marianne S. Noh**

Processes of migration can have significant and lasting effects on immigrants' self-concept. For second-generation immigrants, one's racial/ethnic identity can be deeply impacted by the families' migration experiences. Although the definition and implications of identity are unclear, there is a general consensus that identity plays an instrumental role in the maintenance of mental and physical well-being.[1] A social constructionist analysis of identity, or the self, treats it as created and recreated through text or societal definitions. Our meaning, understanding, intention, and action exist in communication. Identity formation is highly dependent on societal definitions, which categorize groups of people, including racial minorities, as deviants or the Other. And as such, the fluidity of identity formation is influenced by typifications or dominant "successful" definitions that are contested and changed over time.

The social constructionist perspective also accounts for shared experiences, understandings, and meanings.[2] Shared meanings provide the recognition that categorizations are practiced, whether voluntarily or involuntarily. The processes and consequences of categorizing groups of individuals, such as labeling, stigmatizing, and marginalizing, are examined. While the extent of accuracy

* Address correspondence to Marianne S. Noh, PhD, Arthur Labatt Family School of Nursing, H121C Health Sciences Addition, Western University, London, ON N6A 3C1, Canada. Email: mnoh5@uwo.ca.

in interpretation of meaning cannot be evaluated due to ambiguity, discourse creates a certain context in which a pool of meanings and interpretations overlap. Therefore, individuals can share meaning through discourse and have their definitions understood.[3]

Stereotypes can be successfully shared meanings of groups of people. Stereotypes are also used to maintain a larger ideological viewpoint that benefits the dominant group. Case in point, the model minority stereotype is hypothesized to disprove empirical criticisms of racism and hostile immigrant reception in Western societies while also maintaining the subordination of Asians to the dominant group through the notion that pure Americanness and Canadianness means whiteness.[4]

Through a social constructionist lens, we have shared understandings of our own identity as well as the identity of others. Self-concept is both individualistic and shared. The process of developing an identification of Self and Other is collective, imposed by dominant groups. It is important, however, to note that shared meanings are collectively unstable. Societal notions and depictions of belonging and meaning to races, ethnicities, and nationalities are constructed not only by those who have the power to define and take ownership of these notions but also by those who are defined and confined within them. An individual's sense of self is largely based on sweeping generalizations or stereotypes of social groups of peoples.[5] Social constructionist investigations often look at stereotypes, typifications, and other forms of typifying discourse to illustrate identity formation. The social constructionist perspective also conceives typifications as useful tools in developing and communicating the meaning of one's social world and one's self in various settings, expressions, and experiences.

The Model Minority Stereotype and Ethnic Identity Formation

There has been a movement away from essentialist views of identity, in particular racial identity, to an understanding of identity as complex, ambivalent, and filled with a "doubleness" of discourse.[6] Ethnicity, as well, is about the representation of difference. Contemporary race and ethnicity theorists also discuss difference as "sites of power, a power too whereby the dominated come to see and experience themselves as 'Other.'"[7] Based on how the difference between Self and Other are discussed, individuals who belong to a subordinated group are likely to form deviant identities or perceive themselves as the Other. What has grown in prominence is the increasing influence of race and ethnicity dialogue on citizenship and national identity. The use of culture and ethnicity to establish Self and Other has been brought to the fore in race and ethnicity studies. For example, the model minority stereotype construes mixed messages of Self and Other.

To begin, the model minority stereotype refers to the widely accepted belief that Asian Americans live and behave as model citizens, contributing to and working within the dominant ways of the Western society; they are portrayed as Selves and not Others. The most characteristic depictions of the model minority are that Asians are well behaved and are high achievers.[8] There is a common misconception that second-generation Asian immigrants are of privileged status and well adjusted in North American society, lacking financial hardship, assimilative barriers, discrimination, racism, and associated identity issues. These images of Asians have much to do with the ever-present influence of the model minority stereotype.[9] According to the stereotype, Asians in North America are virtually fully assimilated, unaffected by racial or ethnic discrimination. They are perceived to be more successful than European whites when rates of educational attainment and median household income at national levels are observed.[10] However, children of immigrants, regardless of racial background, are surpassing their parents' level of education and occupational status at rates depicted by the model minority stereotype.[11] While the median household incomes among Asians are higher than that of whites, Asians are more likely to have multiple generations of family members with more income earners living under the same roof. As such, a per capita measure would likely yield a different result when comparing the two groups.[12]

Other socioeconomic factors disprove the stereotype that Asians have surpassed their white European counterparts. Asian Americans experience higher rates of poverty than European whites: 11 percent and 10.5 percent, respectively, in 2003.[13] Although Asians are perceived to be "taking over" more professional jobs, Asians in the United States and Canada hold less than 10 percent of top managerial positions.[14] In addition, recent statistics suggest that despite high levels of educational attainment, Korean Canadians (including second-generation immigrants) fall below national rates of labor market participation and personal income.[15] Unlike what the model minority implies, the rates of socioeconomic success require contextualization to be fully understood. The success of Asian immigrants is variable across Asian ethnic groups and dependent on which socioeconomic indicators are considered. Finally, assuming Asian success according to the model minority underestimates the upward economic mobility that second-generation people of other ethnicities and racial backgrounds have achieved.[16]

In addition to misrepresenting racial divides in socioeconomic status, the model minority portrait provides conflicting images of Asian immigrants in the United States and Canada, which encompass both admirable and demeaning qualities.[17] On one hand, the term is presented in a favorable light, framing Asians as insiders, Selves, and honorary whites.[18] The honorary white label depicts Asians as persistent and diligent workers with strong work ethics who were able to overcome discrimination and successfully assimilate. Stories of honorary whites and model minorities have been used to reaffirm the classic assimilation model and the idea that non-native-born nonwhites could realize the "American dream." Depicting Asians as model minorities results in two outcomes that benefit the dominant society. First, the model minority supports the claim that racism does not structure American society and therefore is not the cause of racial inequality. Second, the use of "minority" in the concept reinforces the idea that Asians are not fully American and are a leading example for other nonwhites in Western societies.

The implications of the model minority stereotype on Asian Americans' identity are not fully understood. There are times when being perceived as compliant, intelligent, and emotionally stable is beneficial to individual Asian Americans in legal and work spaces.[19] However, it also enforces restrictive boundaries on the behaviors and roles deemed appropriate for Asians in America. The notion that Asians are naturally quiet, shy, and serious may serve to prevent Asians from being regarded as potential role models and leaders.[20] Zhou and Lee present two significant consequences of the stereotype.[21] First, it "serves to buttress the myth that the United States is a country devoid of racism, and one that accords equal opportunity for all who take the initiative to work hard to get ahead." Second, it creates feelings of "frustration and burden because others judge them by standards different from those of other American youth."

An important element of understanding ethnic identity formation for second-generation Korean immigrants is the use of discourse that deems Asians in the United States and Canada as Others. The development of a deviant identity provides a conceptual tool for understanding ethnic identity formation for second-generation Koreans. As a minority status inherently refers to a deviant status, racial/ethnic minorities are categorized and constructed as social deviants, nongroup members, outsiders, and noncitizens as they are framed in opposition to white American able-bodied men and women. Omi and Winant note that race and sex are the first characteristics one notices and uses to assess, label, and contextualize an individual within a larger societal subgroup.[22] For instance, stereotypes of racial/ethnic minorities and women that are perceived and treated as deviant in turn become internalized to create deviant self-identifications.[23] As ascribed and visible statuses, ethnicity and race are important social markers or implications of citizenship and belongingness.

Among Lee's sample of Hmong high school students, the model minority stereotype provides two opposing negative outcomes.[24] The second-generation Hmong students are depicted as delinquents; they are regarded as rebelling against the model minority image. The 1.5 generation students are described as model minorities: obedient, quiet, and performing well in school. Although Lee finds these depictions to be typified distinctions made by 1.5

and second-generation Hmong, these opposing images are based on the model minority stereotype presented by the dominant group. These second-generation people are possibly changing their identity to rebel against the model minority image.

Tuan finds that the model minority stereotype implies contradictory honorary white and yet forever foreigner statuses.[25] It is implied that Asians are non-Westerners by race and ethnicity. The model minority also implies a set of behaviors and practices for nonwhite American immigrants to endure in white America—that is, to follow the cultural practices of the dominant group while accepting a second class status to whites.

To understand the role of the model minority stereotype in identity formation, it is important to note that deviant identities are both imposed and chosen.[26] The Hmong American students illustrate that the status of honorary white and simultaneously forever foreign results in both a restriction imposed by the dominant group and an enactment by Asians internalizing and utilizing the model minority image to construct their own identities.

Research Methods

The data for this study come from transcribed in-depth interviews with 32 North American second-generation Korean immigrants. In-depth, semistructured, face-to-face interviews were conducted to enhance the depth and richness of the data and to allow for a wide range of themes to be collected.[27] Face-to-face interview methods maximize disclosure of genuine perceptions around social mores such as racist and sexist notions, which may not come out in small group formats.[28] The purpose of the interview was to ask questions that would access the participants' understanding of race/ethnicity, nationality, and belongingness.

Participants for this study were recruited using listservs of Korean-ethnic student organizations of two universities and snowball sampling techniques to recruit outside of the student organization listservs.[29] After screening for eligibility, each participant provided informed consent to participate in this study. Interviews were conducted from 2005 to 2007. Each participant gave consent to have their interviews recorded with a digital voice recorder and transcribed verbatim. The interviews lasted an average of one and half hours, ranging from 45 minutes to 2 hours. Transcriptions were done in Word and imported into NVivo8. The data were analyzed using open coding and emergent themes techniques.[30]

The sample for this study comprises 19 men and 13 women living in the United States or Canada. All participants were enrolled in a full-time undergraduate program at one of the two universities. Participants' ages ranged from

18 to 26 years old. None of the participants identified their sexuality as other than heterosexual. All participants were single, never married, and without children. Most respondents had not heard of the stereotype and were provided with a definition. Model minority discourse was well known among the respondents and they were able discuss their opinions and personal experiences relevant to feelings toward the stereotype once they were given its definition.[31] Pseudonyms are used.

Results: From Model Minority to Second Gen

Two major themes emerged from the interviews. First, the model minority stereotype is associated with identity issues in complex and contradictory ways. There was a tendency to construct confusing notions of the model minority stereotype such as simultaneous feelings of being an honorary white and a forever foreigner. Second, common stressful life events, rather than the model minority image, were presented as factors that influenced, motivated, and led to academic achievement and upward economic mobility. This was used to define the *second gen.*

Unmasking Realities behind the Model Minority Stereotype

An important outcome of the model minority stereotype is the internalization by Asian immigrants of the model minority. Many Asian Americans and Canadians utilize their insider knowledge to align themselves with their personal views of what model minority means. Carrie a 19-year-old Korean American, believed that genetics played a part in an Asian academic superiority type. She also alluded to the framework of the model minority by describing Asians as "culturally programmed for economic success . . . : I think we're kind of trained. I know Asian schools are crazy. They'd never sleep. They'd get hit if they don't study. If [my parents] were raised like that, I'm pretty sure they'll pass on [the same] work ethics to their kids"[32]

Congratulatory yet culturally alien portraits of the model minority mask and tangle the reality of many Asians living in the United States and Canada. The model minority also provides a depiction of all Asian immigrants as integrating and adapting in the same way. Contrary to the narrow depiction of Asians as model minorities, Asians vary across socioeconomic statuses and integration pathways. For example, Dennis, a 19 year-old Korean American, talked about the differences between inner city and middle class suburban schooling and lifestyles. He witnessed large numbers of Korean American youth that mobilized downward. "About 30 percent of [my inner city friends] go to college. Most of them went to the military. They don't turn out right. There's no incentive to go to school . . . [Parents] can barely look after you . . . Parents don't even know what the SATs are [or] how the school system works."

Dennis's quote suggests that social and economic circumstances affect Korean and Asian youth in the same ways that it would affect youth of other ethnic and racial backgrounds. He talks about Korean Americans unlike those illustrated by the model minority stereotype. The model minority narrowly defines and therefore masks the various lived experiences, assimilation paths, and identity issues of Asians in the United States and Canada.

Conflicting images also present hardships for those who feel that they fit the model minority stereotype by entering college and aspiring toward a career in the professional fields. Many of the participants felt that the model minority image accurately described them, although they did not want to take part in reinforcing the stereotype. Others such as Jacob, a 21 year-old Korean American, felt that the stereotype was positive and better than other racial stereotypes but also felt frustrated for being stereotyped or being regarded as a stereotype. "I'm actually complimented [that] people view us like that. We're like the model minority. We're like the best but I don't see all Asians like that so I have to say I disagree with that."

Similar to the results of Tuan's study, the perception and the self-identification of either an honorary white or a forever foreigner were neither dichotomous nor distinct images for the participants.[33] The second-generation Koreans of this study expressed feeling like both an honorary white and a forever foreigner at different times as well as within a single occasion. The model minority stereotype seemed to create confusion and dissatisfaction in the way second-generation Koreans, both American and Canadian, perceived themselves. Jane, for example, had a hard time understanding herself, although she seemed to be well integrated into the dominant US structure and culture. "All of my friends are white . . . Internally, I feel very very Korean . . . I'm into the [Korean] culture and everything . . . I feel like I'm fooling myself. I'm living a double life because everything I do is so [immersed] in the American culture. I ask myself, 'Who are you?'" (Jane, Korean American, 21 years old).

Jane felt that she did not belong with Korean American students on campus and she "naturally" integrated into a group of all-white friends. In university, away from her Korean family and her Korean church, she started to forget that she was Korean and started to think that she was white, "just like them." Jane was starting to feel like an honorary white and felt accepted by her white friends. They regarded her as white or "un-Asian." A white friend told Jane that he perceived Asians to be white, which made her feel "accepted, I guess." At the same time, Jane stated she was proud to be Korean and identified herself as a "Korean American," although in her recent experience she felt that she was acting white.

Jane's experience of identity confusion was a common experience for most participants at some point in their lives. For Jane, she was struggling with her sense of self and belonging in her early adulthood. Most respondents struggled through their "Who am I?" identity crisis in their adolescence. They also interpreted their confused identity as a "developmental stage." It was common for the respondents to explain their feelings as immaturity and that a lack of identity was a regular part of adolescence. However, Jane's quote illustrates the fluidity of identity and its relationship to assimilation experiences. Changing senses of ethnic pride, shame, and belonging across social settings were frequent experiences for all the respondents in adolescence and recent adulthood.

As university students, the participants acknowledged that they were well on their way to achieving economic stability, surpassing their parents' socio-economic status and moving closer to honorary white status. At the same time, they were continuously struggling with the idea that American and Canadian means whiteness. They felt that they were American/Canadian but also recognized that they were not white. As a result, they were unable to escape the sense of feeling forever foreign. Each participant addressed and dealt with their struggle in their own way. Most expressions of confusion came from experiences of subtle or covert racism.

Peter, a 22-year-old Korean Canadian, talked about one of his recent experiences at an internship he had shortly before the interview: "I think for [white interns and employers] it's easier to deal with someone who they can relate to . . . Was it them being racist towards me? . . . it kind of felt that way. Not racist but them just being comfortable with themselves and being able to . . . relate to [each other]."

Peter's example illustrates a confusion and frustration over the inability to avoid and dismantle the model minority stereotype. The majority of the respondents made plans to work in a mainstream occupational sector where such situations would draw attention to the sense of exclusion and being a forever foreigner. For the second-generation Koreans of this study, the messages and the impressions imprinted on their racial status created confusion not only for their implications or implied meanings but also for their own self-concept.

Movement Away from the Model Minority: Defining the Second Gen

While there were unique elements and features in each participant's experience of assimilation, there were also three "hard" life events that were commonly brought up. These life events were expressed not only as hardships but also as resources or motivators for economic achievement, which are not captured by the model minority stereotype. Witnessing their parents' struggles, having difficulty integrating at school, and the complexities in finding comfort from a shared lived experience with other second-generation immigrants (although not necessarily Korean) provided the respondents a typology for the second-generation Korean American/Canadian in contrast to the model minority. Second-generation Koreans in this sample would refer to themselves and other second-generation Koreans as second gen. It appears to be a way of resolving contradictory and unsuitable model minority depictions.

Not every factor was experienced by every participant; however, they were presented as commonly lived experiences and motivations for upward economic mobility. These three factors seemed to function as key influences on self-concept, especially in planning for future upward socioeconomic mobility and ethnic identity formation. Whether they were experienced or not, the respondents perceived these factors as important roles in economic and psychological development. The three difficult life events were described as typical second-gen experiences.

Witnessing Parents' Struggles: "You Know, Your Typical Korean Parents"

"My parents had gotten a stable *gageh* or convenience store, but it was in [town] . . . my dad felt that the education system wasn't challenging us. So he moved me and my brothers back to [city] . . . We knew the reason why we were in [city] . . . So we did study" (Hena, Korean Canadian, 20 years old).

Nearly all participants recounted economic struggles and hardships. Some experienced family unemployment, poverty, and bankruptcy. A common childhood experience associated with financial difficulties was frequent moving across countries, states/provinces, cities, and neighborhoods. The participants were "grateful" to their parents at the time of interview even if they felt resentment at the time of the move. When I asked how it felt to keep moving because of their parents' work, the common response was that of respect for their parents. These children of immigrants felt that their parents were "diligent" and "sacrificial," instilling in them a "good work ethic." This rhetoric is unlike the stereotypical explanation that Asians share a "math gene" that causes academic success. Furthermore, similar patterns of children of immigrants succeeding their parents' socioeconomic status are found across all racial/ethnic groups.[34]

Those participants whose parents attained a professional career in Canada ($n = 1$) and the US ($n = 7$) talked about their parents' "struggle" in terms of difficulties acculturating and assimilating. Part of being second gen meant that their parents faced the challenges of immigrating to a new country such as learning a new language and adapting to a new culture. It appeared that a common second-gen characteristic is to endure difficult times as an immigrant family and to use their struggle as a motivating factor to improve their socioeconomic situation.

Crazy Korean Parents: A Reconceptualization of
High Asian Academic Achievement

> "You know how there's that stereotype: all Asian kids have those crazy parents that make you study all the time" (Jessica, Korean American, 18 years old).

Having "crazy" or "strict" parents that enforce extreme academic achievement was a typical depiction of Korean and Asian American/Canadian parents. For example, Jane had perfect attendance all throughout her elementary school years because of her parents' "strict" views on education. Despite that only one-third ($n = 10$) felt that their parents fit this typification, nearly all 32 participants mentioned that their parents' emphasized the value of education. For the few that did not experience any pressure from their parents, they felt that their parents were exceptions.

Describing nonnormative parental ways was a key element of being second gen and was also regarded as a motivating factor for upward economic mobility. Parents' pressure on their children's academic achievement was portrayed as a dedication to better the lives of their families. Alison's mother used her situation, which entailed long hours of work seven days a week without benefits, to motivate Alison to focus on her studies. Alison's mother did not have a university degree and felt that Alison's future depended on high education attainment, which leads us to the third life event.

Finding Comfort with Other Second Gens
The participants in this study often talked about the feeling of comfort when interacting with other second gens because there was an "unspoken" understanding of second-gen experiences. Understanding or acknowledging experiences of financial hardship, working in a *gageh* (store), Korean forms of corporal punishment, serving as a translator to parents, and "crazy" strict parents were presented as important knowledge to have in developing bonds with other second-generation Koreans. With non-Korean school friends (elementary and secondary schools), participants felt ashamed of their parents and home life and attempted to attain honorary white status. With other second gens, participants felt that they could speak freely about their experiences and "even be proud" of their parents and their Koreanness, possibly developing a second gen, not a model minority, identity.

Church and Christianity: Subculture Formation

All participants except one grew up attending a Korean church. Many told me that the friends they made in church were those that have remained throughout the years while school friends have dissipated within short time periods.

They expressed that part of their understanding of what it means to be second gen came from growing up in a Korean church. Although the churches did not give organized or formal lessons on what it means to be Korean American/ Canadian, they felt comfortable because they could discuss their lived experiences with others who understood them. They found that their network of church peers provided a sense of membership that was not accessible elsewhere. It was not the religion but rather the informal networks that were formed in Korean churches that provided resources for constructing the second-gen identity.

This does not imply that church attendance for second-generation Koreans is mainly for social and not religious purposes. The attendance of Protestant and Catholic churches by second-generation Korean Americans and Korean Canadians is decreasing, which has become a growing concern according to Korean religious leaders. The "silent exodus" is a catch phrase that describes the perceived decline in adult second-generation Korean church membership. Min and Kim examined second-generation Korean church affiliation and attendance in the New York–New Jersey area of the United States. They reported a decline of approximately 33 percent (although religious leaders estimate a 90 percent decline).[35] While the majority of second-generation Korean Americans attends church, Min and Kim's results indicate that Korean churches are not effectively passing on Korean traditions and cultural ways. These second-generation Korean Americans are attending churches predominantly for religious purposes. They also report that attending church for social purposes is less important to them than it is for their parents. The respondents in this study recognized the importance of attending a Korean church in developing a second-gen community and culture.

For 28 out of 31 participants, finding comfort through built connections with other second gens seemed to enhance their sense of ethnic pride and their plans for upward economic mobility. Building connections with other Korean Americans seemed to reinforce motivating factors for upward economic mobility. For example, second gens would meet in the library and "study" together. This was considered a typical second-gen behavior that differentiated them from white Americans/Canadians and from "Korean Koreans" (Korean international students or first-generation Koreans).

Consequences of Honorary Whiteness

Those who did not integrate into a Korean American/Canadian or pan-Asian group expressed a personal struggle in understanding who they were because they had strong Korean family ties but lacked network ties to second-generation Korean American/Canadian friends with whom to share their experiences. This

seemed to be a negative consequence of assimilating upward. Three participants, Caroline, Jane, and Jessica, had all-white friends and no Korean Ameri-
can/Canadian friends. They felt that they were losing their Koreanness and it
worried them. The three stated that they grew out of feeling "ashamed" of their
Korean ethnic status and felt that they could be "proud" of being Korean. At
the same time, they felt that they lacked a sense of authenticity since they did
not have a group of Korean or Asian friends. They explained that their feelings
of loss to be like an ability to feel fully comfortable with their all-white friends.
Through Korean or pan-Asian membership, they felt that they would be able to
develop stronger connections than they could with their white friends. Caroline
told me that although her friends were "good" about it, they "could not understand" the experience of growing up in a Korean household.

While Caroline, Jane, and Jessica's economic and social adjustment
appeared structurally ideal in comparison to coethnically adapted second
gens, their self-concept and sense of belonging seemed more recent and more
problematic than the other 28 participants (who were members of coethnic
groups, formal and informal). For Caroline, Jane, and Jessica, upward assimilation seemed to be negatively affecting their ethnic self-concept. They told
me that being out of their parents' homes gave them the freedom to engage
in more American pastimes such as staying out late, drinking, and going to
house parties. Although Korean Americans on their campuses were engaging
in the same leisure behaviors, they were regarded as a group of people who
spent a lot of time studying in the library. And although there are non-Asian
students who exhibit characteristics of a model minority, they were regarded
as people who party and who are "laid back" about their studies. The three
worried that their deep integration into the dominant mainstream culture was
taking them away from their academic rigorousness and the work ethic their
parents had instilled in them.

These sentiments expressed a significant consequence of upward assimilation
that the classic assimilation model overlooks. Their high average and median
educational attainment, employment, occupation, income, English language
use, and low crime rates imply that Korean Americans and Korean Canadians have integrated successfully. However, socioeconomic measures neglect the
dynamic ethnic identity/self-concept outcome differences among new second-
generation Koreans.[36] This sample revealed that a sense of belonging to a sub-
culture of second-generation Koreans was an important anchor for an ethnic
self-concept.

Summary

There were commonly experienced and recognized life events among the participants of this study. Although they were structural stressors, they were reconciled through individualized reconceptualizations of the events as motivating factors for upward economic mobility. The following three main macrostressors yet micromotivators are discussed here: family hardships, problems integrating at school, and finding comfort with other second-generation Koreans. The respondents in this study regarded and discussed their stressful life events in two ways. The first characteristic included reconstructions of difficult and stressful past experiences into positive motivating factors for successful integration, academic achievement, and upward economic mobility. The second characteristic included the tendency to define lived experiences as "typical" second-generation Korean, or second gen, experiences. These defining characteristics were regarded as uniquely difficult experiences, which factored in their and their parents' diligence to succeed.

Conclusions: Typified Second Gens and Attempted Resolution of the Model Minority Stereotype

An internalization of the model minority stereotype can produce conflicting notions of the self as "honorary white" and "forever foreigner," creating conflicting feelings of wanting to rebel against the stereotype but also to conform to it. The stereotype is used to belittle Asians in the United States and Canada who succeed or achieve middle class status in their host society. It also creates sweeping generalizations about Asians that narrowly define them as socially inept in Western culture. Second gens in the United States and Canada may be internalizing a description of their race and ethnicity that mockingly caricatures the struggle and social exclusion as a more positive stereotype than ones for other racial minorities. At the same time, unsettling feelings of the stereotypes' negativity may be leading second-generation Korean immigrants to attempt to reappropriate the model minority and construct, from within, the second gen.

Notes

1. Samuel Noh et al., "Perceived Racial Discrimination, Depression, and Coping: A Study of Southeast Asian Refugees in Canada," *Journal of Health and Social Behavior* 40 (1999); Richard Lee, "Resilience against Discrimination: Ethnic Identity and Other Group Orientation as Protective Factors for Korean Americans," *Journal of Counseling Psychology* 52 (2005). The results concerning the relationship between a strong ethnic identity and a mental well-being are contradictory; see Kyoung Ja Hyun, "Is an Independent Self a Requisite for Asian Immigrants' Psychological Well-Being in the U.S.? The Case of Korean Americans," *Journal of Human*

Behavior in the Social Environment 3 (2001). For a discussion of the various findings, also see H. C. Yoo and R. M. Lee, "Does Ethnic Identity Buffer or Exacerbate the Effects of Frequent Racial Discrimination on Situational Well-Being of Asian Americans?," *Journal of Counseling Psychology* 55, no. 1 (2008).

2. See Joel Best, "Deviance: The Constructionist Stance," in *Constructions of Deviance: Social Power, Context, and Interaction*, ed. P. A. Adler and P. Adler (Belmont, CA: Wadsworth/Thomson Learning, 2003).

3. Peter L. Berger and Thomas Luckmann, *The Social Construction of Reality: A Treatise in the Sociology of Knowledge* (Garden City, NY: Doubleday & Company Inc., 1966). Best, "Deviance."

4. Sumi K Cho, "Converging Stereotypes in Racialized Sexual Harassment: Where the Model Minority Meets Suzie Wong," in *Critical Race Theory: The Cutting Edge*, ed. R. Delgado and J. Stefancic (Philadelphia, PA: Temple University Press, 1997); Min Zhou, "Growing up American: The Challenge Confronting Immigrant Children and Children of Immigrants," *Annual Review of Sociology* 23 (1997); Min Zhou and Jennifer Lee, "Introduction: The Making of Culture, Identity, and Ethnicity among Asian American Youth," in *Asian American Youth: Culture, Identity and Ethnicity* (New York: Routledge, 2004); Stacey J. Lee, "More Than 'Model Minorities' or 'Delinquents': A Look at Hmong American High School Students," in *Facing Racism in Education*, ed. S. L. Anderson, P. F. Attwood, and L. C. Howard (Cambridge, MA: Harvard Education Review, 2004).

5. Monica Boyd, "Variations in Socioeconomic Outcomes of Second Generation Young Adults," *Canadian Diversity* (2008); Heidi Lasley Barajas and Jennifer L. Pierce, "The Significance of Race and Gender in School Success among Latinas and Latinos in College," *Gender & Society* 15 (2001); Azhou Abu-Ali and Carol A. Reisen, "Gender Role Identity among Adolescent Muslim Girls Living in the U.S.," *Current Psychology* 18 (1999); Karen A. Cerulo, "Identity Construction: New Issues, New Directions," *Annual Review of Sociology* 23 (1997); Stephen Cornell and Douglas Hartmann, *Ethnicity and Race: Making Identities in a Changing World* (Thousand Oaks, CA: Pine Forge Press, 1998); Evelyn Nakano Glenn, "The Social Construction and Institutionalization of Gender and Race: An Integrative Framework," in *Revisioning Gender*, ed. M. Marx Ferree, J. Lorber, and B. B. Hess (Walnut Creek, CA: Alta Mira Press, 2000); Grace Kao, "Group Images and Possible Selves among Adolescents: Linking Stereotypes to Expectations by Race and Ethnicity," *Sociological Forum* 15 (2000); Michael Omi and Howard Winant, *Racial Formation in the United States: From the 1960s to the 1990s*, 2nd ed. (New York: Routledge, 1994); Todd L. Pittinsky, Margaret Shih, and Nalini Ambady, "Identity Adaptiveness: Affect across Multiple Identities," *Journal of Social Issues* 55 (1999); Karen D. Pyke, "Asian American Women's Accounts of Asian and White Masculinities: An Example of Internalized Gendered Racism," Department of Sociology (Riverside, CA 92521-0419: University of California, 2004); Karen D. Pyke and Denise L. Johnson, "Asian American Women and Racialized Femininities 'Doing' Gender across Cultural Worlds," *Gender & Society* 17 (2003); L. Susan Williams, Sandra D. Alvarez, and Kevin S. Andrade Hauck, "My Name Is Not Maria: Young Latinas Seeking Home in the Heartland," *Social Problems* 49 (2002).

6. Stuart Hall, "Old and New Identities, Old and New Ethnicities," in *Theories in Race and Racism*, ed. S. Hall, L. Back, and J. Solomos (New York: Psychology Press, 1999).

7. Martin Bulmer and John Solomos, "Introduction: Re-thinking Ethnic and Racial Studies," *In Ethnic and Racial Studies* 21 (1998).

8. Desiree Boalia Qin, Niobe Way, and Preetika Mukherjee, "The Other Side of the Model Minority Story," *Youth and Society* 34 (2008).

9. Nazli Kibria, *Becoming Asian American: Second-Generation Chinese and Korean American Identities* (Baltimore, MA: Johns Hopkins University Press, 2002); Stacey J. Lee, *Unraveling the "Model Minority" Stereotype: Listening to Asian American Youth* (New York: Teachers College Press, 1996); Stacey J. Lee, "Additional Complexities: Social Class, Ethnicity, Generation, and Gender in Asian American Student Experiences," *Race, Ethnicity and Education* 9 (2006).

10. Boyd, "Variations in Socioeconomic Outcomes of Second Generation Young Adults"; Lee, "Additional Complexities: Social Class, Ethnicity, Generation, and Gender in Asian American Student Experiences."

11. Roger Waldinger and Renee Reichl, "Today's New Second Generation: Getting Ahead or Falling Behind?," in *Securing the Future: US Immigrant Integration Policy, A Reader*, ed. M. Fix (Washington, DC: Migration Policy Institute, 2007).

12. The US Census Bureau provides 1993–2004 per capita income by race group statistics. Up to 2004, Asian per capita income was less than white per capita income.

13. Carmen DeNavas-Walt, Bernadette D. Proctor, and Cheryl Hill Lee, "U.S. Census Bureau, Current Population Reports," in *Income, Poverty, and Health Insurance Coverage in the United States: 2004 U.S.* (Washington, DC: Government Printing Office, 2005).

14. Terrance J. Reeves and Claudette E. Bennett, "We the People: Asians in the United States," in *Census 2000 Special Reports* (US Census Bureau, 2004); Statistics Canada, "Canadian Statistics: Visible Minority Population, by Provinces and Territories (2001 Census)," http://www40.statcan.ca/l01/cst01/demo52a.htm.

15. Jungwee Park, "A Demographic Profile of Koreans in Canada," in *Korean Immigrants in Canada: Perspectives on Migration, Integration, and the Family*, ed. S. Noh, A. H. Kim, and M. S. Noh (Toronto, ON: University of Toronto Press, 2012).

16. Waldinger and Reichl, "Today's New Second Generation: Getting Ahead or Falling Behind?"

17. Zhou and Lee, "Introduction: The Making of Culture, Identity, and Ethnicity among Asian American Youth."

18. Mia Tuan, *Forever Foreigners or Honorary Whites* (New Brunswick, NJ: Rutgers University Press, 1998).

19. Pittinsky, Shih, and Ambady, "Identity Adaptiveness: Affect across Multiple Identities"; Morrison G. Wong, "Model Students: Teachers' Perceptions and Expectations of Their Asian and White Students," *Sociology of Education*, no. 53 (1990).

20. Charles R. Taylor and Barbara B. Stern, "Asian-Americans: Television Advertising and the 'Model Minority' Stereotype," *Journal of Advertising* 26 (1997).

21. Zhou and Lee, "Introduction," 18

22. Omi and Winant, *Racial Formation in the United States*.

23. Edwin M. Schur, *Labeling Women Deviant: Gender, Stigma, and Social Control* (New York: Random House, 1984).

24. Lee, "More than 'Model Minorities' or 'Delinquents': A Look at Hmong American High School Students."

25. Tuan, *Forever Foreigners or Honorary Whites.*

26. Bulmer and Solomos, "Introduction: Re-thinking Ethnic and Racial Studies."

27. Kathy Charmez, "Grounded Theory," in *Approaches to Qualitative Research: A Reader on Theory and Practice*, ed. S. N. Hesse-Biber and P. Leavy (New York: Oxford University Press, 2004).

28. H. J. Rubin and I. S. Rubin, *Qualitative Interviewing: The Art of Hearing Data* (London: Sage, 1995).

29. Previous studies have been careful to interview both members and nonmembers to capture a broader understanding of ethnic identity; Kibria, *Becoming Asian American.*

30. Charmez, "Grounded Theory"; Barney G. Glaser, *Theoretical Sensitivity: Advances in the Methodology of Grounded Theory* (Mill Valley, CA: Sociology Press, 1978); A. Strauss and J. Corbin, *Basics of Qualitative Research: Grounded Theory Procedures and Techniques* (Newbury Park: Sage, 1990).

31. The question "Have you ever felt like you were expected to behave like a model minority?" was officially added to the guide after reviewing the Canadian respondents' responses to feeling like a model minority as they would tend to make a distinction between feeling like a model minority and feeling like they were expected to behave according to the stereotype.

32. Kibria, *Becoming Asian American,* 11

33. Tuan, *Forever Foreigners or Honorary Whites.*

34. Waldinger and Reichl, "Today's New Second Generation."

35. Pyoung Gap Min and Dae Young Kim, "Intergenerational Transmission of Religion and Culture: Korean Protestants in the U.S.," *Sociology of Religion* 66 (2005).

36. Nancy Lopez, "Disentangling Race-Gender Work Experiences: Second-Generation Caribbean Young Adults in New York City," in *Gender and U.S. Immigration: Contemporary Trends*, ed. P. Hondagneu-Sotelo (Los Angeles, CA: University of California Press, 2003).

Bibliography

Abu-Ali, Azhou, and Carol A. Reisen. "Gender Role Identity among Adolescent Muslim Girls Living in the U.S." *Current Psychology* 18 (1999): 185–92.

Barajas, Heidi Lasley, and Jennifer L. Pierce. "The Significance of Race and Gender in School Success among Latinas and Latinos in College." *Gender & Society* 15 (2001): 859–78.

Berger, Peter L., and Thomas Luckmann. *The Social Construction of Reality: A Treatise in the Sociology of Knowledge.* Garden City, NY: Doubleday & Company, 1966.

Best, Joel. "Deviance: The Constructionist Stance." In *Constructions of Deviance: Social Power, Context, and Interaction*, edited by P. A. Adler and P. Adler, 90–94. Belmont, CA: Wadsworth/Thomson Learning, 2003.

Boyd, Monica. "Variations in Socioeconomic Outcomes of Second Generation Young Adults." *Canadian Diversity 6* (2008): 20-24.

Bulmer, Martin, and John Solomos. "Introduction: Re-Thinking Ethnic and Racial Studies." *In Ethnic and Racial Studies* 21 (1998): 819–37.

Cerulo, Karen A. "Identity Construction: New Issues, New Directions." *Annual Review of Sociology* 23 (1997): 385–409.

Charmez, Kathy. "Grounded Theory." In *Approaches to Qualitative Research: A Reader on Theory and Practice*, edited by S. N. Hesse-Biber and P. Leavy, 496–521. New York: Oxford University Press, 2004.

Cho, Sumi K. "Converging Stereotypes in Racialized Sexual Harassment: Where the Model Minority Meets Suzie Wong." In *Critical Race Theory: The Cutting Edge*, edited by R. Delgado and J. Stefancic, 532–42. Philadelphia, PA: Temple University Press, 1997.

Cornell, Stephen, and Douglas Hartmann. *Ethnicity and Race: Making Identities in a Changing World*. Thousand Oaks, CA: Pine Forge Press, 1998.

DeNavas-Walt, Carmen, Bernadette D. Proctor, and Cheryl Hill Lee. "U.S. Census Bureau, Current Population Reports." In *Income, Poverty, and Health Insurance Coverage in the United States: 2004 U.S.*, 60–229. Washington, DC: Government Printing Office, 2005.

Glaser, Barney G. *Theoretical Sensitivity: Advances in the Methodology of Grounded Theory*. Mill Valley, CA: Sociology Press, 1978.

Glenn, Evelyn Nakano. "The Social Construction and Institutionalization of Gender and Race: An Integrative Framework." In *Revisioning Gender*, edited by M. Marx Ferree, J. Lorber, and B. B. Hess, 3–43. Walnut Creek, CA: Alta Mira Press, 2000.

Hall, Stuart. "Old and New Identities, Old and New Ethnicities." In *Theories in Race and Racism*, edited by S. Hall, L. Back, and J. Solomos, 144–53. New York: Psychology Press, 1999.

Hyun, Kyoung Ja. "Is an Independent Self a Requisite for Asian Immigrants' Psychological Well-Being in the U.S.? The Case of Korean Americans." *Journal of Human Behavior in the Social Environment* 3 (2001): 179–200.

Kao, Grace. "Group Images and Possible Selves among Adolescents: Linking Stereotypes to Expectations by Race and Ethnicity." *Sociological Forum* 15 (2000): 407–30.

Kibria, Nazli. *Becoming Asian American: Second-Generation Chinese and Korean American Identities*. Baltimore, MA: Johns Hopkins University Press, 2002.

Lee, Richard. "Resilience against Discrimination: Ethnic Identity and Other Group Orientation as Protective Factors for Korean Americans." *Journal of Counseling Psychology* 52 (2005): 36–44.

Lee, Stacey J. "Additional Complexities: Social Class, Ethnicity, Generation, and Gender in Asian American Student Experiences." *Race, Ethnicity and Education* 9 (2006): 17–28.

———. "More Than 'Model Minorities' or 'Delinquents': A Look at Hmong American High School Students." In *Facing Racism in Education*, edited by S. L. Anderson, P. F. Attwood, and L. C. Howard, 95–117. Cambridge, MA: Harvard Education Review, 2004.

————. *Unraveling the "Model Minority" Stereotype: Listening to Asian American Youth*. New York: Teachers College Press, 1996.

Lopez, Nancy. "Disentangling Race-Gender Work Experiences: Second-Generation Caribbean Young Adults in New York City." In *Gender and U.S. Immigration: Contemporary Trends*, edited by P. Hondagneu-Sotelo, 174–93. Los Angeles, CA: University of California Press, 2003.

Min, Pyoung Gap, and Dae Young Kim. "Intergenerational Transmission of Religion and Culture: Korean Protestants in the U.S." *Sociology of Religion* 66 (2005): 263–82.

Noh, Samuel, Morton Beiser, Violet Kaspar, Feng Hou, and Joanna Rumens. "Perceived Racial Discrimination, Depression, and Coping: A Study of Southeast Asian Refugees in Canada." *Journal of Health and Social Behavior* 40 (1999): 193–207.

Noh, Samuel, and Violet Kaspar. "Perceived Discrimination and Depression: Moderating Effects of Coping, Acculturation, and Ethnic Support." *American Journal of Public Health* 93 (2003): 232–38.

Omi, Michael, and Howard Winant. *Racial Formation in the United States: From the 1960s to the 1990s*. 2nd ed. New York: Routledge, 1994.

Park, Jungwee. "A Demographic Profile of Koreans in Canada." In *Korean Immigrants in Canada: Perspectives on Migration, Integration, and the Family*, edited by S. Noh, A. H. Kim, and M. S. Noh, 19–34. Toronto, ON: University of Toronto Press, 2012.

Pittinsky, Todd L., Margaret Shih, and Nalini Ambady. "Identity Adaptiveness: Affect across Multiple Identities." *Journal of Social Issues* 55 (1999): 503–18.

Pyke, Karen D. "Asian American Women's Accounts of Asian and White Masculinities: An Example of Internalized Gendered Racism," Department of Sociology. Riverside, CA 92521-0419: University of California, 2004.

Pyke, Karen D., and Denise L. Johnson. "Asian American Women and Racialized Femininities 'Doing' Gender across Cultural Worlds." *Gender & Society* 17 (2003): 33–53.

Qin, Desiree Boalia, Niobe Way, and Preetika Mukherjee. "The Other Side of the Model Minority Story." *Youth and Society* 34 (2008): 480–506.

Reeves, Terrance J., and Claudette E. Bennett. "We the People: Asians in the United States." In *Census 2000 Special Reports*. US Census Bureau, 2004.

Rubin, H. J., and I. S. Rubin. *Qualitative Interviewing: The Art of Hearing Data*. London: Sage, 1995.

Schur, Edwin M. *Labeling Women Deviant: Gender, Stigma, and Social Control*. New York: Random House, 1984.

Statistics Canada. "Canadian Statistics: Visible Minority Population, by Provinces and Territories (2001 Census)." http://www40.statcan.ca/l01/cst01/demo52a.htm.

Strauss, A., and J. Corbin. *Basics of Qualitative Research: Grounded Theory Procedures and Techniques*. Newbury Park: Sage, 1990.

Taylor, Charles R., and Barbara B. Stern. "Asian-Americans: Television Advertising and the 'Model Minority' Stereotype." *Journal of Advertising* 26 (1997): 47–61.

Tuan, Mia. *Forever Foreigners or Honorary Whites*. New Brunswick, NJ: Rutgers University Press, 1998.

Waldinger, Roger, and Renee Reichl. "Today's New Second Generation: Getting Ahead or Falling Behind?" In *Securing the Future: Us Immigrant Integration Policy, a Reader*, edited by M. Fix. Washington, DC: Migration Policy Institute, 2007.

Williams, L. Susan, Sandra D. Alvarez, and Kevin S. Andrade Hauck. "My Name Is Not Maria: Young Latinas Seeking Home in the Heartland." *Social Problems* 49 (2002): 563–84.

Wong, Morrison G. "Model Students: Teachers' Perceptions and Expectations of Their Asian and White Students." *Sociology of Education*, no. 53 (1990): 236–46.

Yoo, H. C., and R. M. Lee. "Does Ethnic Identity Buffer or Exacerbate the Effects of Frequent Racial Discrimination on Situational Well-Being of Asian Americans?" *Journal of Counseling Psychology* 55, no. 1 (2008): 63.

Zhou, Min. "Growing up American: The Challenge Confronting Immigrant Children and Children of Immigrants." *Annual Review of Sociology* 23 (1997): 63–95.

Zhou, Min, and Jennifer Lee. "Introduction: The Making of Culture, Identity, and Ethnicity among Asian American Youth." In *Asian American Youth: Culture, Identity and Ethnicity*, 1–32. New York: Routledge, 2004.

CHAPTER 8

Social Exclusion and the Welfare State

Effects of Distributive Conflicts on Immigrants in Germany

Marcella Myers[*]

In October 2010 German chancellor Angela Merkel declared multicul-turalism a failure. Merkel's comments came on the heels of the con-troversy over Thilo Sarrazin's comments regarding the negative impact Muslims have on the German welfare state. A study done by the *Friedrich Ebert Stiftung*[1] found that 30 percent of Germans agree that foreigners come to Germany to exploit the welfare state, that there are too many foreigners in Germany, and that the number of foreigners in Germany is dangerous. These attitudes persist in spite of countervailing evidence showing that the number of foreign born (individuals not holding German citizenship) in Germany has remained stable, even falling almost imperceptibly, from 8.8 percent of the total population in 1995 to 8.2 percent in 2007.[2] Most often discussions about immigration and anti-immigrant sentiment are framed in terms of eth-nicity and race. Framing the debate in this way is important and appropriate; I suggest another rationalization for anti-immigrant attitudes. I argue that there is an economic basis for anti-immigrant attitudes that manifests as wel-fare chauvinism and is expressed through conflicts over the distribution and redistribution of resources in society.

The perception on the part of Germans regarding the exploitation of the welfare state by immigrants is representative of redistributive conflicts that

[*] Address correspondence to Marcella Myers, PhD, Department of History and Political Science, 131 Buller Hall, Andrews University, Berrien Springs, MI 49104-0010. Email: marcellm@andrews.edu.

occur within most welfare states. The conflict over distribution and redistribution may lead to the exclusion of immigrants not only from social benefits but also from the labor market as well. If the purpose of the welfare state is to provide equity, social justice, and a level playing field to all members of society, social exclusion violates these basic principles. I argue that these violations disproportionately and negatively affect immigrants. This chapter presents a discussion of exclusion, how exclusion may violate the welfare state principles of social justice, and the ways in which the conflict over redistribution negatively affects immigrants in Germany.

Exclusion

Exclusion occurs in multiple contexts. In the case of Germany, the issue of social exclusion is of interest due to the nature of its immigration policy. Legal immigrants in Germany obtain social rights; however, they do not have access to political rights. Thus immigrant communities must rely on external associations for the political articulation of their needs. Without civic rights, social rights become more precarious. The question is whether public policy reinforces and/or expands social exclusion.

It is generally agreed that social exclusion is a multidimensional phenomenon and, for this reason, is complicated.[3] Large-scale exclusion implies that "people, although they are being cared for, no longer have an obligatory commitment to an important social institution."[4] This undermines social institutions and may be compounded by perceptions on the part of nonrecipients that individuals are taking advantage of welfare services to which they are not entitled, leading to a further lack of confidence in institutions. Most advanced industrialized countries have persons living on the fringes of society, outside traditional labor and social patterns. These marginalized persons may be excluded for a variety of reasons, including but not limited to social welfare policies pursued by governments and the consequences of those policies. How distribution to and/or integration of these marginalized populations is an important issue for welfare states. Marginalized persons frequently depend on government for some form of social assistance. Social exclusion may not necessarily be economic in nature; however, economically marginalized populations tend to include higher numbers of immigrants.

Social Exclusion

According to Vleminckx and Berghman, social exclusion has four main characteristics. The first, "social exclusion implies one is not like others in the society in which one lives";[5] on this point the implications for immigrants may vary depending on the immigrants' country of origin. For example, Germany has seen an increase in the number of Polish immigrants. Arguably integration for a Pole might be more easily achieved than for an individual from Turkey or Vietnam. Second, social exclusion is multidimensional. As with the first dimension, multidimensional exclusion disproportionately affects immigrants. In immigrant communities there tend to be lower levels of education that in turn means individuals have lower job skills, resulting in lower pay and less secure employment. Lower income also affects consumption, housing, and educational choices. Third, social exclusion is dynamic, "an action or series of actions developing over time."[6] These characteristics present a picture of social exclusion as a dynamic process in which processes are mutually reinforcing. A final distinguishing feature of social exclusion is that the processes leading to exclusion are, as a series of events, unpredictable.

These processes are not provided for "by the conventional safety nets created by existing systems of social protection, or the aid granted by these systems turns out to be inadequate for dealing with the problem."[7] Social exclusion is not only a process but also a limiting of social and economic opportunities of "those who are different in one of several respects such as race, language, religion, local or social origin, and ethnicity."[8] Social exclusion and poverty may be related but are not the same thing. One may live in poverty but have social inclusion as a member of a social group. The converse is also true; one may be excluded socially based on language or social skills but may have a high socioeconomic status.[9]

Labor Market Exclusion

Exclusion from the labor market is important because it undermines an individual's ability to participate in other market sectors. This exclusion may be characterized by unemployment, underemployment, or losses in wages and benefits. The concern is that unemployment will develop into long-term unemployment and prolonged dependence on welfare supports. Exclusion from employment may occur from the lack of qualifications or training to secure employment in the first place. Therein lies the problem for immigrants who have less education and job training. The transformation of labor from manufacturing to a knowledge-based economy plays a part. First, it creates a new set of standards for employment; second, labor markets are becoming more selective.[10] Where employers demand efficiency, the qualifications of the employee must exactly match the task requirements specified by management. "Those who do not have the qualifications are not hired, and those who are employed but do not adapt to the change in standards of their tasks are fired."[11] New standards of employment and more selective hiring practices mean that growing numbers of adults are excluded from the labor market and many young people are unable to enter it.[12] In this way education becomes important because the type of labor market determines the best education to pursue, assuming one is not excluded from educational opportunities.

When workers remain employed, they also face risks through the loss of benefits, formerly paid by their employer. The individual who has lost his or her job may find another job but at reduced pay or benefits, which may result in or lead to underemployment.[13] The transformation to postindustrial economies, from manufacturing to service base, contributes to exclusion through the emergence of low-paying jobs that lead to dependency on family income supports and do not enable workers to earn enough to become completely independent.[14] Low-paying and/or part-time service employment creates a different set of problems than straightforward unemployment.

Many low-paying, part-time jobs are concentrated in immigrant communities, specifically toward single parent, working families where skills are low. If the conditions precarious jobs offer are "below the threshold for social insurance," these jobs can "store up problems for future entitlements, compromising the very form of personal entrepreneurial investment in life that is advocated" by policymakers.[15] These people, though they may be employed, often live at or below the subsistence level.[16] Pierson writes that where policies encourage the expansion of the low-wage private sector employment, the "costs include maintaining poverty and inequality, large gaps in the support for human capital development, and a host of associated social problems."[17] Underemployment may mean social exclusion because of income reduction, but it may also include exclusion from consumption.[18] The inability to secure housing and transportation can make finding or maintaining employment difficult. Further, underemployment makes securing better housing, a higher-paying job, or an education for children difficult, thus trapping individuals in an excluded category, potentially for generations.

Social Justice

Barry argues that social exclusion violates the values of social solidarity and social justice. Principles of social justice provide a way to assign "rights and duties in the basic institutions of society and they define the appropriate distribution of the benefits and burdens of social cooperation."[19] In a just society basic liberties are "taken for granted and the rights secured by justice are not subject to political bargaining or the calculus of social interests."[20] The consequence of the relationship between social justice and social exclusion are profound. Advanced industrial societies are approaching a norm of "social politics organized around flexible labor markets and structural exclusion."[21] Structural exclusion fundamentally alters the environment of individuals, altering the access to social inclusion through education and employment as well as a potential alteration in geographical space that limits access to resources. As a result, the choice set of individuals that enables people to live lives they value is limited.

There are social costs to injustices, structural or otherwise. First is the undermining of the individual's self-respect; the "denial of justice to another is to either refuse to recognize him as an equal" or to be willing to exploit natural "fortunes and happenstance for our own advantage."[22] In any case, "deliberate injustice invites submission or resistance. Submission arouses contempt of those who perpetuate injustice and confirms their intention, whereas resistance cuts the ties of community."[23] Powerless, people or institutions automatically arouse contempt, the desire to attack, the desire to dominate, and the desire to humiliate.[24] The consequences for society are negative. Submission excludes the powerless through injustice perpetrated by those in power; the resulting contempt of those more powerful undermines individual self-worth. Thus a downward spiral of contempt and submission reinforce the position of excluded individuals.

The implications for institutions perceived to be powerless are also serious. If the institutions of the welfare state are perceived to be powerless or ineffective, individuals in positions of power may exploit those institutions for their own benefit. In "flexible capitalism," the economic environment in which low-wage, junk jobs are the rule rather than the exception, there is a massive resource transfer to the "most affluent, the capitalists and the comprador new superclass."[25] The gains are economic, political, and social; those benefiting from these gains control resources and the determination of who should receive those resources, in what quantity and how.

The Welfare State

"One of the classic aspirations of the welfare state is that their policies should have a uniform state-wide reach" with the aim to ensure the "equity of provision for all citizens irrespective of where they live within the state."[26] It further "provides its beneficiaries with freedom from want"[27] and to "even out differences in life chances" with programs that are meant to "help people reallocate income over the life cycle, to insure against events which cause income loss, and to provide a sense of security to all citizens."[28] Ultimately the welfare state makes public policies intended to level the playing field for all residing within its borders. In effect this is the practice of social justice, and social exclusion is a violation of not only social justice but also the principles of the welfare state. Social justice allows individuals to make legitimate claims, maintaining that "disadvantages for which people cannot reasonably be made responsible should give rise to legitimate claims for aid, redress, or compensation (as appropriate)."[29]

The welfare state offers help to individuals in need and provides an equality of opportunity. However, how the welfare state is structured to deliver the distribution of benefits is important. As welfare states have come under increased budgetary pressures, conflicts over distribution are likely to increase. These distributive conflicts have the potential to further marginalize individuals already at risk and deepen existing cleavages between groups in society. Concerns regarding redistribution are not only about the distribution of resources but also about the inequality in the distribution of risks associated with the economic and labor transformation that has taken place in advanced industrialized countries. "These developments arouse strong feelings of vulnerability, uncertainty, and even anxiety, reinforced by the observation that there is no longer good correspondence between individual achievement and the distribution of rewards."[30] In this politicized conflict over distribution, those individuals without civic rights are particularly at risk. Without a strong advocate acting on their behalf, individuals and communities with only social rights are at the mercy of politicians and populations that may be hostile.

Redistributive conflicts often become centered on the issue of immigration. In the wake of the collapse of the Soviet Union, German reunification, and the Yugoslav civil war, the advanced industrial countries of Western Europe experienced the influx of large numbers of refugees and immigrants, adding to existing immigrant communities. Immigrant communities have suffered some of the same problems experienced by native populations, specifically as these problems relate to the labor market. Immigrants recruited to work in Western Europe have generally come to work in industries that have been most severely affected by economic downturns and restructuring.[31] The problems for immigrants are compounded because they often lack education and/or training so that "the number of foreigners who fall below the poverty line is considerably higher than is the proportion of the native population."[32] A higher rate of poverty among immigrants contributes to the perception on the part of the native population that immigrants are taking advantage of the programs and benefits offered by the host country.

When the welfare state programs are based on insurance principles in which benefits are received in proportion to the individual contribution, public acceptance of social programs is not undermined.[33] When the welfare state goes beyond the insurance principle, redistributing funds from contributors to beneficiaries, ethnic balance plays a role in the public acceptance of social programs and specifically programs that extend benefits to immigrants.[34] Means-tested, targeted, or selective benefit programs are an alternative. In means-tested programs eligibility is based on categorical or income requirements. "Means-tested or targeted systems are designed to separate the 'needy' from the well-to-do, the deserving from the undeserving, and so on,"[35] "the distributive rational is one of targeting the poor."[36] This distributive rational then directs benefits to those who are "already disadvantaged in terms of income and education"; means testing also tends to "establish hierarchies, accentuate differences, highlight inequalities, and denigrate the self-esteem of welfare recipients."[37]

This policy structure requires the confirmation of eligibility and runs the risk of promoting stigmatization by imposing predefined administrative or sociopolitical categories[38] leading to selective distribution and differentiation. Selective distribution implies low levels of standardization, local administration reinforced by decentralization.[39] A decentralized benefit structure allows multiple access points in policymaking and for program administration. Vague or general guidelines for implementation made at higher levels of government may result in local administrators or proxy bureaucracies interpreting those guidelines leading to or resulting in gate keeping. Gate keeping occurs when program applicants or recipients are not aware or made aware of their full rights or eligibility for programs and assistance.

How legislation defines benefits also plays a role in how the welfare state administers programs. Where benefit structures are vaguely defined, it would "enable states to do very little that was new and let them find some part of existing policy that was having a positive impact."[40] Vague definitions allow states to choose facts regarding policies that fit their interests and act on them without imposing a particular social model on states.[41] The vagueness of legislation is of particular interest in Germany, where federal authorities determine the basic services and benefits that regional governments should provide. In the end programs selectively distributing benefits make program recipients more visible to all members of society. Because immigrants are already visible, their dependency on social programs only serves to highlight how different they are.

In policymaking differentiation often relies on the "notion of 'different needs' which feeds the belief in cultural, essential differences."[42] An environment of stigmatization develops in which immigrants on welfare confirm for the native population that minorities are more dependent and more parasitical than other members of society. The "moral logic of 'exclusion' stigmatizes foreigners as undeserving others" and should result in "higher levels of welfare chauvinism, less trust, and more fractious relations between natives and newcomers."[43]

Welfare chauvinism is the notion that welfare services should be restricted to the native population; immigrants receiving welfare grants coincide with smaller benefits for the native population with "real" problems.[44] Welfare chauvinism is not based in traditional racism and xenophobia; rather, it is a "rational consideration of alternative options to preserve social club goods."[45] It appeals particularly to those who expect "to gain from the redistributive welfare state but fear a welfare state backlash, if the number of beneficiaries swells due to the special needs of immigrants."[46] The message to immigrants is that they are not welcome. The cleavage that develops is not only between haves and have-nots but also between those who have rights, civil and political, and those who do not or are not aware of their rights.[47] Welfare chauvinism "captures the material dimension of conflict, in the sense that immigrants are attracted to a country because of its generous welfare benefits, do not pay taxes, take away the jobs of natives, depress wages, and abuse healthcare, education, and other public services."[48]

The belief in essential differences feeds the perception that "they" are taking advantage of the system leads to welfare chauvinism. If immigrants are viewed as a threat to what Kitschelt calls "club goods," citizens will be more likely to support the exclusion or expulsion of immigrants to preserve national "club goods" and limit redistributive expenses.[49] "Club goods" may include low costs of crime, high social stability, and low levels of poverty. Members of the "club" may be defined as the native population of the country. Who is native in part depends on how national identities are formed. In France this has traditionally referred to those holding French citizenship; in Germany this has traditionally referred to those of German descent.

In order for the cleavage to develop between who receives benefits and who does not, the differences between groups must be discernible. The structure of the welfare state plays an important role. Crepaz and Damron have argued that in universal welfare states, there is little possibility of labeling recipients of welfare benefits. In these universal systems, "almost everyone contributes and almost everyone receives, making it more difficult to stigmatize receivers of government support as 'other.'"[50] Furthermore, the universalist model fights inequality through universal social policies, targeting socioeconomic inequalities rather than ethnic inequalities. However, in doing so, universalism also denies ethnic inequalities, "constructing a socioeconomic problem of 'exclusion' or a problem of 'integration' and not recognizing the existence of ethnic discrimination and racism."[51]

Redistributive Conflicts

Conflicts over redistribution are important, not only in terms of who benefits and who does not, but also because these conflicts shape and are shaped by politics and policy choices. There are also important economic consequences because redistributive conflicts have a negative impact on economic growth. The more equitable the distribution of income in the economy, the higher capital endowment of the median voter, which results in a lower equilibrium level of capital taxation and a higher economic growth.[52] In less equal societies more redistribution is sought by a majority of the population, but these policies reduce economic growth by introducing economic distortions.

There are at least two conditions in which redistributive conflicts may take place. First, there may be "situations in which otherwise attractive policy purposes can only be attained at the expense of identifiable individuals or groups"; second, the existing distribution of assets or life chances may become the policy issue.[53] How the conflict develops from one or both of these basic conditions and the nature of the conflict are affected by a number of factors, which include but may not be limited to an individual's position in the labor market, income, education, and age. These factors are of particular importance to immigrants or migrants, who are often identifiable groups with lower educational attainment and higher levels of unemployment and underemployment than native populations.

Distributional conflicts are about not only the formal welfare state but also the informal welfare as well (e.g., tax expenditures, "corporate welfare," regulated monopolies). Sheltered firms prefer the "wholesale elimination of publicly socialized health, education, and labor market risks to lower their tax burden."[54] The effect on public policy and redistributive conflicts is noticeable in pressures on government by protected firms to privatize social programs. The shift of risk to the individual "allows sheltered firms to pass social costs onto larger firms that face organized labor and so must provide a wide range of benefits to buy labor peace."[55]

This differential shift in the risk structure has a dampening effect on spending, especially when spending is redistributive.[56] The slow down or reduction in spending may also result in intense redistributive battles between those in secure and insecure labor market positions. "If people in secure positions know that they are highly unlikely to end up in insecure ones, i.e. face low labor market risks, they have less reason to be solidaristic with those in insecure positions."[57] These shifts in redistribution raise concerns, amplified by the inequalities in the distribution of risks in transition economies.

Redistributive choices are political and expressed through choices voters make when voting their partisan preferences. The evidence suggests preferences or support for redistribution are in part dependent on an individual's position in the labor market. There is strong evidence too that income is an important factor in the formation of redistributive preferences.[58] Individuals with higher incomes are less supportive of redistributive policies, specifically regarding public pension schemes.[59] Moene and Wallerstein argue that if the majority of the electorate receives a below-average income and if an increase in inequality causes above-average incomes to rise and below-average incomes to fall, then it is reasonable to think that demands for public policies to reduce the gap between rich and poor will increase.[60] In this model the demand for welfare spending comes from those who never work and low-wage workers who may lose their employment. High-wage workers, who by assumption face no risk of income loss, oppose spending on social insurance to the extent that they vote in a self-interested way. However, in reality the risk of income loss rises gradually as individuals move up the income scale.[61]

Implications for Immigrants

The expectations regarding redistributive conflicts and the effect on immigrants are within the context of the corporatist/Christian democratic welfare state. As a Christian democratic country, Germany pursues goals of equality and budgetary restraint.[62] Therefore, the government will encourage egalitarian labor markets by encouraging associational inclusion and heavy regulation of the labor and product markets;[63] this means that workers must belong to labor associations or unions and an egalitarian earning structure.[64] If there is income equality, we should expect attitudes toward immigrants to be more favorable. However, due to the emphasis on union membership, there is a "failure to provide employment opportunities for all who want to work," which results in exclusion and resentment among "outsider classes."[65]

Immigrants do experience higher levels of unemployment, lower incomes, and lower levels of education. This makes the issue of education for them all the more important. The German vocational education system has come under some criticism. First, it has been argued that the German system creates skilled workers whose qualifications and identities are rooted in traditional and rigid occupational categories, preventing German manufacturing from adapting to innovations and more flexible manufacturing techniques. The second weakness is the "relative underdevelopment of continuing vocational education and training."[66] It may be, however, that this weakness is not due to underdevelopment of continuing vocational education and training but rather the type of skills "from which workers derive their income,"[67] making continuing vocational education and training a secondary problem related to skill specificity.

Although these criticisms are legitimate, it is also clear that the creation of skilled workers contributes to a population of workers with high productivity and higher incomes while decreasing the risks of unemployment and income inequality for some individuals.[68] This lack of skills in the population of foreign residents in Germany is a primary contributing factor to not only higher rates of low educational attainment but also higher levels of poverty and unemployment leading to higher levels of immigrant dependence on social welfare services, like income supports, housing subsidies, and cash benefits.

The issue of unskilled labor concentrated in the immigrant population is in part a result of labor policy in post–World War II Germany. Immigrant guest workers recruited to Germany were primarily blue-collar, unskilled laborers,[69] and the decades between 1960 and 2000 were characterized by an increasing foreign population.[70] The demographics of the foreign population in Germany have changed since 2000. The proportion of unskilled workers has fallen, while the numbers of skilled workers, supervisors, masters (the higest skill level), and qualified senior employees have increased.[71] At the same time levels of education among foreigners have increased and individuals completing vocational training or retraining has risen.[72] Skills, employment, and income are linked. As employment rises and more immigrants gain higher skills and education, their ability to find employment and their incomes will rise. This in turn should reduce the number of immigrants receiving welfare state benefits, and in turn we should expect a reduced antipathy toward immigrants.

As immigrants find less opposition to their presence in Germany, there should also be a greater willingness on their part to integrate; negative attitudes on the part of the native population may pose a significant threat to the willingness of immigrants to integrate into the German society.[73] Natives' attitudes toward foreigners have been found to have a negative and significant effect on citizenship aspirations. "Importantly, the association is robust . . . indicating that perceived and objective negative attitudes have independent (negative) effects on citizenship acquisition."[74] The willingness of immigrants to integrate based on perceived and objective negative attitudes may become a cyclical problem. Demands on the part of the native population for groups to integrate are related to a higher degree of hostility toward foreigners.[75]

Low educational attainment combined with higher levels of poverty and unemployment among foreigners are factors that shape the perception on the part of the native population that foreigners are a problem. These perceptions on the part of native populations are important, in part because they may lead to demands for the exclusion of foreigners receiving the benefits of the welfare state. These perceptions on the part of the native population are also shaped by demographics. Individuals with higher levels of education tend to have less hostility toward foreigners; additionally, as income rises, hostility toward foreigners lessens.[76] The social/political climate also influences attitudes toward foreigners when the social climate is characterized by individual's attitudes, political actors, the media, or other social norms; discrimination against ethnic minorities tends to emerge in everyday situations (e.g., school, employment, and housing).[77] Finally, although economic deprivation is considered important in the formation of anti-immigrant attitudes, Zick et al. found that this explanation is rather limited. Instead, they found that two factors most relevant to group-focused hostility are income and a sense of deprivation of their own group.[78] Those with low incomes are more likely to represent derogatory attitudes toward vulnerable groups.[79]

Conclusion

Officially, the German government pursues a policy of integration for foreigners through a number of education and social assistance programs. Although the success of these programs may not be obvious, evidence suggests there is some success in terms of rising education, income, and employment rates for immigrants. It should be noted that the rising employment and income of foreigners is also influenced by the relatively strong German economy, which results in rising employment.

Existing research also suggests that the social climate characterized by individual attitudes, political actors, media, and social norms invites discrimination.[80] This finding should give pause to political leaders and those expressing discriminatory attitudes publicly in a national forum. Such expressed attitudes only reinforce discrimination and hostility toward foreigners, giving "permission" to listeners and citizens to discriminate. Expressed hostility on the part of the native population reduces the desire on the part of immigrants to integrate.

The welfare state is an important component in the perception and expression of discrimination and how the redistributive conflict is shaped; where the German welfare state remains within the insurance scheme, there is less opposition to the inclusion of immigrants.[81] This applies for all governments; those welfare regimes in which universal systems are in place reduce conflict by eliminating one point of differentiation between groups. Where conflict may develop is in public and social policy that reinforces differentiation between groups. Therefore, where the welfare state engages in means testing, we should expect that there will be more conflict regarding those policies and the immigrants that benefit from them.

The negative consequences of the redistributive conflict for immigrants in Germany may not be found in formal government policy. However, in terms of perceptions on the part of the native population, the consequences are discrimination and bearing the "blame" for what is wrong with society. The facts reflect something different. Although immigrants are indeed as a percentage of their population more often dependent on the welfare state, the reasons for this are complex.

Notes

1. Andreas Zick, Beate Küpper, and Andreas Hövermann, *Die Abwertung der Anderen: Eine europäische Zustandsbeschreibung zu Intoleranz, Vorurteilen und Diskriminierung* (Berlin: Friedrich-Ebert Stiftung, 2011), 62.
2. OECD Factbook, "Economic, Environmental and Social Statistics," accessed November 12, 2010, http://www.oecd-ilibrary.org.

3. Gilles Raveaud and Robert Salais, "Fighting against Social Exclusion in a European Knowledge-Based Society: What Principles of Action," in *Social Exclusion and European Policy,* ed. David Mayes, Jos Berghman, and Robert Salais (Cheltham, UK: Edward Elgar, 2001), 47–71.

4. Bram Steijn, Jan Berting, and Mart-Jan de Jong, eds. *Economic Restructuring and the Growing Uncertainty of the Middle-Class* (Dordrecht: Kluwer Academic Publishers, 1998), 16.

5. Koen Vleminckx and Jos Berghman, "Social Exclusion and the Welfare State: An Overview of Conceptual Issues and Implications," in *Economic Restructuring and the Growing Uncertainty of the Middle-Class,* ed. Bram Steijn, Jan Berting, and Mart-Jan de Jong (Dordrecht: Kluwer Academic Publishers, 1998), 36.

6. Ibid., 36.

7. Raveaud and Salais, "Fighting against Social Exclusion," 50.

8. Jan Berting, "Rise and Fall of Middle-Class Society: How the Restructuring of Economic and Social Life Creates Uncertainty, Vulnerability, and Social Exclusion," in *Economic Restructuring and the Growing Uncertainty of the Middle-Class,* ed. Bram Steijn, Jan Berting, and Mart-Jan de Jong (Dordrecht: Kluwer Academic Publishers, 1998), 17.

9. David Mayes, "Introduction," in *Social Exclusion and European Policy*, ed. David Mayes, Jos Berghman, and Robert Salais (Cheltham, UK: Edward Elgar, 2001), 1–25.

10. Raveaud and Salais, "Fighting against Social Exclusion," 55.

11. Berting, "Rise and Fall of Middle-Class Society," 13.

12. Nicholas Deakin, Ann Davis, and Neil Thomas, *Public Welfare Services and Social Exclusion: The Development of Consumer Oriented Initiatives in the European Union* (Ireland: Laughlinstown House, 1995), 8.

13. Torben Iversen, "The Dynamics of Welfare State Expansion," in *The New Politics of the Welfare State,* ed. Paul Pierson (New York: Oxford University Press, 2001), 45–79.

14. Deakin, Davis, and Thomas, *Public Welfare*, 9.

15. Steen Mangen, "Political Transition, Social Transformation and the Welfare Agenda," in *The New Germany in the East: Policy Agendas and Social Developments since Unification,* ed. Chris Flockton, Eva Kolinsky, and Rosalind Pritchard (London: Frank Cass, 2000), 41.

16. Berting, "Rise and Fall of Middle-Class Society," 20.

17. Paul Pierson, "Coping with Permanent Austerity," in *The New Politics of the Welfare State,* ed. Paul Pierson (New York: Oxford University Press, 2001), 85.

18. Anthony B. Atkinson, *Poverty in Europe* (Oxford: Blackwell Publishers, 1998).

19. John Rawls, *A Theory of Justice: revised edition* (Cambridge, MA: Harvard University Press), 4.

20. Ibid., 25.

21. David Byrne, *Social Exclusion* (Buckingham, England: Open University Press, 1999), 70.

22. Rawls, *Justice*, 337.

23. Ibid.

24. Erich Fromm, *Escape from Freedom* (New York: Holt and Company, 1994), 167.
25. Byrne, *Social Exclusion*, 101.
26. Charlie Jeffrey, "Balancing Territorial Politics and Social Citizenship in Germany and Britain: Constraints in Public Opinion," *German Politics* 16 (2007): 58.
27. Raveaud and Salais, "Fighting against Social Exclusion," 49.
28. Atkinson, *Poverty in Europe*, 6.
29. Brian Barry, "Social Exclusion, Social Isolation, and the Distribution of Income" (Oxford: Oxford University Press, 2002), 19.
30. Berting, "Middle-Class Society," 20.
31. Deakin, Davis, and Thomas, *Public Welfare,* 11.
32. Hans-Georg Betz, *Radical Right-Wing Populism in Western Europe* (New York: St. Martin's Press, 1994), 88.
33. Herbert Kitschelt with Anthony J. McGann, *The Radical Right in Western Europe: A Comparative Analysis* (Ann Arbor: University of Michigan Press, 1995).
34. Kitschelt, *Radical Right*, 261.
35. Markus M. L. Crepaz and Regan Damron, "Constructing Tolerance: How the Welfare State Shapes Attitudes about Immigrants," *Comparative Political Studies* 42 (2009): 445.
36. Steffan Blomberg and Jan Peterson, "Stigma and Non-take Up in Social Policy: Reemerging Properties of Declining Welfare State Programs?" in *Social Exclusion in Europe: Problems and Paradigms,* ed. Paul Littlewood with Ignace Glorieux, Sebastian Herkommer, Ingrid Jönsson (Aldershot: Ashgate, 1999), 164.
37. Crepaz and Damron, "Constructing Tolerance," 445.
38. Raveaud and Salais, "Fighting against Social Exclusion," 52.
39. Blomberg and Peterson, "Stigma and Non-take Up in Social Policy," 164.
40. David Mayes, Jos Berghman, and Robert Salais, *Social Exclusion and European Policy* (Cheltham, UK: Edward Elgar, 2001), 5.
41. Ibid.
42. Valérie Sala Pala, "Differentialist and Universalist Antidiscrimination Policies on the Ground: How Far They Succeed, Why They Fail: A Comparison between Britain and France," *American Behavioral Scientist* 53 (2010): 1791.
43. Crepaz and Damron, "Constructing Tolerance," 446.
44. Jogen Goul Andersen and Tor Bjørklund, "Structural Changes and New Cleavages: The Progress Parties in Denmark and Norway," *Acta Sociologica* 33 (1990): 195–217.
45. Kitschelt, *Radical Right*, 262.
46. Ibid.
47. Sophie Body-Genderot and Marco Martiniello, "Introduction: The Dynamics of Social Integration and Social Exclusion at the Neighborhood Level," in *Minorities in European Cities: The Dynamics of Social Integration and Social Exclusion at the Neighborhood Level,* ed. Sophie Body-Genderot and Marco Martiniello (New York.: St. Martin's Press, 1990), 1–10.
48. Crepaz and Damron, "Constructing Tolerance," 439.
49. Kitschelt, *Radical Right*, 262.
50. Crepaz and Damron, "Constructing Tolerance," 449.
51. Sala Pala, "Differentialist and Universalist," 1792.

52. Alberto Alisina and Dani Rodrik, "Distributive Politics and Economic Growth," *Quarterly Journal of Economics* 109 (1994): 465–90.

53. Fritz Scharpf, *Games Real Actors Play: Actor Centered Institutionalism in Policy Research* (Boulder, CO: Westview Press, 1997), 70.

54. Herman Schwartz, "Round Up the Usual Suspects: Globalization, Domestic Politics, and Welfare State Change," in *The New Politics of the Welfare State,* ed. Paul Pierson (New York: Oxford University Press, 2001), 39.

55. Ibid.

56. Torben Iversen, "The Dynamics of the Welfare State Expansion," in *The New Politics of the Welfare State,* ed. Paul Pierson (New York: Oxford University Press, 2001), 69.

57. Iversen, "The Dynamics of the Welfare State Expansion," 78.

58. Marius R. Busemeyer, Achim Goerres, and Simon Weschle, "Attitudes towards Redistributive Spending in an Era of Demographic Ageing: The Rival Pressures from Age and Income in 14 OECD Countries," *Journal of European Social Policy* 19 (2009): 195–212; Torben Iversen and David Soskice, "An Asset Theory of Social Policy Preferences," *American Political Science Review* 95 (2006): 875–93.

59. Busemeyer, Goerres, and Weschle, "Attitudes towards Redistributive Spending," 195–212.

60. Karl Ove Moene and Michael Wallerstein, "Inequality, Social Insurance, and Redistribution," *American Political Science Review* 95 (2001): 859.

61. Moene and Wallerstein, "Inequality, Social Insurance, and Redistribution," 871.

62. Torben Iversen and Ann Wren, "Equality, Employment, and Budgetary Restraint: The Trilemma of the Service Economy," *World Politics* 50 (1997): 514.

63. Ibid., 516.

64. Ibid., 517.

65. Ibid., 518.

66. Kathleen Thelen, *How Institutions Evolve: The Political Economy of Skills in Germany, Britain, the United States, and Japan* (Cambridge, UK: Cambridge University Press, 2004), 270.

67. Iversen and Soskice, "An Asset Theory," 876.

68. Torben Iversen and John D. Stephens, "Partisan Politics, the Welfare State, and Three Worlds of Human Capital Formation," *Comparative Political Studies* 41 (2008): 600–37; Marius Busemeyer, "Social Democrats and Education Spending: A Refined Perspective on Supply-Side Strategies" (Max-Planck-Institut für Gesellschaftsforschung Working Paper 07/2, 2007).

69. Martin Kahanec and Mehmet Serkan Tosun, "Political Economy of Immigration in Germany: Attitudes and Citizenship Aspirations," *International Migration Review* 43 (2009): 263.

70. Christian Babka von Gostomski, *Fortschritte der Integration: Zur Situation der fünf größten in Deutschland lebenden Ausländergruppen* (Berlin: Bundesamt für Migration und Fluchtlinge, 2010), 30.

71. Ibid., 34.

72. Ibid.

73. Kahanec and Tosun, "Political Economy," 287.

74. Ibid., 282.

75. Zick, Küpper, and Hövermann, *Die Abwertung der Anderen*, 142.
76. Ibid., 106.
77. Ibid., 120.
78. Ibid., 184.
79. Ibid.
80. Ibid., 120.
81. Kitschelt, *Radical Right*, 261.

Bibliography

Alisina, Alberto, and Dani Rodrik. "Distributive Politics and Economic Growth." *Quarterly Journal of Economics* 109 (1994): 465–90.

Andersen, Jogen Goul, and Tor Bjørklund. "Structural Changes and New Cleavages: The Progress Parties in Denmark and Norway." *Acta Sociologica* 33 (1990): 195–217.

Atkinson, Anthony Barnes. *Poverty in Europe*. Oxford: Blackwell Publishers, 1998.

Barry, Brian. "Social Exclusion, Social Isolation, and the Distribution of Income." In *Understanding Social Exclusion*, edited by John Hills, Julian Le Grand, and David Piachaud, 13–29. Oxford: Oxford University Press, 2002.

Berting, Jan. "Rise and Fall of Middle-Class Society? How the Restructuring of Economic and Social Life Creates Uncertainty, Vulnerability and Social Exclusion." In *Economic Restructuring and the Growing Uncertainty of the Middle-Class*, edited by Bram Steijn, Jan Berting, and Mart-Jan de Jong, 7–24. Dordrecht, The Netherlands: Kluwer Academic Publishers, 1998.

Betz, Hans-Georg. *Radical Right-Wing Populism in Western Europe*. New York: St. Martin's Press, 1994.

Blomberg, Steffan, and Jan Peterson. "Stigma and Non-take Up in Social Policy: Reemerging Properties of Declining Welfare State Programs?" In *Social Exclusion in Europe: Problems and Paradigms*, edited by Paul Littlewood with Ignace Glorieux, Sebastian Herkommer, and Ingrid Jönsson, 157–174. Aldershot, UK: Ashgate, 1999.

Body-Genderot, Sophie, and Marco Martiniello. "Introduction: The Dynamics of Social Integration and Social Exclusion at the Neighborhood Level." In *Minorities in European Cities: The Dynamics of Social Integration and Social Exclusion at the Neighborhood Level*, edited by Sophie Body-Genderot and Marco Martiniello, 1–10. New York: St. Martin's Press, 2000.

Busemeyer, Marius. "Social Democrats and Education Spending: A Refined Perspective on Supply-Side Strategies." Max-Planck-Institut für Gesellschaftsforschung Working Paper 07/2, 2007.

Busemeyer, Marius, Achim Goerres, and Simon Weschle. "Attitudes towards Redistributive Spending in an Era of Demographic Ageing: The Rival Pressures from Age and Income in 14 OECD Countries." *Journal of European Social Policy* 19 (2009): 195–212.

Byrne, David S. *Social Exclusion*. Buckingham, England: Open University Press, 1999.

Castles, Francis, and Herbert Obinger. "Social Expenditure and the Politics of Redistribution." *Journal of European Social Policy* 17 (2007): 206–22.

Crepaz, Markus M. L., and Regan Damron. "Constructing Tolerance: How the Welfare State Shapes Attitudes about Immigrants." *Comparative Political Studies* 42 (2009): 437–63.

Deakin, Nicholas, Ann Davis, and Neal Thomas. *Public Welfare Services and Social Exclusion: The Development of Consumer Oriented Initiatives in the European Union.* Dublin, Ireland: Loughlinstown House, 1995.

Esping-Andersen, Gøsta. *Three Worlds of Welfare Capitalism.* Princeton, NJ: Princeton University Press, 1990.

Fromm, Erich. *Escape from Freedom.* New York: Holt and Company, 1994.

Gostomski, Christian von Babka. *Fortschritte der Integration: Zur Situation der fünf größten in Deutschland lebenden Ausländergruppen.* Berlin: Bundesamt für Migration und Fluchtlinge, 2010.

Huber, Evelyn, and John D. Stephens. "The Social Democratic Welfare State." In *Social Democracy in Neo-liberal Times: The Left and Economic Policy Since 1980,* edited by Andrew Glyn, 276–311. Oxford, UK: Oxford University Press, 2001.

Jeffrey, Charlie. "Balancing Territorial Politics and Social Citizenship in Germany and Britain: Constraints in Public Opinion." *German Politics* 16 (2007): 58–78.

Kahanec, Martin, and Mehmet Serkan Tosun. "Political Economy of Immigration in Germany: Attitudes and Citizenship Aspirations." *International Migration Review* 43 (2009): 263–91.

Kersbergen, Kees van. *Social Capitalism: A Study of Christian Democracy and the Welfare State.* London: Routledge, 1995.

Kitschelt, Herbert, with Anthony J. McGann. *The Radical Right in Western Europe: A Comparative Analysis.* Ann Arbor: University of Michigan Press, 1995.

Iversen, Torben. *Capitalism, Democracy, and Welfare.* New York: Cambridge University Press, 2005.

———. "The Dynamics of the Welfare State Expansion: Trade Openness, De-industrialization, and Partisan Politics." In *The New Politics of the Welfare State,* edited by Paul Pierson, 45–79. New York: Oxford University Press, 2001.

Iversen, Torben, and David Soskice. "An Asset Theory of Social Policy Preferences." *American Political Science Review* 95 (2006): 875–93.

Iversen, Torben, and John D. Stephens. "Partisan Politics, the Welfare State, and Three Worlds of Human Capital Formation." *Comparative Political Studies* 41 (2008): 600–37.

Iversen, Torben, and Anne Wren. "Equality, Employment, and Budgetary Restraint: The Trilemma of the Service Economy." *World Politics* 50 (1997): 507–46.

Lijphart, Arendt, and Markus Crepaz. "Notes and Comments—Corporatism and Consensus Democracy in Eighteen Countries: Empirical and Conceptual Linkages." *British Journal of Political Science* 21 (1991): 235–56.

Mangen, Steen. "Political Transition, Social Transformation and the Welfare Agenda." In *The New Germany in the East: Policy Agendas and Social Developments since Unification,* edited by Chris Flockton, Eva Kolinsky, and Rosalind Pritchard, 27–47. London: Frank Cass, 2000.

———. "Social Policy: One State, Two-Tier Welfare." In *Developments in German Politics*, edited by Gordon Smith, William E. Paterson, Peter H. Merkl, and Stephen Padgett, 208–26. Durham: Duke University Press, 1992.

Mayes, David. "Introduction." In *Social Exclusion and European Policy*, edited by David Mayes, Jos Berghman, and Robert Salaism, 1–25. Cheltham, UK: Edward Elgar, 2001.

Mayes, David, Jos Berghman, and Robert Salais. *Social Exclusion and European Policy*. Cheltenham, UK: Edward Elgar, 2001.

Moene, Karl Ove, and Michael Wallerstein. "Inequality, Social Insurance, and Redistribution." *American Political Science Review* 95 (2001): 859–74.

OECD Factbook. *Economic, Environmental and Social Statistics*. Accessed November 12, 2010, http://www.oecd-ilibrary.org.

Pierson, Paul. "Coping with Permanent Austerity." In *The New Politics of the Welfare State*, edited by Paul Pierson, 410–56. Oxford, NY: Oxford University Press, 2001.

Raveaud, Gilles, and Robert Salais. "Fighting against Social Exclusion in a European Knowledge-Based Society: What Principles of Action." In *Social Exclusion and European Policy*, edited by David Mayes, Jos Berghman, and Robert Salais, 47–71. Cheltham, UK: Edward Elgar, 2001.

Rawls, John. *A Theory of Justice: revised edition*. Cambridge, MA: Harvard University Press, 1999.

Sala Pala, Valérie. "Differentialist and Universalist Antidiscrimination Policies on the Ground: How Far They Succeed, Why They Fail: A Comparison between Britain and France." *American Behavioral Scientist* 53 (2010): 1788–1805.

Scharpf, Fritz. *Games Real Actors Play: Actor Centered Institutionalism in Policy Research*. Boulder, CO: Westview Press, 1997.

Schwartz, Herman. "Round Up the Usual Suspects: Globalization, Domestic Politics, and Welfare State Change." In *The New Politics of the Welfare State*, edited by Paul Pierson, 17–44. New York: Oxford University Press, 2001.

Steijn, Bram, Jan Berting, and Mart-Jan de Jong, eds. *Economic Restructuring and the Growing Uncertainty of the Middle Class*. Dordrecht: Kluwer Academic Publishers, 1998.

Thelen, Kathleen. *How Institutions Evolve: The Political Economy of Skills in Germany, Britain, the United States, and Japan*. Cambridge, UK: Cambridge University Press, 2004.

Vleminckx, Koen, and Jos Berghman. "Social Exclusion and the Welfare State: An Overview of Conceptual Issues and Implications." In *Social Exclusion and European Policy*, edited by David Mayes, Jos Berghman, and Robert Salais, 27–46. Cheltham, UK: Edward Elgar, 2001.

Zick, Andreas, Beate Küpper, and Andreas Hövermann. *Die Abwertung der Anderen: Eine europäische Zustandsbeschreibung zu Intoleranz, Vorurteilen und Diskriminierung*. Berlin: Friedrich-Ebert Stiftung, 2011.

PART III

Toward Justice

CHAPTER 9

Somewhere over the Rainbow (Nation)

Zimbabweans in South Africa

*Susan Smith-Cunnien**

It was 2005, barely more than a decade since the emergence of the "new" South Africa, and the signs of the ten-year anniversary celebrations were everywhere. The ubiquitous graphic designs based on the South African flag—with its rainbow-like array of six colors—adorned street lamps, buildings, vehicles, and even product packaging. Upon stepping outside the Johannesburg airport, I was greeted by a giant mural joyously declaring, "44 million people, 9 indigenous languages and not a single word for stranger. Welcome." Although I was admittedly skeptical of the linguistic assertion, I smiled. It was a wonderful way to welcome new arrivals, and I applauded the skill of the public relations team—or politicians—behind this salutation.

Like most tourists, I saw evidence of this welcoming in many other venues as well. I almost always felt welcomed personally, of course, but I attributed that to the graciousness that is part of the various cultures of the nation and to the fact that I was clearly happily contributing to the South African economy in as many ways as I could afford. I was most struck, though, by my experience with a guide, "James," whom I had hired to take me through Hillbrow, a neighborhood in Johannesburg that was known in the late apartheid era as a "gray area"; was a progressive center for those who embraced the integration of Europeans and Africans; and is known now mainly for its poverty, violence, and high crime rate. James pointed up at the high-rises, with colorful laundry

* Address correspondence to Susan Smith-Cunnien, Ph.D., Department of Sociology and Criminal Justice, University of St. Thomas, 2115 Summit Avenue, Mail #4318, St. Paul, MN 55105-1096, USA. Email: slsmithcunni@stthomas.edu.

flapping off the balconies and out of the windows as far up as I could see. "These used to be luxury flats," he said sadly and sighed. "Now the owners have left," he continued, "and it is the poor who live here, mostly immigrants, mostly Zimbabweans." But for James, the sadness came from the fact that people were living in the high-rises without services—no elevators, no running water, no plumbing—not from the fact that the neighborhood was now populated with poor immigrants. For James, a steadily employed, black South African in his forties, the Zimbabweans were just another element in the delightful mix of the rainbow nation.

And so it was with sorrow that I, like the many millions of others who had been cheering for the new South Africa, read the May 2008 headlines screaming of xenophobia and read of the violence against the immigrants, many of whom were Zimbabwean, as well as the ensuing 62 deaths, the destruction of homes and businesses, and the deployment of government troops to quell the disturbances.[1] "What on earth has happened to the rainbow nation?" wondered the world.

But in South Africa, and for those who follow South Africa closely, the outburst of xenophobia was surprising in scale but otherwise not very surprising at all. Xenophobic violence has occurred sporadically in the new South Africa from its inception. The Southern African Migration Project has been tracking xenophobic attitudes and actions since the 1990s.[2] Indeed, many social scientists trace the roots of this xenophobia to the policies and practices of the colonialists, which were reproduced by the postapartheid government in South Africa.[3] From this perspective, "rainbow-ism" was always more aspirational than real. It is in this context of xenophobia that Zimbabweans in South Africa must be understood.

The story of these Zimbabwean immigrants and the South African response to them is understandably complex, for the immigrants themselves are a varied group, the response to them is multifaceted and sometimes contradictory, and there have, of course, been changes in all these aspects over time. I have organized my attempt to tell this story into three sections: first, an overview of current issues related to the migration of Zimbabweans to South Africa and the social, historical, political, and economic context within which this migration has taken place; second, an examination of South Africa's multifaceted and sometimes contradictory response to what is now seen as a crisis of immigration; and finally, a consideration of alternative ways of conceptualizing the situation as South Africa continues to move toward social justice for all who live within its bounds.

An Overview: Zimbabwean Immigrants in South Africa

It would be appropriate to begin with an accounting of how many Zimbabwean immigrants there are in South Africa, but no one knows that number. The porous border allows for much migration to occur outside official channels, many people overstay visas originally acquired legally, some use false documents, and the official accounting procedures are less than perfect. Moreover, the number has become politicized. Those who wish to emphasize the seriousness of the immigration crisis claim the number is huge. Many use the figure that there are five to eight million immigrants in South Africa, a number first cited by the Human Sciences Research Council (HSRC) in 1995 although officially withdrawn in 2001.[4] The majority of these immigrants are presumed to be Zimbabweans, with the French NGO Doctors without Borders, for example, claiming that 4.1 million Zimbabweans were in South Africa in 2009,[5] although others say this is unlikely.[6] Researchers at the Forced Migration Studies Programme at the University of the Witwatersrand claim that there are a maximum of 1.5 million Zimbabweans in South Africa, and Human Rights Watch offers a similar estimate of 1 to 1.5 million.[7]

Zimbabwe is both a sender and a receiver of migrants, today as well as historically, and it also serves as a transit point for migration. HSRC data from 2001 to 2002 indicates that of the migrants to South Africa coming from Zimbabwe, roughly half were born in Zimbabwe (3,448), and half were born elsewhere (3,983).[8] The United Nations High Commissioner for Refugees (UNHCR) notes that today Zimbabwe is a major stopover point for those migrating from the Great Lakes region and Somalia to South Africa.[9] Additionally, it is worth noting that South Africa is not the only destination for migrants from Zimbabwe; more migrants, particularly those with resources, head for Great Britain, and many others head for neighboring Botswana and other southern African nations.[10]

Why Are So Many Zimbabweans in South Africa?

Zimbabweans come to South Africa for a variety of reasons. Some come in crisis, escaping the horrors of starvation or persecution, while others come as part of the mundane routine of their lives. Zimbabwe shares a border with South Africa, and Zimbabweans have been traveling to South Africa for eons. Many people living on either side of the Limpopo River, the border between Matabeleland South and Masvingo Provinces in Zimbabwe and the Limpopo Province in South Africa, share some of the same heritage and languages, among them Sotho, Venda, and Tsonga. There is a long history of cross-border trading, with people moving back and forth across the border sometimes daily, sometimes for a month or two, if travel to the interior is required. A survey of a representative sample of Zimbabweans in 1997 found that those who had visited South Africa in the last five years (22 percent of the sample) had traveled to South Africa an average of six times in the last five years (with a high of fifty visits).[11] The most frequently reported primary purpose for the visit was shopping or the buying and selling of goods (true for 65 percent of the females and 32 percent of the males).[12] In the past two decades, there has generally been more cross-border movement from Zimbabwe to South Africa and back, and since 2000 there has been an increase in "day-trippers" from Zimbabwe who cross the border to buy food, fuel, mechanical parts, and the many other necessities that have been difficult to find in Zimbabwe or, as during the period of hyperinflation, have not been affordable.[13]

Getting to South Africa: The Push and Pull Factors

A great deal of the population movement from Zimbabwe to South Africa involves longer-term migration. There are some obvious "push and pull" factors that have contributed to these migratory patterns. South Africa is a relatively rich country, and Zimbabwe has become a comparatively poor one. Additionally, Zimbabwe has experienced episodic political violence and repression during the last three decades. South Africa has recruited workers from various southern African nations since colonial times, primarily unskilled labor for mining and commercial farming, with skilled professionals added to the mix in the last few decades. Labor migration in southern Africa is typically temporary and circular, with people journeying to work and returning home at the end of a specified period or agricultural season. The "pull" here is not just an abstract sociological construct but comprises concrete policies and procedures that facilitate the movement of Zimbabweans and others to South Africa to meet its labor needs.

Zimbabweans have been recruited for unskilled work in South African mines since the 1890s, but Zimbabwe has been an "episodic supply country" for these mines since then.[14] Mining was and continues to be very difficult and dangerous work, often taking place under almost slave-like conditions, and migrants are generally contracted by employment agencies to work in the mines for periods of up to three years, living in single-sex hostels at the mines and returning to their families at the end of the contract period. A typical miner might have a dozen stints in the mines over his lifetime.[15] In colonial times, the need for cash to pay colonial taxes was a primary motivation for these labor migrants, although sometimes men signed mining contracts to avoid forced labor, and sometimes recruitment to the mines was itself forced. The draw today is above-average wages (though they are still low by US standards).

Seasonal agricultural workers from Zimbabwe have been traveling to South Africa "since the earliest colonial times."[16] Commercial farming is extremely difficult work under poor conditions, and the pay is usually less than minimum wage.[17] Since 2005, commercial farm operators have been able to apply for corporate permits, which then ease the process of securing individual work permits.[18] The majority of commercial farms are in northeastern South Africa, in Limpopo, which borders Zimbabwe, and undocumented Zimbabweans are widely thought to constitute a majority of commercial farm workers. Some say South Africans refuse to do this tough work for such low pay, but others argue that farm operators prefer a workforce of undocumented migrants, who are unlikely to complain and can be exploited with impunity. Most of these workers are seasonal and return to Zimbabwe regularly, but others have lived in northern South Africa for years.[19]

In the last few decades, skilled labor has become a more important part of the migrant stream from Zimbabwe to South Africa. The International Labour Organization (ILO) reported that from 1982 to 1988, 90 percent of the skilled and professional migrants coming to South Africa from other African nations were from Zimbabwe.[20] In 1998, the ILO reported that an estimated sixty thousand Zimbabwean professionals were working in South Africa.[21] South Africa experienced "brain drain" in the years just before and after the new government was launched in 1994, and South Africa still has a need for highly skilled labor, as evidenced by its preferential quotas for immigrants with scarce professional skills (such as physicians, teachers, and engineers).[22] Since 2005, however, skilled and professional Zimbabweans appear to compose a declining percentage of the migrant stream.[23]

During the colonial era, migration from Zimbabwe to South Africa was primarily due to the "pull" of economic opportunities in South Africa. In fact, the then–Southern Rhodesian government prohibited native workers from being recruited to South African mines in an attempt to make sure there was adequate labor at home.[24] In recent decades, however, political and economic push factors have become the major forces driving Zimbabweans from their country.

Political atrocities have been part of postindependence Zimbabwe almost from its inception in 1980. For more than two decades, political violence seemed to follow the cycle of elections, but in the last few years it appears to have become endemic. Zimbabwe's first presidential election was won by Robert Mugabe of the Zimbabwe African National Union—Patriotic Front (ZANU-PF) party and his Shona-speaking supporters. The ensuing starvation and slaughter of ten thousand civilians in Matabeleland and Midlands Provinces in the early to mid-1980s, in retribution against the Ndebele-speaking supporters of rival candidate Joshua Nkomo, were the first of many acts of violence by the government and ZANU-PF supporters against their foes.[25] When it appeared that ZANU-PF might lose the parliamentary elections in 2000 to the new Movement for Democratic Change (MDC) opposition party, a campaign of threat and force was initiated. Government security forces, ZANU-PF supporters, and allies threatened and engaged in the detention, torture, and killing of many who were accused of opposing the government, and white farm owners and their employees were attacked throughout Zimbabwe.[26] As the 2002 presidential elections loomed, another cycle of intimidation and violence began. In 2005 there was a terrible campaign to clean up the "filth," as Mugabe phrased it, by destroying informal marketplaces and informal housing in all the major urban areas of Zimbabwe, displacing seven hundred thousand people and indirectly affecting another two million.[27] In the period leading up to the 2008 presidential runoff elections, violence against the MDC opposition was even more excessive.[28] Under the current power-sharing arrangements between MDC's Morgan Tsvangirai and Mugabe, it is Mugabe who controls the nation's police and the military organizations, and allegations of intimidation by police and ZANU-PF supporters continue to surface.

Economic factors have played an even greater role in pushing Zimbabweans out of their country. At the time of independence, Zimbabwe was an exporter of food and natural resources. In the last three decades, it has become an importer of food, and a few years ago it was generally known as having the fastest shrinking economy in the world. Part of the recent difficulties started with the 1991 structural adjustment policies that the Zimbabwean government agreed to at the behest of the World Bank and International Monetary Fund. Between 1991 and 1997, 23,000 jobs were retrenched in the public sector and at least 50,000 jobs were lost in the private sector.[29] Unsustainable government spending continued, massive amounts of money "disappeared" in apparently corrupt land reform programs and Congo war financing, and the country was spending more than 40 percent of its export earnings to pay for its debt.[30] By the turn of the century, Zimbabwe was in a downward spiral of inflation and unemployment, with the economy reduced by one-third from 1999 to 2004.[31] In a 2002 land seizure, many commercial farms were closed as lands were redistributed through patronage, resulting in massive food shortages. Hyperinflation hit in the middle of the decade and skyrocketed in 2008.[32] Many workers were not paid, and supplies for consumers and businesses were not available even for those who had the money to buy them. Episodic drought conditions in several areas throughout southern Africa exacerbated the economic devastation.

Asylum Seekers

Zimbabweans filing for asylum in South Africa have the lowest likelihood in the world of qualifying for refugee status, with 5 percent accepted in 2006, 14 percent accepted in 2007, and less than 1 percent accepted in 2009.[33] In

2009, there were 171,700 Zimbabwean asylum-seeker applications filed in South Africa.[34] In 2010, South Africa received more asylum applications than anywhere else in the world, and the majority of these were submitted by Zimbabweans.[35] To say the asylum-seeking processing centers are overwhelmed is an understatement. Even in 2006, when there were "only" 19,000 applications for asylum, a scant 2,000 were processed, and those were from the backlog from previous years.[36] Now there is a backlog of more than 300,000 applications.[37]

Mixed Migration and Economic Migrants

Recent surveys of Zimbabwean immigrants corroborate the role played by both economic and political factors and confirm the increasingly common conflation of economic and political motivations captured by the term "mixed migration." But in this case it appears that the conflation of motivations often exists within a given individual migrant rather than just having different types of migrants present in the migrant flow. A 2004 survey of five hundred Zimbabwean immigrants in South Africa found that they had migrated primarily for economic reasons: 35 percent said the economic situation was the main reason, 20 percent said the lack of employment was the main reason, and 8 percent said their main reason was to work abroad.[38] But 37 percent of these migrants reported that the political situation in Zimbabwe was an additional reason.[39] The Southern African Migration Programme's surveys of Zimbabweans who travel to South Africa generally do not ask about multiple motivations for entrance to the country; however, these surveys confirm that the bulk of Zimbabweans come to South Africa for economic reasons.[40] In their 2010 survey, only 10 percent of a sample of Zimbabweans in Cape Town and Johannesburg who had arrived after 2005 said their main reason for coming to South Africa was related to political asylum, even though slightly over half the sample had asylum or refugee permits.[41]

South African Response to the "Immigration Crisis"

While immigrants both regular and irregular are estimated to constitute only about 4 to 5 percent of the South African population,[42] immigration has been an issue of concern to both the government and the populace since 1990.[43] The Immigration Act of 2002 (No. 13 of 2002) and the Refugee Act of 1998 (No. 130 of 1998) were both recently amended, and to the relief of some and the disappointment of others, the changes were primarily procedural and did not dramatically further constrain immigration.[44] South Africa is a signatory to the 1951 United Nations Refugee Convention and the 1967 Protocol, as well as the 1969 Organization of African Unity Convention Governing the Specific Aspects of the Refugee Problems in Africa. On paper then, even though South

Africa has not signed the Draft Protocol on the Free Movement of Persons in Southern Africa Development Community (SADC),[45] it has a reasonable, if exclusionary, immigration law and adequate legal protections for asylum seekers. The problems arise in implementation, with the focus on control and deportation. Additionally, the foreign policy objectives of South Africa, which have dictated a "hands-off" policy toward Zimbabwe, if not outright support of Zimbabwe's President Mugabe, have artificially bound the hands of the government, making it impossible to have an effective policy regarding the large influx of Zimbabwean nationals.[46]

Ironically, South Africa is one of the few countries in the region that does not encamp those who have been granted refugee status or are seeking asylum. While such a lack of constraint usually promotes the integration of immigrants into society and allows them to achieve a higher standard of living, the xenophobia in South Africa has altered these typical social processes. According to the UNHCR, many Zimbabweans prefer to live in inner-city areas, rather than in townships or rural areas, for safety reasons.[47] The largest number of Zimbabweans, between 600,000 and 650,000, are believed to be living in Johannesburg,[48] where there is insufficient available housing. The highly publicized case of the Johannesburg Central Methodist Church illustrates the housing problem. At the end of 2008, this church was providing nighttime sleeping accommodations for at least two thousand people, 80 percent of whom were Zimbabwean immigrants.[49] About 1,000 people continue to sleep in the church today.[50]

South African law allows for deportation of immigrants who are found to be in the country illegally, but this law was enforced only sporadically until recently. Throughout the 1990s, Zimbabweans constituted only 8 to 12 percent of deportations from South Africa.[51] Although the Department of Home Affairs (DHA) does not report the nationality of those being deported, Human Rights Watch reports that it reviewed an unpublished DHA memo indicating that in 2006 Zimbabweans composed almost half of those deported (81,289 of 165,270 deportations), with a deportation rate of 18,000 per month by 2007,[52] a number confirmed by the 2007 International Organization for Migration (IOM) report stating that 3,900 Zimbabweans were being deported per week.[53] In the most recent reporting year, 2010–11, the DHA reported that there were a total of 55,825 deportations, significantly less than the target number of 224,000 deportations, because of a special dispensation program discussed in the next paragraph.[54] Despite the large number of deportees, South Africa has only one official holding facility for those awaiting deportation or awaiting status determination: the infamous Lindela Repatriation Centre outside Johannesburg, which has been criticized for overcrowding, inhumane treatment, lack of medical care, and corrupt correctional officers.[55]

After deporting more than two hundred thousand immigrants for two years in a row and reeling from the violence against immigrants in 2008, the government declared a Special Dispensation for Zimbabwean immigrants in April 2009. There was be a moratorium on deportations, and plans were made for special permits to be issued for Zimbabweans. In September 2010, the DHA announced the Documentation of Zimbabweans Project (DZP).[56] Under this program, permits were issued at no charge to undocumented Zimbabweans who could provide proof that they were working, studying, or conducting business in South Africa and could provide a Zimbabwean passport.[57] The DZP also provided amnesty from criminal prosecution for migrants who surrendered their fraudulent documents. The DZP registered 275,762 applications, 6,243 of which were amnesty applications in which fraudulent documents were surrendered.[58] The project was completed at the end of September[59] and deportations resumed in October, with nearly 15,000 Zimbabweans deported between October 2011 and the beginning of March 2012,[60] which was actually many fewer than predicted.[61]

The majority of the people in South Africa—though certainly not all—have negative opinions about immigrants and immigration, and these negative opinions abound among people of all social classes, all population groups (races), all ages, and all regions.[62] Often denigrated as *makwerekwere*, a derogatory term for immigrants, Zimbabweans and other immigrants have been demonized. They are blamed for crime, unemployment, and the spread of disease and are resented for usurping housing and other resources.[63] Perhaps because of these attitudes, societal resources are often denied to both regular and irregular migrants.[64]

While xenophobic beliefs were widely considered to be behind the violence against immigrants that exploded in 2008, national government officials from then–President Mbeki on down have generally attributed the violence to a much more limited number of criminals.[65] This is somewhat ironic since South African sociologist Michael Neocosmos and others have documented the numerous ways in which South African national leaders have led the charge in demonizing immigrants.[66] Additionally, Sabelo Ndlovu-Gatsheni has pointed out how the current promotion of "nativism" and the "new nationalism" by elites in South Africa has started to move the nation to a more parochial and limited view of who belongs.[67] Seeing immigrants as the source of so many of South Africa's problems appears to be a "frame" being promoted by those at the top of South African society, a frame that then guides actions at both national and local levels.[68]

Local governmental officials were not so quick to condemn the violence and reported that they needed to be careful in addressing the needs of the victims of the xenophobic violence because they did not want it to appear that the victims were getting more help than South Africans.[69] This response is not surprising given that local leaders, official or otherwise, were more likely to be directing the violence than working to stop it, according to Jean Pierre Misago and his colleagues, who studied seven poor communities in areas near Cape Town and Johannesburg, five of which were sites of violence.[70]

South Africa has the strongest economy in southern Africa, but it is a society fraught with economic inequality. The massive influx of Zimbabweans comes at a time when the majority of South Africans are struggling economically and are worse off today than 15 years ago. However, poverty alone does not explain why immigrants are scapegoated; it explains the frustration of feeling "cheated of the promises of liberation," says Neocosmos, but not the target of this frustration.[71] For that, he argues, one must go back to the creation of the new South Africa, with the defeat of the Pan-Africanist inclusive democratic vision and the success of the rights-based liberal democratic vision, with its exclusionary vision of citizenship: citizens have rights, others do not.[72] Alternative conceptions about citizenship are needed, he concludes, or South Africa will be headed toward what John Sharp has called "Fortress SA."[73]

Conclusion

The DHA has declared it a priority to devise a process to distinguish those who are economic migrants from those who are "genuine" asylum seekers in order to make the process more manageable.[74] The reality is that so many thousands of permit applications were received from 2007 onward that any system anywhere in the world would likely have faltered. However, the issues here are much broader than simply streamlining bureaucratic procedures. As Jonathan Crush and his colleagues at the Southern African Migration Project have suggested, a more "migrant-centered" approach is needed.[75]

While a simple and clear differentiation among migrants—asylum seeker or economic migrant, forced or voluntary—is understandably preferred by agencies working within existing human rights and legal regimes, a migrant-centered approach not only acknowledges the "fluidity" of migrant status at different points in time,[76] but it guides us to focus on the complexity of motivations that can initiate and maintain migration.[77] As is so frequently the case when we examine how people think and behave, it makes more sense to look at Zimbabwean immigrants as falling somewhere along one or more continuums, ranging from "economic reasons only" at one end to "escaping personal persecution" at the other, for example.

Those who have been successful in gaining asylum-seeking status or refugee status are sometimes surprised to learn that they cannot return to Zimbabwe even for a quick visit to family. Again, thinking about this from a "migrant-centered" approach helps us to understand the refugee and human rights regime in a different way: as a system bound to unintentionally create law violators when the long-standing patterns of circular movement, the particular need to use informal channels of remittance, and the connections to family push these migrants to occasionally cross back into Zimbabwe, even at great personal risk. Again, it can be helpful to think of this variable on a continuum, where at one end are immigrants who see no possibility of safely returning to Zimbabwe and at the other are migrants who feel perfectly comfortable moving back and forth across the border, with perhaps the vast majority of migrants falling somewhere in between.

Neocosmos and Sharp both argue for a more flexible notion of citizenship, not in the sense that we should all be citizens of the world, but in the sense that citizenship is not an either-or phenomenon.[78] It is not a static category that, if granted, gives the passive citizen certain rights. In reality, citizens must actively claim rights, and depending on age, income, and gender, these rights may be denied "on the ground" even if they are given on paper.[79] In light of the fact that the majority of Zimbabweans in South Africa do not appear to hold citizenship or even permanent residence as their goal, the linking of rights to citizenship constrains how the issues are framed and may needlessly exacerbate xenophobia and deprive this population of inalienable rights.

Zimbabweans in South Africa are caught in the historical moment, but they are a varied group, and it would be a mistake to see them only as "migrants," only in terms of citizenship, only as outsiders, or as any other single category. As Blair Rutherford observed in his study of Zimbabwean farm workers in Musina,[80] Zimbabweans in South Africa are agents, not victims; they are people who not only figure out ways to feed themselves and their families but engage in the whole gamut of human activities, from the glorious to the shameful. This is not unexpected. As Francis B. Nyamnjoh states, "The bulk of ordinary people in Africa refuse to celebrate victimhood."[81] But the people in South Africa who engaged in violence against immigrants are also caught in the historical moment, and as Misago and his colleagues noted, they are also trying to feed themselves and their families and are engaged in the whole gamut of human activities, from the glorious to the shameful.[82]

Daniel Hopkins has observed that, "as far as immigrants are concerned, threatened responses are best thought of as a product of exceptional times, and not as the norm."[83] The exceptional times of this historical moment will pass, but the next moment will be one of greater social justice for both South Africans and the Zimbabweans in their midst only if South Africa reconsiders its exclusive policies as it continues to restructure itself both economically and politically. It is time to get back to "the norm."

Notes

1. Barry Bearak, "Anti-Immigrant Violence in Johannesburg," *New York Times*, May 19, 2008, accessed July 12, 2012, http://www.nytimes.com/2008/05/19/world/africa/19safrica.html; Scott Baldauf, "Zimbabweans Face Hate in South Africa," *Christian Science Monitor* (Boston), May 20, 2008, accessed July 12, 2012, http://www.csmonitor.com; Megan Lindow with Alex Perry, "Anti-Immigrant Terror in South Africa," *Time*, May 20, 2008, accessed July 12, 2012, http://www.time.com/time/world/article/0,8599,1808016,00.html.

2. Jonathan Crush, David A. McDonald, Vincent Williams, Kate Lefko-Everett, David Dorey, Don Taylor, and Roxanne la Sablonniere, *The Perfect Storm: The Realities of Xenophobia in Contemporary South Africa*, Migration Policy Series No. 50 (Cape Town: SAMP, 2008), accessed June 20, 2012, http://www.queensu.ca/samp/sampresources/samppublications.

3. Mahmood Mamdani, *Citizen and Subject* (Princeton, NJ: Princeton University Press, 1996); Michael Neocosmos, *From "Foreign Natives" to "Native Foreigners,"* 2nd ed. (Dakar, Senegal: CODESRIA, 2010).

4. Crush et al., *Perfect Storm*, 44.

5. "How Many Zimbabweans in SA?" *News24* (Cape Town), June 23, 2009, accessed July 12, 2012, http://www.news24.com/SouthAfrica/News/How-many-Zimbabweans-in-SA-20090621.

6. Center for Development and Enterprise, *Migration from Zimbabwe: Numbers, Needs and Policy Options* (Johannesburg: CDE, 2008), 9, accessed June 8, 2012, http://www.cde.org.za.

7. Tara Polzer, *Regularizing Zimbabwean Migration to South Africa*, Migration Policy Brief (Johannesburg: CoRMSA and FMSP, University of the Witwatersrand, 2009), 3, accessed July 11, 2012, http://www.cormsa.org.za; Human Rights Watch, *Neighbors in Need: Zimbabweans Seeking Refuge in South Africa* (New York: HRW, 2008), 23, accessed August 10, 2012, http://www.hrw.org/reports/2008/06/18/neighbors-need.

8. Cited in John O. Oucho, "Cross Border Migration and Regional Initiatives in Managing Migration in Southern Africa," in *Migration in South and Southern Africa*, ed. Pieter Kok, Derik Gelderblom, John O. Oucho, and Johan van Zyl (Cape Town: HSRC Press, 2006), 54.

9. UNHCR, *2012 Regional Operations Profile—Southern Africa*, accessed August 10, 2012, http://www.unhcr.org.

10. Lazarus Zanamwe and Alexandre Devillard, *Migration in Zimbabwe: A Country Profile 2009* (Harare, Zimbabwe: Zimbabwe National Statistical Agency and International Organization for Migration, 2010), 36, accessed July 11, 2012, http://www.publications.iom.int.

11. Lovemore Zinyama, "Cross-Border Movement from Zimbabwe to South Africa," in *Zimbabweans Who Move: Perspectives on International Migration in Zimbabwe*, ed. Daniel Tevera and Lovemore Zinyama. Migration Policy Series No. 25, Southern African Migration Project (Cape Town: Idasa and Queen's University, Canada: Southern African Research Centre, 2002), 33, 36, accessed September 9, 2011, http://www.queensu.ca/samp/sampresources/samppublications.

12. Ibid., 29.

13. There were more than one hundred thousand day-trippers at Beitbridge, the official Limpopo crossing on the Zimbabwe side in 2007. Zanamwe and Devillard, *Migration in Zimbabwe*, 51.

14. Marie Wentzel and Kholadi Tlabeda, "Historical Background to South African Migration," in *Migration in South and Southern Africa*, ed. Kok et al. (Cape Town: HSRC Press, 2006), 74.

15. Aderanti Adepoju, "Internal and International Migration within Africa," in *Migration in South and Southern Africa*, ed. Kok et al. (Cape Town: HSRC Press, 2006), 33.

16. Wentzel and Tlabela, "Historical Background," 80.

17. Blair Rutherford, "The Politics of Boundaries: The Shifting Terrain of Belonging for Zimbabweans in a South Africa Border Zone," *African Diaspora* 4 (2011): 216.

18. Ibid., 214, 219.

19. Blair Rutherford, "The Uneasy Ties of Working and Belonging: The Changing Situation for Undocumented Zimbabwean Migrants in Northern South Africa," *Ethnic and Racial Studies* 34 (2011): 1303–19.

20. Cited in Wentzel and Tlabela, "Historical Background," 78.

21. As reported in Zinyama, "Cross-Border Movement," 29.

22. Loren B. Landau and Aurelia Wa Kabawe Segatti, "Human Development Impacts of Migration South Africa Case Study," Human Development Research Paper 2009/05 (UNDP, 2009), 26–28, accessed September 8, 2011, http://hdr.undp.org/en/reports/global/hdr2009/papers/HDRP_2009_05.pdf.

23. Jonathan Crush, Abel Chikanda, and Godfrey Tawodzera, *The Third Wave: Mixed Migration from Zimbabwe to South Africa*, Migration Policy Series No. 59 (Cape Town: SAMP, 2012), 30, accessed June 20, 2012, http://www.queensu.ca/samp/sampresources/samppublications.

24. Wentzel and Tlabela, "Historical Background," 75.

25. Martin Meredith, *The Fate of Africa: A History of Fifty Years of Independence* (New York: Public Affairs, 2005), 131, 325, 610.

26. Ibid., 636–37.

27. United Nations, *Report of the Fact-Finding Mission to Zimbabwe to Assess the Scope and Impact of Operation Murambatsvina by the UN Special Envoy on Human Settlement in Zimbabwe* (July 18, 2005), accessed August 10, 2012, http://www.unhabitat.org/content.asp?cid=10018&catid=463&typeid=3&subMenuId=0&AllContent=1.

28. Human Rights Watch, *Perpetual Fear: Impunity and Cycles of Violence in Zimbabwe* (New York: 2011), 19–20, accessed April 28, 2012, http://www.hrw.org/reports/2011/03/08/perpetual-fear-0; Rhoda E. Howard-Hassmann, "Mugabe's Zimbabwe, 2000–2009: Massive Human Rights Violations and the Failure to Protect," *Human Rights Quarterly* 32 (2010): 898–920.

29. As reported in Zinyama, "Cross-Border Movement," 27–28. The number for private sector jobs lost is a conservative figure that only includes those for which governmental permission for retrenchment had been obtained.

30. David Moore, "Neoliberal Globalisation and the Triple Crisis of 'Modernisation' in Africa: Zimbabwe, the Democratic Republic of the Congo and South Africa," *Third World Quarterly* 22 (2001): 915.

31. Meredith, *Fate of Africa*, 645.

32. See Hanke, *Zimbabwe: From Hyperinflation to Growth* (Washington, DC: Cato Institute, 2008), as cited in Crush et al., *Third Wave*, 13.

33. UNHCR data cited in Crush et al., *Third Wave*, 22–23.

34. UNHCR, *2012 UNHCR Country Operations Profile—South Africa*, accessed August 10, 2012, http://www.unhcr.org.

35. Ibid.

36. Michael Wines, "Influx from Zimbabwe to South Africa Tests Both," *New York Times*, June 23, 2007, accessed September 8, 2011, http://www.nytimes.com.

37. UNHCR, *2012 UNHCR Country Operations Profile—South Africa*, accessed August 10, 2012, http://www.unhcr.org.

38. Alice Bloch, "Emigration from Zimbabwe: Migrant Perspectives," *Social Policy and Administration* 40 (2006): 72–73.

39. Ibid., 73.

40. Crush et al., *Third Wave*, 8–9, 14–16, 24.

41. Ibid., 23–24.

42. Official 2001 census figures indicate that 2.3 percent of the population was not born in South Africa. Statistics South Africa, *Census 2001: Census in Brief*, Report No. 03-02-03 (2001) (Pretoria, South Africa: Statistics South Africa, 2003), 21, accessed September 8, 2011, http://www.statssa.gov.za/census01/html/CInBrief/CIB2001.pdf.

43. Neocosmos (*Foreign Natives*, 18) argues that this begins in 1990, not 1994.

44. Immigration Amendment Act No. 13 of 2011, *Government Gazette*, August 26, 2011, section 15, page 18, accessed July 9, 2012, http://www.gov.za; Refugees Amendment Act No.12 of 2011, *Government Gazette*, August 26, 2011, accessed July 9, 2012, http://www.gov.za.

45. Francis Nwonwu, "The Neo-Liberal Policy, Free Movement of People and Migration," *Africa Insight* 40 (2010): 150.

46. James Barber, "The New South Africa's Foreign Policy: Principles and Practice," *International Affairs* 81 (2005): 1079–96; Linda Freeman, "South Africa's Zimbabwe Policy: Unravelling the Contradictions," *Journal of Contemporary African Studies* 23 (2005): 147–72, accessed June 4, 2012, doi:10.1080/0258900042000229999.

47. UNHCR, *2012 UNHCR Country Operations Profile—South Africa*, accessed August 10, 2012, http://www.unhcr.org.

48. Christa L. Kuljian, "2010 Annual Ruth First Memorial Lecture, University of the Witwatersrand: Making the Invisible Visible: A Story of the Central Methodist Church," *African Studies* 70 (2011): 168, accessed June 4, 2012, doi:10.1080/00020184.2011.559383.

49. Ibid., 172.

50. John Campbell, "The Central Methodist Mission in Johannesburg," *John Campbell Africa in Transition* (blog), March 29, 2012, accessed July 19, 2012, http://blogs.cfr.org/campbell/2012/03/29/the-central-methodist-mission-in-johannesburg.

51. Lovemore Zinyama, "International Migration and Zimbabwe: An Overview," in *Zimbabweans Who Move: Perspectives on International Migration in Zimbabwe*, ed. Daniel Tevera and Lovemore Zinyama, Migration Policy Series No. 25, Southern African Migration Project (Cape Town: Idasa; Queen's University, Canada:

Southern African Research Centre, 2002), 22, accessed September 9, 2011, http://www.queensu.ca/samp/sampresources/samppublications.

52. Human Rights Watch, *Neighbors in Need*, 22n4.

53. Cited in Wines, "Influx from Zimbabwe."

54. *Department of Home Affairs Annual Report 2010/2011* (Pretoria, South Africa: Department of Home Affairs, 2011), 42, accessed June 8, 2012, http://www.gov.za.

55. South African Human Rights Commission, *Lindela: At the Crossroads for Detention and Repatriation* (Johannesburg: SAHRC, 2000), accessed July 19, 2012, http://www.gov.za/view/DownloadFileAction?id=70338.

56. "Home Affairs Director-General, Mkuseli Apleni's Statement on the Implementation Plan for the Documentation of Zimbabweans," Speeches and Statements (Pretoria, South Africa: South African Government Information, September 10, 2010), accessed June 9, 2012, http://www.gov.za.

57. Zanamwe and Devillard (*Migration in Zimbabwe*, 80) argue that one of the main reasons there are so many irregular Zimbabwean migrants is that few Zimbabweans have passports and that recent government upheaval has made it more difficult to obtain one.

58. Jacob Mamabolo, "Speaking Notes for Briefing Media by the Head of the Zimbabwe Documentation Project, Jacob Mamabolo," Speeches and Statements (Pretoria, South Africa: South African Government Information, June 30, 2011), accessed July 9, 2012, http://www.gov.za.

59. "Zimbabwean Documentation Project: Briefing by Department of Home Affairs," Parliamentary Monitoring Group (Cape Town), September 19, 2011, accessed July 16, 2012, http://www.pmg.org.za/report/20110920-department-home-affairs-zimbabwean-documentation-project.

60. "Latest Stats on Deportation of Zim Illegals," *Zoutnet* (South Africa), March 13, 2012, accessed July 16, 2012, http://www.zoutnet.co.za/details/13-03-2012/laest_stats_on_deportation_of-zim_illegals/12127.

61. Kathleen Chaykowski, "Zimbabweans Brace for Deportation," *Mail and Guardian Online* (South Africa), July 29, 2011, accessed July 16, 2012, http://mg.co.za.

62. Crush et al., *Perfect Storm*, 24–38; Steve Gordon, Ben Roberts, and Jarè Struwig, "Foreign Exchange," *HSRC Review* 10 (2012), accessed July 23, 2012, http://www.hsrc.ac.za/HSRC_Review_Article-300.phtml.

63. Human Sciences Research Council, *Citizenship, Violence and Xenophobia in South Africa: Perceptions from South African Communities* (Cape Town: HSRC Press, 2008), accessed July 23, 2012, http://www.hsrc.ac.za/Research_Publication-20635.phtml.

64. Landau and Segatti, "Human Development Impacts of Migration," 39–45.

65. Thabo Mbeki, "Shameful Actions Blemish South Africa," South African Government News Agency (Pretoria, South Africa), May 27, 2008, accessed July 9, 2012, http://www.sanews.gov.za; Essop Phahd (Minister in the Office of the President), "Xenophobia Has No Place in South Africa," Government Communication and Information System (Pretoria, South Africa), May 29, 2008, accessed July 9, 2012, http://www.sanews.gov.za; "Minister Mthethwa Condemns and Cautions These Thugs to Refrain from Threats," Speeches and Statements (Pretoria, South Africa:

South African Government Information, July 1, 2010), accessed July 9, 2012, http://www.gov.za.

66. Neocosmos, *Foreign Natives*, 61–104; Rutherford, "Politics of Boundaries," 209–10.

67. Sabelo J. Ndlovu-Gatsheni, "Africa for Africans or Africa for 'Natives' Only? 'New Nationalism' and Nativism in Zimbabwe and South Africa," *Africa Spectrum* 1 (2009), 61–78.

68. Daniel J. Hopkins, "Politicized Places: Explaining Where and When Immigrants Provoke Local Opposition," *American Political Science Review* 104 (2010): 56.

69. Vicki Igglesden, Tamlyn Monson, and Tara Polzer, *Humanitarian Assistance to Internally Displaced Persons in South Africa: Lessons Learned Following Attacks on Foreign Nationals in May 2008: Executive Summary and Recommendations* (Johannesburg: University of the Witwatersrand Forced Migration Studies Programme, 2009), 9, accessed July 19, 2012, http://atlanticphilanthropies.org/sites/default/files/uploads/FMSP_Disaster_Response_Evaluation_FINAL_09-01-25exec_sum_recs.pdf.

70. Jean Pierre Misago, Loren B. Landau, and Tamlyn Monson, *Towards Tolerance, Law and Dignity: Addressing Violence against Foreign Nationals in South Africa* (Arcadia, South Africa: IOM Regional Office for South Africa, 2009), accessed July 23, 2012, http://iom.org.za.

71. Neocosmos, *Foreign Natives*, 148.

72. Ibid., 18. South African human rights activists argue that the South African constitution links rights to "all people," not citizens.

73. Ibid., 140; John Sharp, "Fortress SA: Xenophobic Violence in South Africa," *Anthropology Today* 24 (2008): 1–3.

74. *Department of Home Affairs Strategic Plan 2010/2011–2012/2013* (Pretoria, South Africa: Department of Home Affairs, March 27, 2011), 11, accessed July 9, 2012, http://www.info.gov.za.

75. Crush et al., "Third Wave," 4–5.

76. Katherine M. Donato and Amanda Armenta, "What We Know about Unauthorized Migration," *Annual Review of Sociology* 37 (2011): 529–43.

77. Nicholas Van Hear, Rebecca Brubaker, and Thais Bessa, "Managing Mobility for Human Development: The Growing Salience of Mixed Migration," Human Development Research Paper 2009/20 (UNDP, 2009).

78. Neocosmos, *Foreign Natives*, 129–30; Sharp, "Fortress SA," 3.

79. Neocosmos, *Foreign Natives*, 129.

80. Rutherford, "Uneasy Ties."

81. Francis B. Nyamnjoh, "Globalization, Boundaries and Livelihoods: Perspectives on Africa," *Identity, Culture and Politics* 5 (2004): 39, accessed July 19, 2012, http://www.codesria.org.

82. Misago, Landau, and Monson, *Towards Tolerance, Law and Dignity*.

83. Hopkins, "Politicized Places," 56.

Bibliography

Adepoju, Aderanti. "Internal and International Migration within Africa." In *Migration in South and Southern Africa: Dynamics and Determinants*, edited by Kok, Pieter, Derik Gelderblom, John O. Oucho, and Johan van Zyl, 26–45. Cape Town: HSRC Press, 2006.

Apleni, Mkuseli. "Home Affairs Director-General, Mkuseli Apleni's Statement on the Implementation Plan for the Documentation of Zimbabweans," Speeches and Statements. Pretoria, South Africa: South African Government Information, September 10, 2010. Accessed June 9, 2012. http://www.gov.za.

Barber, James. "The New South Africa's Foreign Policy: Principles and Practice." *International Affairs* 81 (2005): 1079–96.

Bloch, Alice. "Emigration from Zimbabwe: Migrant Perspectives." *Social Policy and Administration* 40 (2006): 67–87.

Campbell, John. "The Central Methodist Mission in Johannesburg." *Africa in Transition* (blog). http://blogs.cfr.org/campbell/2012/03/29/the-central-methodist-mission-in-johannesburg.

Center for Development and Enterprise. *Migration from Zimbabwe: Numbers, Needs and Policy Options*. Johannesburg: CDE, 2008. Accessed June 20, 2012. http://www.cde.org.za.

Crush, Jonathan, Abel Chikanda, and Godfrey Tawodzera. *The Third Wave: Mixed Migration from Zimbabwe to South Africa*. Migration Policy Series No. 59. Cape Town: SAMP, 2012. Accessed June 20, 2012. http://www.queensu.ca/samp/sampresources/samppublications.

Crush, Jonathan, David A. McDonald, Vincent Williams, Kate Lefko-Everett, David Dorey, Don Taylor, and Roxanne la Sablonniere. *The Perfect Storm: The Realities of Xenophobia in Contemporary South Africa*. Migration Policy Series No. 50. Cape Town: SAMP, 2008. Accessed June 20, 2012. http://www.queensu.ca/samp/sampresources/samppublications.

Department of Home Affairs. Department of Home Affairs Annual Report 2010/11. Pretoria, South Africa: Department of Home Affairs, 2011. Accessed June 8, 2012. http://www.info.gov.za.

Department of Home Affairs. Department of Home Affairs Strategic Plan 2010/2011–2012/2013. Pretoria, South Africa: Department of Home Affairs, March 27, 2011. Accessed July 9, 2012. http://www.info.gov.za.

Donato, Katharine M., and Amanda Armenta. "What We Know about Unauthorized Migration." *Annual Review of Sociology* 37 (2011): 529–43. Accessed June 21, 2012. doi:10.1146/annurev-soc-081309-150216.

Freeman, Linda. "South Africa's Zimbabwe Policy: Unravelling the Contradictions." *Journal of Contemporary African Studies* 23 (2005): 147–72. doi:10.1080/0258900042000229999.

Gordon, Steve, Ben Roberts, and Jarè Struwig. "Foreign Exchange." *HSRC Review* 10 (2012). Accessed July 23, 2012. http://www.hsrc.ac.za/HSRC_Review_Article-300.phtml.

Hopkins, Daniel J. "Politicized Places: Explaining Where and When Immigrants Provoke Local Opposition." *American Political Science Review* 104 (2010): 40–60. doi:10.1017/S0003055409990360.

Howard-Hassmann, Rhoda E. "Mugabe's Zimbabwe, 2000–2009: Massive Human Rights Violations and the Failure to Protect." *Human Rights Quarterly* 32 (2010): 898–920. doi:10.1353/hrq.2010.0030.

Human Rights Watch. *Neighbors in Need: Zimbabweans Seeking Refuge in South Africa.* New York: HRW, 2008. Accessed August 10, 2012. http://www.hrw.org/reports/2008/06/18/neighbors-need.

———. *Perpetual Fear: Impunity and Cycles of Violence in Zimbabwe.* New York: HRW, 2011. Accessed April 28, 2012. http://www.hrw.org/reports/2011/03/08/perpetual-fear-0.

Human Sciences Research Council. *Citizenship, Violence and Xenophobia in South Africa: Perceptions from South African Communities.* Cape Town: HSRC Press, 2008. Accessed July 23, 2012. http://www.hsrc.ac.za/Research_Publication-20635.phtml.

Igglesden, Vicki, Tamlyn Monson, and Tara Polzer. *Humanitarian Assistance to Internally Displaced Persons in South Africa: Lessons Learned Following Attacks on Foreign Nationals in May 2008: Executive Summary and Recommendations.* Johannesburg: University of the Witwatersrand Forced Migration Studies Programme, 2009. Accessed July 19, 2012. http://atlanticphilanthropies.org/sites/default/files/uploads/FMSP_Disaster_Response_Evaluation_FINAL_09-01-25exec_sum_recs.pdf.

Kok, Pieter, Derik Gelderblom, John O. Oucho, and Johan van Zyl, eds. *Migration in South and Southern Africa: Dynamics and Determinants.* Cape Town: HSRC Press, 2006. Accessed June 29, 2012. http://www.hsrcpress.ac.za.

Kuljian, Christa L. "2010 Annual Ruth First Memorial Lecture, University of the Witwatersrand: Making the Invisible Visible: A Story of the Central Methodist Church." *African Studies* 70 (2011):167–74. Accessed June 4, 2012. doi:10.1080/00020184.2011.559383.

Landau, Loren B., and Aurelia Wa Kabwe Segatti. "Human Development Impacts of Migration South Africa Case Study." Human Development Research Paper 2009/05, United Nations Development Programme, 2009. Accessed September 8, 2011. http://hdr.undp.org/en/reports/global/hdr2009/papers/HDRP_2009_05.pdf.

Mamabolo, Jacob. "Speaking Notes for Briefing Media by the Head of the Zimbabwe Documentation Project, Jacob Mamabolo." Speeches and Statements. Pretoria, South Africa: South African Government Information, June 30, 2011. Accessed July 9, 2012. http://www.gov.za.

Mamdani, Mahmood. *Citizen and Subject.* Princeton, NJ: Princeton University Press, 1996.

Mbeki, Thabo. "Shameful Actions Blemish South Africa." Pretoria, South Africa: South African News Agency. Accessed July 9, 2012. http://www.sanews.gov.za.

Meredith, Martin. *The Fate of Africa: A History of Fifty Years of Independence.* New York: Public Affairs, 2005.

Misago, Jean Pierre, Loren B. Landau, and Tamlyn Monson. *Towards Tolerance, Law and Dignity: Addressing Violence against Foreign Nationals in South Africa.* Arcadia,

South Africa: IOM Regional Office for South Africa, 2009. Accessed July 23, 2012. http://iom.org.za.

Moore, David. "Neoliberal Globalisation and the Triple Crisis of 'Modernisation' in Africa: Zimbabwe, the Democratic Republic of the Congo and South Africa." *Third World Quarterly* 22 (2001): 909–29.

Mthethwa, Nathi. "Minister Mthethwa Condemns and Cautions These Thugs to Refrain from Threats." Speeches and Statements. Pretoria, South Africa: South African Government Information, July 1, 2010. Accessed July 9, 2012. http://www.gov.za.

Ndlovu-Gatsheni, Sabelo J. "Africa for Africans or Africa for 'Natives' Only? 'New Nationalism' and Nativism in Zimbabwe and South Africa." *Africa Spectrum* 1 (2009): 61–78.

Neocosmos, Michael. *From "Foreign Natives" to "Native Foreigners."* 2nd ed. Dakar, Senegal: CODESRIA, 2010. Accessed June 19, 2012. http://www.codesria.org.

Nwonwu, Francis. "The Neo-Liberal Policy, Free Movement of People and Migration." *Africa Insight* 40 (2010): 149–68.

Nyamnjoh, Francis B. "Globalization, Boundaries and Livelihoods: Perspectives on Africa." *Identity, Culture and Politics* 5 (2004): 37–59. Accessed July 19, 2012. http://www.codesria.org.

Oucho, John O. "Cross-Border Migration and Regional Initiatives in Managing Migration in Southern Africa." In *Migration in South and Southern Africa: Dynamics and Determinants*, edited by Kok, Pieter, Derik Gelderblom, John O. Oucho, and Johan van Zyl, 47–70. Cape Town: HSRC Press, 2006

Parliamentary Monitoring Group. "Zimbabwean Documentation Project: Briefing by Department of Home Affairs." Cape Town: Parliamentary Monitoring Group, September 19, 2011. Accessed July 16, 2012. http://www.pmg.org.za/report/20110920-department-home-affairs-zimbabwean-documentation-project.

Phahd, Essop. "Xenophobia Has No Place in South Africa." Pretoria, South Africa: Government Communication and Information System, May 29, 2008. Accessed July 9, 2012. http://www.sanews.gov.za.

Polzer, Tara. *Regularizing Zimbabwean Migration to South Africa*. Migration Policy Brief. Johannesburg: CoRMSA and FMSP, University of the Witwatersrand, 2009. Accessed July 11, 2012. http://www.cormsa.org.za.

Rutherford, Blair. "The Politics of Boundaries: The Shifting Terrain of Belonging for Zimbabweans in a South Africa Border Zone." *African Diaspora* 4 (2011): 207–29. doi:10.1163/187254611X606346.

———. "The Uneasy Ties of Working and Belonging: The Changing Situation for Undocumented Zimbabwean Migrants in Northern South Africa." *Ethnic and Racial Studies* 34 (2011): 1303–19. doi:10.1080/01419870.2010.535551.

Sharp, John. "Fortress SA: Xenophobic Violence in South Africa." *Anthropology Today* 24 (2008): 1–3.

South African Human Rights Commission. *Lindela: At the Crossroads for Detention and Repatriation*. Johannesburg: SAHRC, 2000. Accessed July 19, 2012. http://www.info.gov.za/view/DownloadFileAction?id=70338.

Statistics South Africa. Census 2001: Census in Brief. Report No. 03-02-03 (2001). Pretoria, South Africa: Statistics South Africa, 2003. Accessed September 8, 2011, http://www.statssa.gov.za/census01/html/CInBrief/CIB2001.pdf.

United Nations. *Report of the Fact-Finding Mission to Zimbabwe to Assess the Scope and Impact of Operation Murambatsvina by the UN Special Envoy on Human Settlement in Zimbabwe.* July 18, 2005. Accessed August 10, 2012. http://www.unhabitat.org/content.asp?cid=10018&catid=463&typeid=3&subMenuId=0&AllContent=1.

United Nations High Commissioner for Refugees. 2012 Regional Operations Profile – Southern Africa. 2012. Accessed August 10, 2012. http://www.unhcr.org.

United Nations High Commissioner for Refugees. 2012 UNHCR Country Operations Profile – South Africa. 2012. Accessed August 10, 2012. http://www.unhcr.org.

Van Hear, Nicholas, Rebecca Brubaker, and Thais Bessa. "Managing Mobility for Human Development: The Growing Salience of Mixed Migration." Human Development Research Paper 2009/20, United Nations Development Programme, 2009. Accessed July 19, 2012. http://hdr.undp.org/en/reports/global/hdr2009/papers/HDRP_2009_20.pdf.

Wenzel, Marie, and Kholadi Tlabela. "Historical Background to South African Migration." In *Migration in South and Southern Africa: Dynamics and Determinants*, edited by Kok, Pieter, Derik Gelderblom, John O. Oucho, and Johan van Zyl, 71–95. Cape Town: HSRC Press, 2006

Zanamwe, Lazarus, and Alexandre Devillard. *Migration in Zimbabwe: A Country Profile 2009.* Harare, Zimbabwe: Zimbabwe National Statistical Agency and International Organization for Migration, 2010. Accessed July 11, 2012. http://www.publications.iom.int.

Zinyama, Lovemore. "Cross-Border Movement from Zimbabwe to South Africa." In *Zimbabweans Who Move: Perspectives on International Migration in Zimbabwe*, edited by Daniel Tevera and Lovemore Zinyama, 26–41. Migration Policy Series No. 25. Southern African Migration Project. Cape Town: Idasa, 2002. Accessed September 9, 2011. http://www.queensu.ca/samp/sampresources/samppublications.

———. "International Migration and Zimbabwe: An Overview." In *Zimbabweans Who Move: Perspectives on International Migration in Zimbabwe*, edited by Daniel Tevera and Lovemore Zinyama, 7–25. Migration Policy Series No. 25. Southern African Migration Project. Cape Town: Idasa, 2002. Accessed September 9, 2011. http://www.queensu.ca/samp/sampresources/samppublications.

CHAPTER 10

Comparative Religious Freedom
The Right to Wear Religious Dress

*Anthony Gray**

In recent years, the issue of the extent to which an individual has or should have the right to religious freedom has become more contentious. In July 2012, controversy arose when a German court found that the circumcision of a child at the (Muslim) parents' request could amount to bodily harm and a breach of international norms.[1] Part of religious freedom is the ability to manifest that freedom by wearing particular items of clothing. Some nations have seen fit to ban the wearing of particular items of clothing thought to have religious significance, at least in some contexts. Courts from a range of jurisdictions have sought to grapple with these issues, involving a range of values and sometimes competing interests. They have done so in different ways, and some of the results are, at first blush, somewhat surprising. Religious freedoms have been protected to a lesser extent than one might have imagined.

Freedom of religion is recognized as fundamental in various international human rights documents. A feature of the First Amendment, it is also included in Article 9(1) of the *European Convention on Human Rights*, protecting the right to freedom of religion and to manifest that religion in worship or practice, subject to limited exceptions.[2] Similar provisions appear in Article 18 of the *International Covenant on Civil and Political Rights* and Article 18 of the *Universal Declaration of Human Rights*. These rights protections have been borne out of a long history of violence and persecution in relation to religion, oppression of religious minorities, and imposition of religion by states. The United States Supreme Court noted, "A large proportion of the early settlers of this country came here from Europe to escape the bondage of laws which compelled them to support and attend government

---

* Address correspondence to Professor Anthony Gray, deputy head of school, University of Southern Queensland, Sinnathamby Boulevard, Springfield 4300. Email: Anthony.gray@usq.edu.au.

favoured churches. The centuries immediately before and contemporaneous with the colonization of America had been filled with turmoil, civil strife, and persecutions, generated in large part by established sects determined to maintain their absolute political and religious supremacy."[3]

Despite these provisions, some jurisdictions have recently moved to ban forms of religious expression.[4] For example, Law 2004-228, passed in France, prohibits in public elementary schools, colleges, junior high schools, and high schools the wearing of signs and behaviors by which the pupils express openly a religious membership. Facially the article does not single out a particular religion; however, in practice it has been applied almost exclusively to require that the *hijab* and *burqa* not be worn at these venues.[5] In 2010, the French government moved to extend the ban beyond educational settings. In terms of topicality, it seems reasonable to focus in more detail on the ban of hijab and burqa, though the principles involved are, of course, of universal application.

The Meaning of the Hijab and Burqa

The fundamental question arises whether a banning of either or both the hijab and burqa interferes with the person's right to freedom of religion and their right to manifest that religion. An important consideration here is the relevant provisions of the Qur'an. Typically, the following passage is quoted: "And say to the believing women that they should lower their gaze and guard, their modesty; that they should not display their beauty and ornaments except what (must ordinarily) appear thereof; that they should draw their veils over their bosoms and not display their beauty except to their husbands, their fathers, their husband's fathers, their sons, their brothers or their brother's sons, or their women."[6]

As with many issues in religion, this passage has been interpreted in different ways. A specific challenge with Islam is that, as Baker notes, there is no central authority figure, and followers adhere to different forms and interpretations of Islamic tenets.[7] Opinions differ as what "guarding their modesty" might mean; some interpret this strictly to require the full-body garment (burqa) be worn; others see the headscarf as being sufficient; others argue that the woman merely cannot wear clothing showing the outline of her bosom.[8] Others say that the headscarf is a cultural tradition that has nothing to do with Islam, and the hijab referred to in the Qur'an is a curtain Muhammad used to separate his wives from male visitors and is not a piece of clothing at all.[9]

Some suggest the hijab or burqa are more significant culturally than theologically. Tiefenbrun summarizes these views of the garments as including (1) a positive symbol designating the cultural and religious source of protection, respect, and virtue; (2) a positive sign signifying Muslim identity, which might (arguably) be seen as opposition to Western civilization; (3) a positive sign allowing Muslim women to freely participate in public life, preventing women from "tempting men and corrupting morality";[10] and/or (4) a negative symbol of Islam's power over women.[11]

Studies based on interviews with Muslim women suggest that while some Muslim women adopt the veil to comply with family values and expectations, more commonly women choose to wear the headscarf themselves, often without pressure and often against their parents' wishes. It is sometimes argued by Muslim women that the veiling forces males to deal with them on a mental level as equals rather than sexual objects.[12] A multitude of reasons is plausible.[13] Given this range of views, it would be difficult for a court to determine emphatically that the wearing of the hijab or burqa was or was not the manifestation of a religious practice. The courts have sometimes expressed their reluctance to judge the "validity" of an asserted religious belief, acknowledging that religious belief is intensely personal.[14]

The Fate of Bans on Religious Dress on Both Sides of the Atlantic

Europe

In some parts of Europe veiling has not created difficulty.[15] However, in 2004 France banned the wearing of symbols or clothing denoting religious affiliation in schools. The legislation was, on its face, applicable to all religions; however, the intention apparently was, and the practice has been, that the legislation has overwhelmingly been applied in relation to the wearing of the hijab and burqa.[16]

France has a long and complex history concerning the relation between church and state, and a formal separation that occurred in a 1905 act, confirming the state's impotence in regulating religious matters, arguably completed the separation that commenced in 1789.[17] This principle of secularism, also known as *laicite*, has become associated with French identity and notions of equality, such that differences based on culture, ethnicity or religion, or things that symbolize such differences may be seen as problematic.

Questions have arisen as to the extent to which the wearing of religious dress infringes laicite. In a 1989 opinion, the Conseil d'Etat, one of the three high courts of France, found that laicite and the wearing of religious dress could be compatible, provided it did not constitute an act of pressure, provocation, proselytism, or propaganda impinging upon the freedom of others.

However, a very different approach was evident in a report by the Stasi Commission, set up to study the French concept of laicite. The commission concluded in 2003 that a tension existed between laicite and the wearing of religious dress or symbols, justifying a ban on wearing them in public institutions such as schools. As discussed earlier, this recommendation was legislated into existence in the following year. One reason the commission provided to justify this recommendation was that the wearing of religious dress or symbols often represented an involuntary act: "Pressures exert themselves on young girls, forcing them to wear religious symbols. The familial and social environment sometimes imposes on them a choice that is not theirs. The Republic cannot remain deaf to the cries of distress from these young women."[18]

Critics of such findings counter that the reasons why an individual might wear religious dress or symbol are often complex and multiple, alluded to earlier. The Stasi Commission did not commission research to support its assertion that the wearing of religious dress was usually or often the product of pressure from others, and there is evidence to the contrary, as has been noted earlier.[19] Further, the ban implemented is far from complete; it only bans the wearing of such dress in a (public) school environment but not in society more generally. If it really were about avoiding the oppression of people who might feel forced to wear religious dress or symbols, why is the ban confined to the wearing of such dress at (public) school? Why does it not apply to students in private schools? Or banned in any context?[20] Further, as Custos notes, the ban is confined to expressions of religious affiliations through the wearing of dress or symbols; in contrast, oral or written expressions of religious affiliation are not prohibited or confined, whether at school or elsewhere.[21] It may have the effect of alienating Muslim youth, denying young women an education, and discouraging integration within French society.[22]

The French government may have been emboldened in its decision to ban the wearing of religious dress in schools by some decisions interpreting the right to freedom of religion in this context. Somewhat surprisingly, several European Court of Human Rights decisions have apparently condoned such restrictions on the right of an individual to manifest their religious views, despite the strong protection given to religion by Article 9 of the convention. In *Dahlab v. Switzerland*,[23] the court considered a Swiss law restricting the wearing of religious clothing, in this case applied against a teacher who wished to wear an Islamic headscarf. The court found that although there was an interference with the right to freedom of religion espouses in Article 9(1), it was justified within the "margin of appreciation" granted to member states. Here allowing a teacher to wear the scarf would violate the notion of institutional neutrality associated with public schools. It was relevant that the teacher taught students ages four to eight, where their vulnerability was high. (However, the court acknowledged there was no evidence that the teacher had attempted to indoctrinate her students in any way.) Further, the court concluded that the wearing of the Islamic scarf "is hard to square with the principle of gender equality," and "it appeared difficult to reconcile the wearing of an Islamic headscarf with the message of tolerance, respect for others and, above all, equality and non-discrimination that all teachers in a democratic society must convey to their pupils."[24]

In *Sahin v. Turkey*, the court considered a ban on the wearing of an Islamic headscarf at a Turkish University.[25] Sahin was excluded from the university because she refused to comply with the ban. Her arguments to the European Court of Human Rights were unsuccessful. By a majority of 16 to 1, the Grand Chamber dismissed her case. They held that although there was an interference with Sahin's right to freedom of religion, the ban fell within the Turkish government's "margin of appreciation," necessary to combat the headscarf's threat to secularism and gender equality, important values in the Turkish Republic. The court reiterated the value of secularism to protect equality and liberty. The majority found the headscarf was "difficult to reconcile with the message of tolerance, respect for others . . . and non-discrimination."[26] Referring to the *Dahlab* case, the majority noted that the court had stressed the "powerful external symbol" that the wearing of the headscarf represented and questioned whether it might have a proselytizing effect, given it was worn as a religious precept that was difficult to reconcile with equality.[27] The majority claimed that "in such a context, where the values of pluralism, respect for the rights of others and, in particular, equality before the law of men and women are being taught and applied in practice, it is understandable that the relevant authorities should wish to preserve the secular nature of the institution concerned and so consider it contrary to such values to allow religious attire, including, as in the present case, the Islamic headscarf to be worn."[28]

The dissentient, Judge Tulkens, noted there was no evidence of Sahin's reasons for wearing the headscarf or that she was seeking to make any particular statement or achieve any particular purpose by wearing it. There was no evidence that Sahin's wearing of the scarf had caused, or would likely cause, disruption on the campus.[29]

The judge noted that Sahin in her evidence said she wore the headscarf of her own free will, giving the lie to the suggestion of the majority that allowing Sahin to wear it would be perpetuating inequality or intolerance. The judge asked what the connection was between the ban and sexual equality, accusing the majority judgment of paternalism.[30] As has been noted, if the government really was serious about promoting equality and really did believe that a ban was necessary to promote or preserve it, the ban actually implemented was grossly inadequate to the task—the ban should have been applied to all of Turkish society rather than in schools and government.[31] Further, the effect of such laws may be, in effect, to deny Islamic women the right to education, a result actually exacerbating inequality rather than addressing it. According to one estimate, the result of the Sahin case has been that thousands of Turkish Islamic women have dropped out of Turkish universities.[32]

At the national level, courts have considered similar issues in the context of both convention rights and rights under more general discrimination/equality legislation. A student complaint was upheld in *The Queen on the Application of Watkins-Singh and the Governing Body of Aberdare Girls' High School and Rhondda Cynon Taf Unitary Authority*.[33] In this case, argued on the basis of indirect discrimination on the ground of race rather than the European Convention on Human Rights, a student complained about a school decision to refuse her permission to wear the kara, a plain steel bangle that was very significant to the student as a Sikh. The student stated that she wore the kara out of a sense of duty as well as an expression of her race and culture. An expert testified as to the importance of the bangle, reminding Sikhs of God's infinity and that followers were handcuffed to God. The school argued that its uniform policy prohibited the wearing of jewelry and that it would be discriminatory to allow an exception to this particular student.

The court found that the school had unlawfully discriminated against the student on the grounds of race and religion. The relevant acts under consideration in this case were the Race Relations Act 1976 (UK) and Equality Act 2006 (UK). Section 1 of the Race Relations Act1976 (UK), as amended, set out the key definition of racial discrimination in terms of direct[34] and indirect discrimination.[35] Section 45(3) of the latter act also deals with indirect discrimination, defined to include applying a provision or practice equally to those not of the complainant's religion or belief, such as to place those of the complainant's religion or belief at a disadvantage compared to some or all others (where there is no material difference in relevant circumstances). It includes placing the complainant at a disadvantage compared with those not of their religion or belief, where there is no material difference in circumstances, where the person committing the alleged discrimination cannot justify their actions by reference to matters other than the complainant's religion or belief.

In this case, the court found that the Sikhs comprised both a racial group[36] and a religion. The relevant practice was the school's uniform policy and how it was implemented, specifically a ban on any jewelry apart from a pair of stud earrings, unless it was a compulsory requirement of the student's religion or culture. It was relevant to compare how the practice affected the complainant with those whose religious or racial beliefs were not compromised by the practice. Here the policy caused a particular disadvantage or detriment to the complainant, given the exceptional importance she (genuinely) placed on the wearing of the Kara. The school could not justify its policy. Comparisons with cases in which bans on dress such as the *niqab* and hijab were not valid because these were much more visible, such that arguments about uniformity, coherence, communal spirit, and whether students "stood out" from others were not valid in the current context. The court concluded the defendants had indirectly discriminated against the complainant on the ground of race contrary to the RRA and on the ground of religion under the Equality Act 2006 (UK).

The United Kingdom Supreme Court considered these issues recently *in R v. Governing Body of JFS and the Admissions Appeal Panel of JFS.*[37] There a school policy gave preference in admission to those whose status as Jews was recognized by the Office of the Chief Rabbi (OCR). M. was refused admission because he was not recognized as such by the OCR. His father was recognized as such but his mother was not. She was born in Italy and she had undergone a Jewish conversion process, but it was not recognized as effective by the OCR. As a result of this nonrecognition, M. was not recognized by the school as being Jewish. M. argued that his exclusion from the school on this basis contravened s1 of the Race Relations Act 1976 (UK). The section prohibited both direct discrimination and indirect discrimination. A majority of the court found the actions of the school to be discriminatory contrary to the Race Relations Act 1976 (UK). The majority was satisfied that the discrimination here was due to the person's racial or ethnic origins, such that it contravened the act;[38] for the majority it was artificial to distinguish here between ethnic status (to which the RRA applied) and religious status (to which the RRA did not apply). Some majority judgments considered the extent to which the motive or intention behind the behavior argued to be discriminatory was relevant in considering whether there had been a breach of the act. Members of the majority believed that such a factor was not relevant in assessing the validity of the challenged behavior against the RRA.[39]

The concept of "proportionality" appears in both the Race Relations Act 1976 (UK)[40] and Equality Act 2010 (UK)[41] in the context that discrimination that is otherwise unacceptable may be justified as a proportional means of achieving a legitimate end; this concept is foreign to the ECHR, which provides for strictly limited departures from the rights recognized in Article 9. Further, both the Race Relations Act 1976 (UK) and Equality Act 2010 (UK) require the disadvantage suffered by the complainant be "particular," a concept again foreign to Article 9.[42]

Some (other) important differences should be borne in mind. While Islam is clearly a religion, such that its followers would have a right to bring a complaint under the Equality Act 2006 (UK) and Equality Act 2010 (UK), it would be more difficult to bring a complaint under the Race Relations Act, given its definition of discrimination relates to concepts such as "race" and "ethnic or national origin." Given the standard definition of these concepts in *Mandla*, and the fact that Islam can be described as a "heterogeneous faith" without some of the elements of the *Mandla* definition, unless the definition were adapted, it is arguable whether a follower of the Islamic faith could meet this threshold requirement.[43] The extension in s1(1A), arguably slightly broader than *Mandla*, may not assist.

North America

The United States Supreme Court has noted the history creating the context in which religious freedoms were protected by the First Amendment.[44] In its interpretation of the free exercise of religion and antiestablishment provisions of the First Amendment, the court has moved from a requirement that a law affecting religious practice be justified by a "compelling governmental interest"[45] to a more modest requirement that the law not be directed at specific religious practices or ban the performance of acts solely because of their religious motivation.[46] This approach validates laws that incidentally affect a religious practice but that are of general application and otherwise constitutionally valid.[47] The court considered a religious ban in *Goldberg v. Weinberger, Secretary of Defense*[48] involving an air force regulation prohibiting employees from wearing headgear while indoors as part of the uniform policy. An employee psychologist on an air force base was an Orthodox Jew and ordained rabbi and wore a skullcap (yarmulke) while on duty indoors and under his service cap while outdoors. He was warned he was in breach of the air force uniform regulation and could be the subject of a court martial. The employee claimed the regulation was an infringement of his First Amendment right.

A majority of the Supreme Court upheld the regulation. The majority claimed that great deference should be given to the professional judgment of military authorities concerning the relative importance of a particular military interest. The military had a legitimate interest in ensuring "instinctive obedience, unity, commitment and esprit de corps."[49] The regulation was not aimed at a particular religion.[50] Courts have upheld legislation prohibiting public school teachers from wearing religious clothing in the classroom.[51] Courts have had to grapple with possible inconsistencies between the antiestablishment aspect of the First Amendment in relation to religion and its free exercise.[52] So a decision to suspend a Sikh teacher for wearing white dress and a turban to school was upheld;[53] as was a decision to dismiss a Muslim teacher for wearing a headscarf in the classroom.[54]

Some cases have been argued on the basis of alleged religious discrimination contrary to Title VII of the Civil Rights Act 1964.[55] In *Webb v. City of Philadelphia*, the United States District Court found that the defendant was justified in insisting the plaintiff not wear hijab to work; this was due to the need for uniformity, cohesiveness, cooperation, and esprit de corps among police. Disallowing the hijab here ensured religious neutrality among police and avoided divisiveness.[56]

The leading Canadian case is *Multani v. Commission Scolaire Marguerite-Bourgeoys*.[57] G. was a Sikh student enrolled in a Canadian school. He believed his religion required him to wear a *kirpan* at all times. This is a religious object resembling a dagger and required to be made of metal. The school's governing board claimed that wearing of the kirpan violated the school's code of conduct, which prohibited the carrying of weapons. It cited concerns with safety. It was suggested that G. could wear a kirpan if it was made of a nonmetallic substance. G. refused this; he subsequently brought legal action alleging a breach of the freedom of religion provisions of the *Canadian Charter of Rights and Freedoms*.[58]

The Supreme Court unanimously overturned a finding that the interference with religious freedom was justified by s1 of the charter. The wearing of the kirpan had genuine religious significance to G. G. believed that the wearing of a kirpan made of wood or plastic would not meet his religious obligations. The risk of G. using his kirpan as a weapon was extremely low, and there had been no history of any violent incidents involving kirpans in Canadian schools. While the kirpan could in theory be used as a weapon, it was above all a religious symbol; the word deriving from "kirpa," meaning mercy, kindness, and honor. Although the school's concern with safety was laudable, they were required to provide a reasonable level of safety, not guarantee absolute safety. A ban on metallic kirpans was not a proportional response to the public interest in providing a safe environment in schools given the lack of any history of violence involving them, particularly when Canada had strongly embraced multicultural values.

Conclusion

While religious freedoms are formally recognized in international and domestic human rights instruments, as interpreted by the courts, religious freedoms have been given rather less deference than might have been expected, particularly in Europe and the United States. The courts in Europe and the United States have applied a broad interpretation of the "margin of appreciation" to allow laws that clearly infringe the right to manifest one's religion if the government can present some justification, questionable and poorly researched though it might be. While it is accepted that the right to manifest religion should not be absolute, perhaps courts have generally been too timid in upholding the right against legislative interference.

Notes

1. The practice of circumcision has a religious basis but is often performed for nonreligious reasons.

2. Article 9(2) provides for limits to the freedom if they are prescribed by law and necessary in a democratic society in the interests of public safety, for the protection of the public order, to protect health or morals, or to protect the rights and freedoms of others. Related rights include the right to respect for private and family life (Article 8), right to freedom of expression (Article 10), and the right to freedom from discrimination on the basis of religion (Article 14). The limits are strictly interpreted and must be directly related and proportional to the specific need; they must not be applied in a discriminatory manner: Human Rights Commission *General Comment No 22: The Right to Freedom of Thought, Conscience and Religion* (Article 18, Forty-Eighth Session, 1993). The European Court has found that restrictions on religious freedom call for "very strict scrutiny" by the court since the right is fundamental in nature: *Manoussakis v. Greece*, App. No. 18748/91, 23 European Human Rights Reports 387, 407 (1997).

3. *Everson v. Board of Education* 330 US 1 (1947), in the context of that country's first amendment's antiestablishment clause and Article VI s. 3 forbidding religious tests in order to take office.

4. Links with post-9/11 hysteria have been noted here: "Women who are readily identified as Muslim because they wear a headscarf or veil report that they have often been the target of racist violence and discrimination and that this increased post 9-11 as their clothing is now read to signify religious fundamentalism, danger and terrorism": Margaret Thornton and Trish Luker, "The Spectral Ground: Religious Belief Discrimination," *Macquarie Law Journal* 9 (2009): 83.

5. Mark Levine reports that in the first year following the passage of the French law, 47 Muslim girls had been expelled from French schools for wearing the hijab: "The Modern Crusade: An Investigation of the International Conflict between Church and State," *California Western International Law Journal* 40 (2009): 42.

6. Qur'an 24: 30–31; 24: 60; 33: 59; and 33: 53; Abdullah Yusuf Ali, *The Qur'an Text, Translation and Commentary* (New York: Tahrike Tarsile Qur'an Inc., 2001), 904–5.

7. Christina Baker, "French Headscarves and the United States Constitution: Parents, Children and Free Exercise of Religion," *Cardozo Journal of Law and Gender* 13 (2008): 359.

8. Mukul Saxena, "The French Headscarf Law and the Right to Manifest Religious Belief," *University of Detroit Mercy Law Review* 84 (2007): 779–80; Susan Tiefenbrun, "The Semiotics of Women's Human Rights in Iran," *Connecticut Journal of International Law* 23 (2008): 25.

9. Jeremy Gunn, "Religious Freedom and Laicite: A Comparison of the United States and France," *Brigham Young University Law Review* (2004): 471–72.

10. Aliah Abdo, "The Legal Status of Hijab in the United States: A Look at the Sociopolitical Influences on the Legal Right to Wear the Muslim Headscarf," *Hastings Race and Poverty Law Journal* 5 (2008): 449; "Hijab is not only meant to guard

women from inappropriate leering male attention, but it is considered to be a liberating experience to be free from societal expectations and judgments over a women's body and other physical characteristics"; Mark Levine, "The Modern Crusade" 41.

11. Susan Tiefenbrun, "Semiotics" 22–23; Stefanie Walterick, "The Prohibition of Muslim Headscarves from French Public Schools and Controversies Surrounding the Hijab in the Western World," *Temple International and Comparative Law Journal* 20 (2006): 255: "To many people in France, the hijab is also a symbol of the oppression and subjugation of Muslim women"; Elisabeth Badinter, interview with L. Joffin, *The Nouvel Observateur* (1989): 7–11; Nilufer Gole, "The Voluntary Adoption of Islamic Stigma Symbols," *Social Research* 70 (2003): 817–18.

12. Adrien Wong and Monica Smith, "Critical Race Feminism Lifts the Veil? Muslim Women, France and the Headscarf Ban," *University of California Davis Law Review* 39 (2006): 761–63.

13. Jeremy Gunn, "Commentary: French Secularism as Utopia and Myth," *Houston Law Review* 42 (2006): 98; Yael Barbibay, "Citizenship Privilege or the Right to Religious Freedom: The Blackmailing of France's Islamic Women," *Cardozo Journal of International and Comparative Law* 18 (2010): 201.

14. *R. (Williamson) v. Secretary of State for Education and Employment* (2005) 2 AC 246, 22–23 (Lord Nicholls); *Employment Division, Department of Human Resources of Oregon et al v. Smith et al.* 494 US 872, 887 (1990).

15. In 2003, for instance, the German Federal Constitutional Court held that Muslims could wear their veils while teaching: *Kopftuch-Urteil* [Headscarf Decision], Entscheidungen des Bundesverfassungsgerichts (BVerf GE; Federal Constitutional Court), 108, 282 9/24/03, 2 BvR 1436/02, NJW 2003, 3111 (FRG); Axel Frhr von Campenhausen, "The German Headscarf Debate," *Brigham Young University Law Review* (2004): 665.

16. Nusrat Choudhury notes that 45 of the 48 students expelled in the four months following the implementation of the ban were Muslim girls who refused to remove their headscarves when entering a public school: "From the Stasi Commission to the European Court of Human Rights: L'Affaire Du Foulard and the Challenge of Protecting the Rights of Muslim Girls," *Columbia Journal of Gender and Law* 16 (2007): 201; Stefanie Walterick, "Prohibition of Muslim Headscarves" 251: "The law was enacted with the specific intent to eliminate the Muslim hijab, or headscarf, from French public school classrooms."

17. Dominique Custos, "Secularism in French Public Schools: Back to War? The French Statute of March 15, 2004," *American Journal of Comparative Law* 54 (2006): 345.

18. *Stasi Commission Report*, 4.2.2.1; Dina Alsowayel, "Commentary: The Elephant in the Room: A Commentary on Steven Guy's Analysis of the French Headscarf Ban," *Houston Law Review* 42 (2006): 107; speaking of the French ban, "A young French Muslim girl who was previously shrouded in the hijab removes it to go to school. By removing her cover, she is suddenly more receptive to other ideas regarding matters of faith and can now freely choose among them. This reasoning indicates a woeful lack of understanding about the hijab and Islam."

19. The report has been trenchantly criticized: see Nusrat Choudhury, "From the Stasi Commission" ; Dominique Custos, "Secularism in French Public Schools" 54; Jeremy Gunn, "Religious Freedom and Laicite" 468–73; Mukul Saxena, "The French Headscarf Law".
20. The French government moved to extend the ban in 2010 beyond the educational context.
21. Dominique Custos, "Secularism in French Public Schools" 373.
22. Stefanie Walterick, "The Prohibition of Muslim Headscarves" 252.
23. *Dahlab v. Switzerland* (2001), European Court of Human Rights, 1.
24. The findings have been criticized: see, for example, Ingvill Thorson Plesner, "Legal Limitations to Freedom of Religion or Belief in School Education," *Emory International Law Review* 19 (2005): 572–73: "It is hardly a sign of tolerance to not accept symbols that are carried by women of a particular religious tradition."
25. The Turkish Constitution contains a principle of "laiklik," similar to French laicite, emphasizing the secular nature of the state.
26. [2005] ECHR 819, para. 111.
27. The ban was subsequently lifted in 2008: Frances Raday, "Traditionalist Religious and Cultural Challengers—International and Constitutional Human Rights Responses," *Israel Law Review* 41 (2008): 613.
28. Para. 116.
29. Para. 10.
30. The judge said it was not for the court to make an appraisal of this type on a religion or religious practice. See for further discussion of the case Nusrat Choudhury, "From the Stasi Commission."
31. Benjamin Bleiberg, "Unveiling the Real Issue: Evaluating the European Court of Human Rights' Decision to Enforce the Turkish Headscarf Ban in *Sahin v Turkey*," *Cornell Law Review* 91 (2006): 162; Christopher Belelieu, "The Headscarf as a Symbolic Enemy of the European Court of Human Rights' Democratic Jurisprudence: Viewing Islam through a European Legal Prism in Light of the *Sahin* Judgment," *Columbia Journal of European Law* 12 (2006).
32. Benjamin Bleiberg, "Unveiling the Real Issue," 163.
33. [2008] EWHC 1865 (Admin).
34. Section 1(1)(a) includes within the definition of discrimination treating someone less favorably than another on racial grounds.
35. Section 1(1)(b) includes within the definition of discrimination applying a requirement or condition to those not of the same racial group (group defined by reference to color, race, nationality, or ethnic or national origin s3[1]) as the other but where the proportion of the persons of the same racial group as the complainant who can comply with the requirement is considerably less than the proportion of those not of that racial group who can comply and that is not shown to be justifiable irrespective of the color, race, nationality, or ethnic or national origins of the person to whom it is applied, and as a result the complainant suffers detriment.
36. This concept was discussed in detail in *Mandla v. Dowell Lee* [1983] 2 AC 548, where Lord Fraser discussed essential requirements of a racial or ethnic group to include (1) a long shared history of which the group is conscious as distinguishing it from other groups and the memory of which it keeps alive, (2) a cultural tradition

of its own, including family and social customs and manners, often but not necessarily associated with religious observance. Other relevant factors included a common geographical origin, or descent from a small number of common ancestors, a common language, a common literature peculiar to the group, a common religion differing from neighboring groups, and being a minority or an oppressed group within a larger community.

37. [2009] UKSC 15.
38. Lord Phillips [51], Lady Hale [71], Lord Mance [92], Lord Kerr [123], Lord Clarke [129].
39. Lord Phillips [20], Lady Hale [57], and Lord Mance [81].
40. S1(1A).
41. S19; as does s45 of the Equality Act 2006 (UK).
42. S1(1A) and s19, respectively.
43. The possibility exists, as Ann Blair notes, that a measure affecting Muslims could be challenged if it disproportionately affected people of Asian origin, given high Muslim populations in Indonesia and Malaysia: "Case Commentary—*R (SB) v Headteacher and Governors of Denbigh High School*—Human Rights and Religious Dress in Schools," *Child and Family Law Quarterly* 17, no. 3 (2005). Anne Hewitt agrees that a Muslim would in most cases not be able to meet the definition of "race" or "ethnic group": "Muslims do not satisfy the test as a racial group because they are drawn from too diverse a range of backgrounds": "It's Not Because You Wear Hijab, It's Because You're Muslim—Inconsistencies in South Australia's Discrimination Laws," *Queensland University of Technology Law Journal* 7, no. 1 (2007): 67.
44. *Everson v. Board of Education* (1947) 330 US 1, 8–9; Justice Jackson noted the purpose of religious freedom as indicated in the First Amendment was "broader than separating church and state . . . It was to create a complete and permanent separation of the spheres of religious activity and civil authority" (29) . . . for Madison, as also for Jefferson, religious freedom was the crux of the struggle for freedom in general (34).
45. *Sherbert v. Verner* 374 US 398 (1963). In *Wisconsin v. Yoder* 406 US 205 (1972), Chief Justice Burger wrote for the court that "only those interests of the highest order and those not otherwise served can overbalance legitimate aims to the free exercise of religion" (215). The court has not been impressed with laws that single out particular religions for special treatment: *Church of Lukumi Babalu Aye v. City of Hialeah* 508 US 520 (1993).
46. So for instance, a law prohibiting public school teachers from wearing religious emblems or insignia in the workplace was invalid because the law singled out clothing with religious connotations as opposed to jewelry or clothing more generally: *Nichol v. ARIN* 268 F. Supp 2d 536 (2003).
47. *Employment Division, Department of Human Resources of Oregon et al. v. Smith et al.* 494 US 872 (1990); see also the Religious Freedom Restoration Act 42 USCA 2000bb-1 (1993) in response to the Smith decision and the Supreme Court's rejoinder in *City of Boerne v. Flores* 521 US 527 (1997); Vincent Bonventre, "A Second-Class Constitutional Right? Free Exercise and the Current State of Religious Freedom in the United States," *Albany Law Review* 70 (2007); Steven Green, "Religious Liberty as a Positive and Negative Right," *Albany Law Review* 70 (2007).

48. 475 US 503 (1986).
49. 507.
50. 512.
51. This legislation exists in Oregon, Pennsylvania, and Nebraska. Apparently these kinds of laws, now mostly repealed, were originally designed to prevent Catholic nuns and priests from teaching in public schools, reflecting anti-Catholic sentiment, although they were typically facially neutral in terms of religion: Stefanie Walterick, "The Prohibition of Muslim Headscarves" 264.
52. Wojciech Sadurski, "Neutrality of Law towards Religion," *Sydney Law Review* 12 (1990): 427–47.
53. *Cooper v. Eugene School District* 723 P. 2d 298 (Or. 1986).
54. *United States v. Board of Education for the School District of Philadelphia* 911 F. 2d 882, 893–894 (3d Cir., 1990); however, see *Nichol v. ARIN Intermediate Unit* 28, 268 F. Supp 2d 536 (W.D Pa 2003), where an educational provider's dress code banning teachers from wearing Christian crosses or Stars of David was deemed to violate the free exercise clause. The United States Supreme Court has not yet decided whether the teacher dress statutes in these states is consistent with the First Amendment: see for further discussion Stefanie Walterick, "The Prohibition of Muslim Headscarves" 264–67.
55. 42 USC 2000e-16 (2007).
56. *Webb v. City of Philadelphia* 2007 WL 1866763, 1 (ED Pa, June 27, 2007).
57. [2006] 1 S.C.R 256.
58. S2(a) of the charter, as well as s3 of the Quebec *Charter of Human Rights and Freedoms*. In both cases, as is the case with most human rights provisions, the rights expressed are not absolute—in the case of Canada, the allowance is for "reasonable limits as prescribed by law as can be demonstrably justified in a free and democratic society" (s1 of the *Charter*). Examples where limits on religious freedom were justified include *Ross v. New Brunswick School District No 15* [1996] 1 S.C.R 825 and *B (R) v. Children's Aid Society of Metropolitan Toronto* [1995] 1 S.C.R. 315; see *Amselem v. Syndicat Northcrest* [2004] 2 S.C.R 551.

Bibliography

Abdo, Aliah. "The Legal Status of Hijab in the United States: A Look at the Sociopolitical Influences on the Legal Right to Wear the Muslim Headscarf." *Hastings Race and Poverty Law Journal* 5 (2008): 441–508.

Ali, Abdullah Yusuf. *The Qur'an Text: Translation and Commentary*. New York: Tahrike Tarsile Qur'an, 2006.

Alsowayel, Dina. "Commentary: The Elephant in the Room: A Commentary on Steven Gey's Analysis of the French Headscarf Ban." *Houston Law Review* 42 (2006): 103–120.

Baker, Christina. "French Headscarves and the United States Constitution: Parents, Children and Free Exercise of Religion." *Cardozo Journal of Law and Gender* 13 (2008): 341–368.

Barbibay, Yael. "Citizenship Privilege or the Right to Religious Freedom: The Blackmailing of France's Islamic Women." *Cardozo Journal of International and Comparative Law* 18 (2010): 159–206.

Belelieu, Christopher. "The Headscarf as a Symbolic Enemy of the European Court of Human Rights' Democratic Jurisprudence." *Columbia Journal of European Law* 12 (2006): 573–624.

Blair, Ann. "Case Commentary—*R (SB) v Headteacher and Governors of Denbigh High School*—Human Rights and Religious Dress in Schools." *Child and Family Law Quarterly* 17, no. 3 (2005): 399–414.

Bleiberg, Benjamin. "Unveiling the Real Issue: Evaluating the European Court of Human Rights' Decision to Enforce the Turkish Headscarf Ban in *Sahin v Turkey*." *Cornell Law Review* 91 (2006): 129–170.

Bonventre, Vincent. "A Second Class Constitutional Right? Free Exercise and the Current State of Religious Freedom in the United States." *Albany Law Review* 70 (2007): 1399–1416.

Choudhury, Nusrat. "From the Stasi Commission to the European Court of Human Rights: L'Affaire du Foulard and the Challenge of Protecting the Rights of Muslim Girls." *Columbia Journal of Gender and Law* 16 (2007): 199–296.

Custos, Dominique. "Secularism in French Public Schools: Back to War? The French Statute of March 15, 2004." *American Journal of Comparative Law* 54 (2006): 337–400.

Gey, Steven. "Free Will, Religious Liberty and a Partial Defense of the French Approach to Religious Expression in Public Schools." *Houston Law Review* 42 (2006): 1–80.

Gole, Nilufer. "The Voluntary Adoption of Islamic Stigma Symbols." *Social Research* 70 (2003): 809–828.

Green, Steven. "Religious Liberty as a Positive and Negative Right." *Albany Law Review* 70 (2007): 1453–72.

Gunn, Jeremy. "Commentary: French Secularism as Utopia and Myth." *Houston Law Review* 42 (2006): 81–102.

———. "Religious Freedom and Laicite: A Comparison of the United States and France." *Brigham Young University Law Review* (2004): 419–506.

Hewitt, Ann. "It's Not Because You Wear Hijab, It's Because You're Muslim— Inconsistencies in South Australia's Discrimination Laws." *Queensland University of Technology Law Journal* 7, no. 1 (2007): 57–70.

Kahn, Robert. "The Headscarf as Threat: A Comparison of German and US Legal Discourses." *Vanderbilt Journal of Transnational Law* 40 (2007): 417–44.

Levine, Mark. "The Modern Crusade: An Investigation of the International Conflict between Church and State." *California Western International Law Journal* 40 (2009): 33–54.

Majedi, Azar. *Women's Rights vs. Political Islam: A Series of Political Writings about the Devastating Effects of Political Islam on Women's Situation and the Struggle of Women against It.* 2007.

Plesner, Ingvill Thorson. "Legal Limitations to Freedom of Religion or Belief in School Education." *Emory International Law Review* 19 (2005): 557–86.

Raday, Frances. "Traditionalist Religious and Cultural Challenges—International and Constitutional Human Rights Responses." *Israel Law Review* 41 (2008): 596–634.

Sadurski, Wojciech. "Neutrality of Law towards Religion." *Sydney Law Review* 12 (1990): 420–54.

Saxeng, Mukul. "The French Headscarf Law and the Right to Manifest Religious Belief." *University of Detroit Mercy Law Review* 84 (2007): 765–828.

Stasi Commission Report. *Commission de Reflexion sur l'Application due Principe de Laicite dans Law Republique.* 2003.

Thornton, Margaret, and Trish Luker. "The Spectral Ground: Religious Belief Discrimination." *Macquarie Law Journal* 9 (2009): 71–88.

Tiefenbrun, Susan. "The Semiotics of Women's Human Rights in Iran." *Connecticut Journal of International Law* 23 (2008): 1–82.

Walterick, Stefanie. "The Prohibition of Muslim Headscarves from French Public Schools and Controversies Surrounding the Hijab in the Western World." *Temple International and Comparative Law Journal* 20 (2006): 251–82.

Wing, Adrian, and Monica Smith. "Critical Race Feminism Lifts the Veil? Muslim Women, France and the Headscarf Ban." *University of California Davis Law Review* 39 (2006): 743–86.

CHAPTER 11

We Are All Children of Babel

*Bruce J. Einhorn**

Now the whole earth had one language and few words. And as men migrated from the east, they found a plain in the land of Shinar and settled there. And they said to one another, "Come, let us make bricks, and burn them thoroughly." And they had brick for stone, and bitumen for mortar. Then they said, "Come, let us build ourselves a city, and a tower with its top in the heavens, and let us make a name for ourselves, lest we be scattered abroad upon the face of the whole earth." And the Lord came down to see the city and the tower, which the sons of men had built. And the Lord said, "Behold, they are one people, and they have all one language; and this is only the beginning of what they will do; and nothing that they propose to do will now be impossible for them. Come, let us go down, and there confuse their language, that they may not understand one another's speech." So the Lord scattered them abroad from there over the face of all the earth, and they left off building the city. Therefore its name was called Babel, because there the Lord confused the language of all the earth; and from there the Lord scattered them abroad over the face of all the earth. (Genesis 11:1–9)

You Say Potato . . .

During my almost 17 years as a United States immigration judge (IJ) in Los Angeles, I often felt as if my colleagues and I were still smarting from the curse incurred by the hubris of our common ancestors (who apparently became

* Address correspondence to Judge Bruce J. Einhorn (retired), Pepperdine University School of Law, 7535 Penobscot Drive, West Hills, CA 91304, USA. E-mail bjejudge@aol.com. I would like to thank my senior research assistant and colleague, Kelley Costello, for all her hard work and counsel.

among the first reported refugees). We were fellow judges and friends; we shared our lunches and reveled in our bull sessions caffeinated by twice-cooked coffee only a litigation addict could love. Indeed, among the more than 250 IJs in courts across the United States, I counted many men and women whom I had known, respected, and liked from our days as lawyers to our time on the bench. Notwithstanding my close relations with my fellow judges, or perhaps precisely because of them, I was constantly confounded and confused by our conversations on the subject of asylum law.[1] I was even more lost for words (no small matter, given my nature) by the manner in which many of my colleagues approached asylum applicants and adjudicated their cases.[2] In fairness, I note that my colleagues were just as unable to understand much of what I did in my courtroom in my own proceedings.

Trial judges experience the aloneness and autonomy of adjudication in a way appellate judges do not. The camaraderie that we IJs experienced at rest and in each other's chambers was replaced by a constant scattering of our sensibilities about asylum law when we donned our robes and voluntarily departed to our separate corners of the world, our own tiny principalities, our own courtrooms. We may have shared a taste for good food, bad coffee, and even worse jokes, but we seemed to speak very different legal languages when we heard and decided asylum claims. The curse of Babel was ever present in how we judged others and their alleged fears of persecution abroad.

Our shared war stories, the tall tales we told of our judicial talents, made us seem very similar in our approaches to asylum; but then, people's golf games always improve with the telling of them, far from the fairways and greens and the balls lost in between. The truth was that far more often than not, we judges just did not reason or speak in the same language in the exercise of our role as asylum adjudicators.

The results of this dramatic diversity in the decision-making process were, and continue to be, made clear in the research and conclusions of Professors Ramji-Nogales, Schoenholtz, and Schrag in their exhaustive study "Refugee Roulette: Disparities in Asylum Adjudication."[3] In that study, for example, the writers found that following the new millennium in New York City, one IJ had an 1820 percent greater chance of granting asylum to Albanian litigants than another IJ regarding the same nationality group of litigants in the same courthouse.[4] In another example, the authors found that during this decade, Chinese asylum applicants before the US Immigration Court in Atlanta had only a 7 percent chance of seeing their claims for relief granted, as opposed "to 47 percent nationwide."[5] I share their concerns about the serendipity of asylum adjudication, and admit to being an especially large stakeholder in the future of asylum availability. As a young lawyer with the US Department of Justice engaged in the prosecution of human rights violators, I was assigned to help draft what became the Refugee Relief Act of 1980–the modern law of asylum, codified at Title 8, Sections 1101(a)(42) and 1158 of the Immigration and Nationality Act,[6] as amended.[7] I retain a strong parental interest in the continuing viability of asylum as a form of relief subject to relatively and reasonably consistent (and, I admit, compassionate) parameters of application by the Immigration Courts. I fear that without the changes and reforms proposed by the authors of "Refugee Roulette," the curse of Babel will continue the crazy-quilt method of asylum adjudication for which neither the best prepared lawyers nor the most credible relief applicants could contemplate: that in each case, in each separate courtroom, the "law is what the judge ate for breakfast."[8] Like any dutiful parent, I trust that my contribution to those changes and reforms will help engender health and hardiness in asylum as a rightful remedy for those who seek protection from a broken world, confounded not just by the language but by the practice of persecution.

Variables and Changes in Credibility Determinations

In my experience, and in the frank and frequent conversations I have held with my colleagues from the court, the single most significant factor in an IJ's assessment of an asylum claim is credibility. It has also been my experience that credibility is the single most inconsistently assessed variable in asylum adjudication. In the complex chemistry of credibility determinations, there are a number of free radicals that bedevil and divide judges: "[c]redibility determinations in asylum hearings have always been difficult to make. Reasons for this difficulty include, but are not limited to, differences in cultural norms, the effect of an asylum seeker's past traumatic experiences and flight on her ability to recall events, language barriers, the adversarial nature of the hearing, the asylum seeker's limited access to legal counsel, and the adjudicator's sometimes inaccurate perceptions of foreign culture."[9]

An additional and constant aggravating element in determining credibility is the often crushing caseload of IJs, particularly in large and multicultural cities like Los Angeles or New York, which causes even the best-intentioned adjudicators to lose patience and perspective.[10] It was not unusual for me, and remains standard operating procedure for many of my colleagues, to face "master calendar" sessions of well over 25 or 30 cases. In such master calendar situations, preliminary but critical matters are resolved in removal proceedings, including language determinations, the sufficiency of time for the aliens[11] to seek counsel, the admissions or denials made by aliens to the allegations and charges made against them by the government in the court proceedings, and the submission of relief applications, like those for asylum. Following master calendar hearings, trials or "individual calendar" hearings are scheduled and held. It is often the case that each trial involves three or more hearings on the merits for litigants whose issues of removal, and especially relief, require more than a few minutes of discussion. To continue the metaphor, then, all the aforementioned free radicals make for a most combustible chemistry of credibility determinations that are grossly unpredictable to asylum seekers and their lawyers (should they have any), and injurious to asylum seekers and the reputation of IJs.

Take, for example, the recently decided case of *Mousa v. Mukasey*, 530 F.3d 1025 (9th Cir. 2008). Mousa, an Iraqi Chaldean Christian, was denied asylum by both an IJ and the Board of Immigration Appeals (BIA), despite her testimony "that she and her family members . . . had been harassed and pressured to join [Saddam Hussein's] Ba'ath Party, and that she and her brother [had been] imprisoned in a Ba'ath party compound for forty-seven days," during which time she was raped by the party's representatives (*Id.* at 1026–27). Both the IJ and the BIA found, as a fatal flaw in Mousa's credibility, her failure to mention her rape on her pretestimonial written asylum application (*Id.* at 1027–28). The Ninth Circuit Court of Appeals rejected that finding, however, noting that "the assumption that the timing of a victim's disclosure of sexual assault is a bellwether of truth is belied by the reality that there is often delayed reporting of sexual abuse" (*Id.* at 1027). In remanding the case and finding Mousa's claim of rape to be a credible one, the court of appeals added that "[m]any victims of sexual assault feel so upset, embarrassed, humiliated, and ashamed about the assault that they do not tell anyone that it occurred" (*Id.* at 1027, 1030). The *Mousa* court emphasized that the psychology behind the reluctance to report rape becomes more pronounced when the country of the sexual assault—in this case, Iraq—is one "where reported rapes often go uninvestigated, and where rape victims are sometimes murdered by members of their own families because they have 'dishonored' their families by being raped" (*Id.* at 1028).[12] In sum, the Court of Appeals concluded, in addition to her demonstrated psychological stress, that "Mousa provided a compelling explanation for her failure to mention her rape at an earlier time in the proceedings: her cultural reluctance to admit the fact that it had occurred" (*Id.*).

Another example of convoluted credibility determinations in asylum proceedings may be found in the case of *Zhou v. Gonzales*, 193 F. App'x 98 (2nd Cir. 2006). Petitioner Zhou had applied for asylum because of his opposition to the Chinese government's policies of coercive population control (*Id.* at 99–100). The IJ and the BIA found against Zhou's claim and his credibility (*Id.* at 99, 101). The IJ concluded that Zhou had testified inconsistently about whether he and his wife suffered forced sterilization in China (*Id.*). The Second Circuit Court of Appeals disagreed, however, and in remanding the proceedings found that "this purported inconsistency appeared to be the result of a translation error rather than an attempt to mislead the IJ" (*Id.* at 99). More specifically, the

Second Circuit cited what it regarded as "a nonsensical translation of Zhou's testimony on this exact point: 'I said they forced me to be sterilized and had not been sterilized'" (*Id.*). The Second Circuit went on to criticize the IJ for relying on the translation to reject Zhou's credibility rather than reject the interpreter: "The IJ recognized that the translator was having difficulty, [but] dismissed the problem because Zhou had elected to speak in Mandarin instead of Foo Chow, and subsequently characterized the confusing translation as an example of Zhou's deceitfulness. Under these circumstances, the IJ's finding is based on an 'inaccurate perception of the record' and thus is insufficient. Further, the IJ placed considerable weight on her misapprehension: what she perceived as a lie, as she set forth in her decision, 'flavored the entire hearing'" (*Id.*). The Second Circuit also concluded that the IJ's adverse credibility determinations "seemed to reflect a lack of cultural sensitivity by treating what were obvious translation difficulties as evasiveness that 'flavored the entire hearing'" (*Id.* at 101).

As a last example, consider the case of *Agbor v. Gonzales*, 487 F.3d 499 (7th Cir. 2007). The female copetitioner sought asylum based on her fear of female genital mutilation following her marriage in her native Cameroon (*Id.* at 500). In denying her and her copetitioning spouse asylum relief, the IJ found Agbor not to be credible, in part because of the "alleged implausibility that the petitioners only know Mr. Daniel—the man who provided them shelter and passports—by his first name" (*Id.* at 505). By contrast, the Seventh Circuit cited to the testimony of another witness who told the IJ that Mr. Daniel was a "mere" business acquaintance and not a friend of the petitioners. Furthermore, the circuit court noted the testimony of Ms. Agbor "that in Cameroon it is customary only to know and refer to an acquaintance by his first rather than his full name" (*Id.*). The Seventh Circuit vacated the decisions of the IJ and BIA to deny asylum and related forms of relief, and remanded the Agbors' proceedings (*Id.* at 505–06). Once again, an IJ's failure to incorporate cultural factors into his or her credibility assessment proved to be a fatal flaw that occasioned an Article III appeals court to question the credibility of the IJ rather than the asylum seeker.

The aforementioned examples reveal that from coast to coast and in between, the inability or unwillingness of at least some IJs to let issues of individual psychology, language, lawyerly skills, and, above all, culture[13] inform the content of credibility determinations has created an atmosphere in asylum proceedings that often resembles the crap shoot of a casino more than that of a court of law.

In defense of my former workplace, I should add that some IJs have attempted to recognize both the reality of cultural diversity and the need to pay heed to it in resolving asylum claims. Frankly, the reality of culture clashes between the Byzantine labyrinth of immigration laws and regulations that govern asylum proceedings and the mind-set of the asylum applicants was for me hard to miss. During the first term of the Clinton Administration in the 1990s, as the brave but failed efforts of the US military to bring peace to Somalia became front page news, I had in my courtroom an asylum seeker from that poor and war-torn country. She was single and barely out of her teens with no knowledge of English and understandably no expertise in the workings of the Immigration Court. Despite my urgings to the contrary, the female respondent elected to represent herself and did so with the assistance of a court-contracted Somali language interpreter. In the course of the asylum phase of her deportation proceedings, she produced a document given to her in Kenya after she fled Somalia and before she arrived in the United States. The document appeared to identify the respondent as a refugee from potential persecution in Somalia on account of her tribal (i.e., national and ethnic) origin and thus also appeared to corroborate her reasons for seeking asylum. Government counsel suggested, and I agreed, that the respondent should provide a copy of the document to the court for possible introduction into the evidentiary record of the case. I thereupon asked the respondent whether she would be willing to make a Xerox of the document during a brief recess. In the most polite and straightforward way, the respondent replied in the affirmative, but then added these revealing words: "Excuse me, Your Honor, but what is a Xerox?" This young woman, intelligent but indigent and barely familiar with the gadget-goofy and technology-dependent ways of the West, illustrated better than I ever could the cultural disconnect between her background of desperation—of drought, famine, and internecine tribal warfare unrestrained by the anarchy of the state—and mine. I promptly withdrew my request of her and made the photocopies myself, a practice that I, and indeed almost all my Los Angeles court colleagues, continued in all *pro se* cases.

In another asylum case brought before my court, I was confronted by a Russian-speaking respondent, from the then newly independent state of Estonia. Like the young woman from Somalia, this respondent declined my invitation for her to take some time in order to seek counsel. She too represented herself and claimed that she had been harassed and mistreated by agents of the new government on account of her activities as an organizer and spokesperson for the ethnic Russian minority in Estonia who in turn complained that they became second-class citizens in their own country following the end of Soviet rule. In her written asylum application, prepared through an interpreter before the initiation of her removal proceedings, the respondent contended that Estonian government agents had "raped" her. However, in her courtroom testimony, the respondent swore only that she had been "violated" by the government agents as they fondled her through her clothes. Government counsel argued that the inconsistency evidenced her lack of credibility on a matter central to her asylum claim. I was not persuaded that this was necessarily so; however, never before had I witnessed a case in which an asylum applicant had actually downgraded the degree of abuse she suffered because of her political activities.

I therefore gently pressured government counsel to try to find the interpreter who had assisted the respondent in the preparation of her asylum application. Fortunately, the interpreter was located and testified in my court that the Russian language word for rape—phonetically spelled in Latin letters as "na-seal-a-veats"—may also be used to denote a lesser violation of a woman's body. The interpreter's testimony resolved any reasonable doubts about the respondent's representations, and my grant of asylum to her was not appealed.

Another challenge to which some of my fellow judges and I have been sensitive is gauging the credibility of an asylum applicant through the latter's perception of time. Psychiatric and psychological studies have taught us that traumatic recollections are maintained by the mind in a different way than less jarring memories: the former are saved as fragments, contain a more sensory quality, "do not seem to carry a 'time-stamp," and cannot be "evoked at will" as easily as more routine recollections.[14] The individual stressors that complicate temporally accurate recollections are often aggravated by cultural factors, like the application of non-Western (e.g., Persian and Ethiopian) calendars and systems that measure time based on specific events without reference to any standardized durational units.[15] Some IJs, particularly those without the benefit of expert psychological and cultural experts but burdened by large and looming caseloads, pounce on the difficulty victims of past persecution have in clearly dating their episodes of abuse and, in doing so, conclude that the asylum seeker's credibility is lacking. Some of us have resisted going in that direction, perhaps because some of us as lawyers propounded the testimony of immigrant witnesses (in my case, Holocaust survivors)[16] with similar problems in temporal discussions, however accurate they were in describing people, places, and events critical to their credibility. Federal courts of appeals have often held that discrediting the testimony of a foreign-born asylum seeker because of the difficulty he or she evidences in dating important activities is often based as much on the psychological impatience and cultural ignorance of the IJ as on the weaknesses of the respondent's testimony.[17] Time, therefore, like language, must be considered with psychological and cultural care in assessing asylum seekers' credibility.

In fact, some asylum seekers of non-Western origin perceive time in a different way, and the insistence of judges and other asylum adjudicators on exact timelines and precise chronology of relevant events raises serious problems. Such asylum seekers face a difficult dilemma: either she admits to being unable to answer in the prescribed, Western manner and suffers the frustration and skepticism of the court, or she guesses or speculates about dates and a chronology that may not be correct. In a real sense, however unwittingly, she is being coerced to choose between troublesome truths and reassuring confabulation, "[t]hus cross-cultural differences of time-perception can seriously hinder the accurate assessment of credibility during the asylum hearing."[18]

It is therefore difficult to overstate the extent to which culture differences create variables in credibility determinations to which immigration judges, other asylum adjudicators, and even attorneys for allegedly persecuted persons may not be sensitive. American judges and even defense counsel "filter" the stories of asylum seekers "through the lens of [their] own cultural identity and [their] bundle of preferences and values."[19] What one author has described as the "disciplined naiveté and informed not-knowing" of legally trained but not cross-culturally educated adjudicators and attorneys often give rise to frustration with non-Western asylum seekers: "The client story that seems to make little sense, the strategy direction that you cannot understand, that tactic that you see as self-defeating—each might be perfectly reasonable with another's lens and another's bundle of preferences and values."[20] In order to determine whether cultural dissonance or genuine fabrication is at work in such a situation, multicultural experts are essential to advise attorneys and testify before courts on how asylum seekers and their powers of thought and articulation are informed by the forces of racism, sexism, ethnocentrism, and homophobia to which those allegedly persecuted were exposed in their homelands.[21]

Therapists have come to recognize that in order to effectively understand and then counsel oppressed people from other societies, they must appreciate and factor into their work the cultural indicators that would separate their clients from themselves. The vehicle often used in this regard by psychiatrists and psychologists is a conceptual framework that identifies five stages of development that oppressed people experience as they labor to understand themselves in terms of their own culture, the dominant racial, religious, ethnic, or political culture of their homelands, and the often violent relationship between the two: (1) conformity, (2) dissonance, (3) resistance and immersion, (4) introspection, and (5) integrative awareness.[22] This conceptual framework is known as the "Race/Culture Identity Model."[23] It recognizes a progression of consciousness about a persecuted person's racial, religious, and ethnic backgrounds, and anticipates the psychological implications of each of the five stages of development. Each member of an oppressed people "will constantly cycle through the five levels again and again as new issues are discovered . . . [T]here is no end to development of consciousness as a cultural being."[24] Such a complicated but invaluable conceptual framework needs to be imparted to asylum adjudicators and attorneys through interdisciplinary training and the assistance of expert witnesses. Such a conceptual framework reveals to the bench and bar what therapists have known for some time: that truth is "experiential" and is relative to the narrator's social position, mental health and emotional state[25]. It is imperative to the fair resolution of credibility that adjudicators develop the capacity to imagine a world different than their own and in doing so better interpret and assess the value of narratives of identities and afflictions.

Finally, all the problems that attach themselves to the difficulty in determining credibility in asylum proceedings are made worse by the newness of asylum seekers to the United States and its processes for resolving immigration disputes. While many applicants for relief from removal must establish a considerable number of years of uninterrupted presence in the United States,[26] asylum seekers tend to be more recent arrivals to this country. In fact, INA § 208(a)(2) (B), 8 U.S.C. § 1158(a)(2)(B) (2006) creates a rebuttable presumption that an alien who has filed for asylum more than one year after his arrival in the United States is ineligible to receive the relief. Consequently, because they are newer to the country, asylum applicants tend to be even more "alien" to the psychology, culture, language, and legal profession they encounter than are other foreign-born respondents in Immigration Court. It is therefore not surprising that a significant disparity exists in the way asylum applicants respond to IJs and, more important, vice versa. Nevertheless, while the disparity is explicable, it is not acceptable: the nature and quality of an asylum decision is often literally a matter of life and death. It therefore behooves all of us involved in asylum law and adjudication to discern how best to correct the problems identified by the original authors of "Refugee Roulette;" in doing so, we must implement the reforms proposed by the authors regarding better appointments, improved training regimens, increased resources for IJs, and more and better counsel for asylum seekers.

A New Court, a New Commitment

Old but persistent problems to the body of our legal institutions, and those who operate them, require new prescriptions. My proposal is a new and autonomous United States Asylum Court (USAC). While it would not guarantee (because, indeed, no mortal solution could guarantee) a complete uniformity of results from one trial judge to the next, it could put in place a set of procedures and methods designed to prevent problems of psychology, culture, and language from making it a Herculean task (rather than just a human one) for judges to better understand the newcomers in their courtrooms, and thus decide their cases more on the facts presented and less on the frustrations caused by immigration litigation. A new cure for the problems of Refugee Roulette can come only from a new court invested with new priorities and new resources. Justice, and the sanity of judges, calls for a court tailor-made to adjudicate credibility in cases unlike those that relate to factual issues relating more to events in this country and respondents who have lived here longer.[27]

Essentially, I am calling for two courts to handle removal proceedings brought by the US Department of Homeland Security: an Immigration Court of more general jurisdiction to handle cases that involve non-asylum-based relief claims such as cancellation of removal under INA § 240A(a)–(b), 8 U.S.C. § 1229b(a)–(b), adjustment of status under INA § 245, 8 U.S.C. § 1255, and waivers of inadmissibility under INA § 212(h), 8 U.S.C. § 1182(h); and another handling all removal proceedings where asylum is requested, together with its companion claims of withholding of removal under INA § 241(b)(3) (A), 8 U.S.C. § 1231(b)(3)(A)[28] and relief under the United Nations Convention Against Torture (CAT) pursuant to 8 C.F.R. § 208.16–18.[29] Cases would be assigned to either the General Immigration Court or the USAC by judges at master calendars. Both the General Immigration Court and the USAC could still function within their current agency, the Justice Department's Executive Office of Immigration Review (EOIR), or, as is my preference, within an immigration judiciary independent of the Executive Branch by an act of Congress pursuant to Article I of the US Constitution.[30] Regardless of the conditions for the divorce, a separate USAC would no longer overcook the judicial temperament of its judges by pouring on them all kinds of cases with all kinds of deadlines. The USAC, and for that matter the new General Immigration Court, would enjoy a lighter, if not light, case load to which it could give greater attention in a less hectic and exhausting atmosphere. My proposal would require additional IJ appointments so that each of the two courts would possess approximately the same number of judges as the present malfunctioning Immigration Court.[31] Thus the USAC and the new General Immigration Court would possess the personnel to efficiently adjudicate each of its cases without prejudice to the workload of the other. Such a proposal would cost a significant amount of money, but the problems and embarrassments caused by the current system of Refugee Roulette necessitate a commitment of additional funds and human resources.

Reassignments of current IJs to the USAC and new appointments to the new court would be made, or at least cleared, by a Merits Panel composed of current judges, leaders, specialists in the area of international human rights (both governmental and nongovernmental), and prominent academics and practitioners (both government and private) in the field of immigration law. The result of such a selection system would be the appointment of USAC judges who are truly qualified for and dedicated to the challenges of asylum adjudication. Additionally, all USAC members would be required to participate in an initial and subsequent periodic training in asylum and refugee law, and the psychological, cultural, and other anthropological aspects of examining and assessing asylum claims. Such training would be conducted by incumbent asylum judges, legal scholars, and experts in the aforementioned and related disciplines. Such training would also include review of recent precedent-setting case law on asylum, and at least some review of the legal developments at the international level (e.g., the reports and guidelines provided by the United Nations

High Commissioner for Refugees and his UNHCR Handbook on Procedures and Criteria for Determining Refugee Status), and even review of the decisions of foreign courts in democratic adjudication systems like Canada.[32] Indeed, our adjudication system has much to learn from our neighbors to the north, particularly in the emphasis they accord psychology and culture in credibility determinations. For example, in *Zapata v. Canada* (Minister of Employment and Educ.), the Federal Court of Canada found that "[an expert medical doctor's psychological] report [on an asylum applicant] cannot be rejected solely for the reason that the conclusion made therein is based on what was related to the doctor by the claimant, when it is clear from the report that the doctor's own professional observation of the claimant was material to the conclusion reached" (*Id.*). Canadian courts also emphasize that care be taken to understand that the asylum applicant's "[a]bility to observe and recall events in the course of a hearing: nervousness caused by testifying before a tribunal; the claimant's psychological condition (such as post-traumatic stress disorder) associated with traumas such as detention or torture; the claimant's young age; cognitive difficulties and the passage of time; gender considerations; the claimant's educational background and social position; and cultural factors."[33]

These admonishments comport with very recent studies, conducted both in North America and in Europe that conclude as follows:

> Cultural factors may strongly influence the types of information asylum seekers are comfortable sharing, as well as the pace of disclosure. In many cultures, victims of sexual abuse, rape, or sexual torture experience an overwhelming amount of shame. Because in many cultures it is important to not lose face, these painful experiences would be difficult to share with loved ones, let alone with strangers in a public setting, especially government officials who might evoke memories of the perpetrators in cases where applicants have been terrorized by the agents of the state.
>
> Eye contact is another culturally variable pattern of behavior . . . Lewdness or aggression is associated with prolonged eye contact in many cultures, though not in the U.S . . . Thus, in US culture, ironically, some asylum seekers may arouse suspicion by the aversion of gaze that to them is innately ingrained as a sign of respect or deference.[34]

Thus it is critical that the USAC have regular access to expert witnesses in the disciplines of psychology and culture to mediate between the court and the often difficult-to-understand asylum applicants. To that end, the USAC should have access to its own court-appointed experts with "no dog in the fight," no vested interests, financial or otherwise, in the outcome of asylum litigation. The legal affairs journalist Adam Liptak wrote that, "In most of the rest of the world, expert witnesses are selected by judges and are meant to be neutral and independent. Many foreign lawyers have long questioned the American practice of allowing the parties to present testimony from experts they have chosen and paid."[35] Moreover, by having the experts selected by and responsible to the court, the judges will find it easier and less threatening to inform the content of their decisions, and of the asylum law itself, with the various medical and social disciplines necessary for the proper adjudication of cases based on foreign events and often on complex psychological factors affecting witness credibility. Again, the proposal to have court-appointed experts will cost the government money—indigent and poor asylum applicants often do not have to pay the same as witnesses under the current system. But if the quality and consistency of asylum decisions are to be increased, a capital investment of public funds is appropriate.

On the subject of funds, a new USAC (and for that matter, a separate General Immigration Court) should be allocated more human resources, in the form of additional law clerks, to allow for more research and written decisions regarding those cases that prove more complicated and demanding. Currently, the overwhelming majority of rulings made by IJs are by oral decisions delivered from the bench immediately after respondents' hearings are concluded. Although the immigration laws and regulations do not require oral as opposed to written decisions, the former are actively encouraged by EOIR as a way of accelerating the completion of the hundreds of thousands of pending removal and deportation proceedings. With additional law clerks, written decisions needed to flesh out difficult questions of asylum law and credibility resolution will become more likely.[36] Moreover, judges should be given authority they currently do not have to publish some of their written decisions, even in cases that go unappealed. Then at periodic training sessions, asylum judges could share and discuss their written rulings and what led to them. Additionally, in larger court jurisdictions like Los Angeles, Miami, and New York, IJs might adopt the suggestion of this author that more complex asylum cases be heard and decided by panels of three IJs, who could collaborate in decisions while comparing their approaches to adjudication and perhaps contribute to a more cohesive pattern and practice of decision making. A true and deep dialogue could begin that would lead to a continuing legal education on asylum in general, and credibility resolution in particular, for judges and lawyers alike. A consistent methodology of credibility resolution would surely emerge, and with it, a lessening of extremes in asylum rulings.

Lastly, it is time to allow for a rule that would release public funds for the representation of asylum applicants (and indeed, all indigent respondents) in federal removal proceedings.[37] The better the preparation and representation on both sides in asylum cases, the better informed the asylum judge will be and the better the quality asylum decisions will have. I cannot count the many times my fellow IJs and I have lamented over the inadequacy or even absence of counsel in cases where a better preparation of asylum claims could prevent cultural misunderstandings and enhance the possibility that documentary evidence and corroborating witnesses would be discovered and introduced at trial. Given the time pressures under which most IJs operate, IJs are neither inclined nor encouraged to grant multiple continuances for respondents to seek counsel, or to slow down to a trickle the pace of merits hearings on the possibility that with the unlikely emergence of representation in the midst of proceedings, issues might emerge that could make a relief claim clearer or more credible. Given that the burden of proving asylum eligibility lies with the asylum applicant,[38] the absence of sufficient attorney resources is perceived by IJs as just another problem through which they must muddle and over which they lack control. A civil Gideon standard (see, *Gideon*, 372 U.S. at 344) would solve this problem, empower asylum applicants in their presentations, and allow IJs to adjudicate more thoroughly vetted relief claims in an efficient fashion. Frankly, an adequate supply of competent counsel would make it just as easy for even busy IJs to grant asylum as to deny it.[39]

A New Mentality

We in the West have been conditioned by our religious, political, and economic heritage to believe that all persons are possessed of free and unfettered will, and that all behavior, verbal and physical, should be judged under a theory of strict individual accountability. Thus if an asylum applicant is unable to articulate his claims for relief from removal or deportation, or if his demeanor appears to denote a lack of confidence before a court, then she and she alone is responsible for failing to "measure up" to what a reasonably educated and experienced judge would expect from a reasonably credible litigant. We in the West generally reject the notion that there is a collective response to authority that may determine or at least grossly affect an individual's ability to satisfy her burden of proof on matters of credibility. Our faith in rugged individualism makes it hard for us to embrace testimonial responses rooted in cultural nuances that are based on cultures far more communitarian than our own.

The fact is, however, that just as the Marxist theory that individuals and their behavior are the prisoners of their class is not the Rosetta stone to a fair understanding of history, the Western and especially the American reliance on a triumphant individualism is by itself an insufficient guide to judging the responses of those from very different cultures who face judgment by even the most gifted and earnest robed guardians of our laws. As individual and national nuances must inform any analysis of class conduct, so collective conscience and national nuances should inform the analysis of an asylum seeker's credibility.

We must educated and sensitize ourselves to the others in our midst, just as they must come to our courts of justice, follow our rules of evidence, and tell us the truth, whole truth, and nothing but the truth, in the most respectful and articulate way they can. Removal and deportation hearings in the United States are adversarial, but the testimonial relationship between the asylum seeker as witness and the court as arbiter of credibility should not be equated with the institutional struggle between the litigant (and his lawyer, if any) and the government and its counsel. Judges and other government adjudicators should make every effort to cross cultural divides and meet asylum seekers "on the fifty-yard line."

Conclusion

In August 2008, the United Nations estimated that about 160,000 civilians have been displaced by warfare between Russian and Georgian armed forces on the territory of the former Soviet republic of Georgia.[40] As recently as this spring, some 1,000,000 refugees were reported to have fled the violence and civil unrest of the Maghreb in North Africa in a desperate effort to cross the Mediterranean and seek asylum in Europe (Rights Monitoring News). The cold, hard reality faced by large numbers of refugees, and the humanitarian basis upon which the asylum law was predicated, are very much needed in our difficult world. The key to a more just application of that law and to greater consistency in assessing the credibility of asylum seekers, lies in an interdisciplinary approach to adjudication that gives recognition to the complexities inherent in modern human rights case work: "Let us look the facts of human conduct in the face. Let us look to economics and sociology and philosophy, and cease to assume that jurisprudence is self-sufficient . . . Let us not become legal monks."[41] In the interests of justice, let us shed our shrouds of piety for wisdom, for "[w]isdom is the principal thing; therefore get wisdom; and with all thy getting get understanding."[42]

Notes

1. Immigration and Nationality Act (INA) § 101 (a)(42)(A), 8 U.S.C. § 1101 (a)(42)(A) (2006) (stating that an alien may receive asylum in the United States if he or she establishes that he or she is unable or unwilling to return to his or her home country because of "a well-founded fear of persecution on account of race, religion, nationality, membership in a particular social group, or political opinion"); see *INS v. Cardoza-Fonseca*, 480 U.S. 421, 429 (1987).
2. Pursuant to INA § 240 (a)(1), 8 U.S.C. § 1229 (a)(1) and 8 C.F.R. § 1003.10(a) (2009), US IJs of the Justice Department's Executive Office for Immigration Review (EOIR) are charged with adjudicating whether aliens should be subject to removal from the United States. IJs are also charged with adjudicating whether

such aliens should be granted Asylum in the United States. 8 C.F.R. § 208.2. The decisions of IJs are reviewable by EOIR's Board of Immigration Appeals; Board decisions in asylum cases are in turn reviewable by the US circuit courts of appeals. INA § 242 (a)(5), 8 U.S.C. § 1252 (a)(5); 8 C.F.R. § 1003.1 (b)(1)–(3).

3. *See generally*, Jaya Ramji-Nogales et al., "Refugee Roulette: Disparities in Asylum Adjudication," 60 *Stanford Law Review* 295 (2007).

4. *Id.* at 301, 339

5. *Id.* at 329

6. INA §§ 101 (a)(42), 208; 8 U.S.C. §§ 1101 (a)(42), 1158 (2006).

7. REAL ID Act of 2005, Pub. L. No. 109–13, 119 Stat. 302 (2005). I make no claim to any revisions in the asylum law that occurred after its initial passage. I especially disavow any role in the drafting of the REAL ID Act, which I believe has made it more difficult to grant asylum to credible applicants without in any meaningful way enhancing the nation's post-9/11 security.

8. This less-than-cherished scenario is generally but falsely attributed to the late J. Jerome Frank of the Second Circuit, a philosopher in the school of legal realism. In fact, Frank urged a less flippant and more serious study of the various often extrajudicial elements that affect judicial decisions. In his work, Frank commented: "Many legal scholars, instead of giving serious consideration to that subject, ['the numerous non-rational factors in the decisional process'], resort to derision. Absurdly lumping together all the non-rational, non-logical elements, and describing them as the 'state of the judge's digestion,' these scholars often jeeringly speak of 'gastronomical jurisprudence.' Under the heading of gastronomical ailments, one cannot subsume all the irrationalities of judges." Jerome Frank, *Courts on Trial: Myth and Reality in American Justice* 161 (1949). This article is a small attempt to go beyond the glib analysis of such a theory of jurisprudence to a more realistic analysis of why and how IJs rule as they do in asylum cases.

9. Daniel Forman, "Improving Asylum-Seeker Credibilty Determinations: Introducing Appropriate Dispute Resolution Techniques into the process," 16 *Cardozo J. Int'l and Comp. L.* 207, 209 (2008) (emphasis added).

10. *See*, Michele Benedetto, "Crisis on the Immigration Bench," 73 *Brook. L. Rev.* 467, 467–68 (2008) (*citing, Tun v. Gonzales*, 485 F.3d 1014, 1027–30 (8th Cir. 2007)).

11. The term "alien" is not one I would choose to use in immigration law. It implies beings of an extraterrestrial origin, instead of fellow flesh-and-blood humans. Unfortunately, the general term applied to the foreign born who are in the United States but not citizens or nationals of the United States is "alien." INA § 101 (a)(3); 8 U.S.C. § 1101 (a)(3) (2006). The immigration law's selection of the term "alien" is, in my view, a powerful example of a long-running theme that "[a] citizen democracy can only work if most of its members are convinced that their political society is a common venture of considerable moment" that "requires . . . a special sense of bonding among the people working together." Charles Taylor, *Why Democracy Needs Patriotism* 119, 120 (Joshua Cohen ed., 199). The theme was put more bluntly by Thomas Jefferson, on the subject of immigration, that newcomers to the United States would bring their "principles, with their language, [which] they will transmit to their children," and that as to America, "[t]hey will infuse into it their spirit, warp and bias is direction, and render it a heterogeneous, incoherent,

distracted mass." Frederic G. Whelan, "Citizenship and Freedom of Movement: An Open Admission Policy," in *Open Borders? Closed Societies? The Ethical and Political Issues* 17, 18 (Mark Gibney ed., 1988). It is no great wonder that the chemistry of credibility determinations in asylum cases are poisoned by a culture of paranoia, aggravated by a culture of misunderstanding and caseload crunching.

12. *Mousa* at 1028 (citing European Council on Refugees and Exiles, "Guidelines on the Treatment of Iraqi Asylum Seekers and Refugees in Europe," 18 *Int'l J. Refugee L.* 452, 458 (2006)). There is no evidence in the record of proceedings in Mousa that her attorneys ever submitted the previously cited journal piece, which the court of appeals understandably found so persuasive and that it apparently found for itself. The failure of Mousa's counsel, particularly at her removal hearing, to address and advance the issue of culture as a basis for understanding her reluctance to admit her rape, clearly did not help her case for relief, and delayed her procurement of the same.

13. By "culture," I mean "all the customs, values, and traditions that are learned from one's environment. [I]n a culture there is a "a set of people who have common and shared values, customs, habits, and rituals; systems of labeling, explanations, and evaluations; social rules of behavior; perceptions regarding human nature, natural phenomena, interpersonal relationships, time and activity; symbols, art, and artifacts; and historical developments." Gargi Roysicar Sadowsky, E. W. M. Lai, and B. S. Plake, "Moderating Effect of Sociocultural Variables on Acculturation Variables of Hispanic and Asian Americans," 70 *Journal of Counseling and Development* 194 (1991). It is sadly ironic that persecuted peoples may have an easier time making themselves clear to their tormentors in their homelands than to adjudicators in a democracy like the United States where the persecuted seek refuge.

14. Jane Herlihy, "Evidentiary Assessment and Psychological Difficulties," in *Pro-of, Evidentiary Assessment and Credibility in Asylum Procedures* 123, 126 (Gregor Noll ed., 2005)

15. Walter Kalin, "Troubled Communication: Cross-Cultural Misunderstandings in the Asylum-Hearing," *20 Int'l Migration Rev.* 230, 236–37 (1986).

16. As a prosecutor and as Chief of Litigation for OSI, I interviewed, deposed, and took the testimony of thousands of refugees from Nazi persecution and from Nazi collaborators who agreed to serve as witnesses against the subjects of my office's investigations and court proceedings. Many of the most credible witnesses, especially among Holocaust survivors, described the murderous and/or violent actions of the OSI defendants as if those actions had been "frozen in time." Oftentimes, the more convincing the recollections of the survivors, the more convoluted seemed their ability to "date-stamp" those memories. With the patience of the witnesses and the courts who heard them, and the aid of experts on psychology and on foreign cultures, the credibility of these brave and good survivors survived and even flourished in the course of the trials. OSI taught me much about building bridges of communication between individuals from other times and places and those lawyers and judges who dwell in the very different, more neat and tidy world of the Anglo-American courtroom. But for my work at OSI, I may well have become one of those overworked, insufficiently assisted IJs, who suffered excoriation at the hands of US courts of appeals.

17. See, for example, *Fiadjoe v. Attorney Gen.*, 411 F.3d 135, 137, 145–47, 153–55 (3d Cir. 2005) (holding that the lower court's conclusion regarding the credibility of plaintiff's testimony was unsupported by reasonable evidence and, after noting the cruel, crude, and insensitive nature of the IJ's decision and interrogation of the plaintiff, remanding the case for review by a different IJ).

18. Walter Kalin, "Cross-Cultural Misunderstandings in the Asylum Hearing," *International Migration Review,* vol. 20, no. 2, Special Issue: "Refugees: Issues and Directions" (Summer 1986) 230–41 at 237.

19. Paul R. Tremblay, "Interviewing and Counseling Across Cultures: Heuristics and Biases," *Clinical Law Review* 9, 373, 412 (2002).

20. *Id.*

21. David Sue and Derald Wing Sue, *Counseling the Culturally Different* (3rd ed. 1999).

22. David Sue and Derald Wing Sue, *Counseling the Culturally Different* (2nd ed. 1990)

23. Ibid.

24. Harold Cheatham, Allan E. Ivey, Mary Bradford Ivey, Paul Pedersen, Sandra Ragazio-DiGilio, Lynn Simek-Morgan, and Derald Wing Sue, *Multicultural Counseling and Therapy II: Integrative Practice in Counseling and Psychotherapy* (4th ed.) 133, 163.

25. Laurence J. Kirmayer, "Failures of Imagination: The Refugee's Narrative in Psychiatry," *Anthropology and Medicine*, vol. 10, no. 2 (2003).

26. For example, INA § 240A (b)(1)(A); 8 U.S.C. § 1229b (b)(1)(A) (2006) allows for the possible cancellation of an alien's removal (and his resulting procurement of lawful permanent residence) if, inter alia, he proves that he has maintained continuous physical presence in the United States for at least ten years from the date of his relief application.

27. For example, under INA § 240A(a)(1)–(3), 8 U.S.C. § 1229b(a)(1)–(3), a lawful permanent resident of the United States may obtain a grant of cancellation of his removal if, despite his or her criminal convictions (almost always ones recorded in the United States), he or she demonstrates that he or she (1) has been an alien lawfully admitted [to the United States] for not less than five years, (2) has resided in the United States continuously for seven years after having been admitted in any status, and (3) has not been convicted of an any aggravated felony. *Id.* "Aggravated felony" is a term of art defined at INA § 101(a)(43), 8 U.S.C. § 1101(a)(43), which generally excludes all but the most serious offenses, like rape and murder. INA § 240A(b), 8 U.S.C. § 1229b(b) provides a form of relief within the sound discretion of an IJ to grant or deny, by weighing the criminal record of the alien in the United States against his or her time, family contacts, rehabilitation, personal and filial hardships, and the positive achievements he or she has accomplished here. Thus the critical issues to be weighed are domestic ones usually well within the common understanding of the respondent, the attorneys for both sides, and the judge. The stress on asylum proceedings brought on by culture shock is therefore far less severe in a cancellation of removal case and other litigation that involves aliens who have lived in the United States for more significant periods of time.

28. INA § 241(b)(3)(A), 8 U.S.C. § 1231(b)(3)(A) prohibits the removal of an alien to a country where "the alien's life or freedom would be threatened in that country because of the alien's race, religion, nationality, membership in a particular social

group, or political opinion." *Id.*; see *INS v. Stevic*, 467 U.S. 407, 429–30 (1984) (noting that eligibility for a withholding of removal must "be supported by clear and convincing evidence establishing that it is more likely than not that the alien [will] be subject to persecution"); but see *INS v. Cardoza-Fonseca*, 480 U.S. 421, 423, 449 (1987) (stating that asylum eligibility may be proven by a lower standard of "a well-founded fear of persecution on account of race, religion, nationality, membership in a particular social group, or political opinion").

29. 8 C.F.R. § 208.16(a) (2009) ("[A]n immigration judge may adjudicate both an asylum claim and a request for withholding of removal whether or not asylum is granted."); id. § 208.16(c)(2) (specifying that relief from removal under CAT is available if the alien "establish[es] that it is more likely than not that he or she would be tortured if removed to the proposed country of removal").

30. It is unseemly for a supposedly impartial court of such consequence for hundreds of thousands of litigants to be subject to control by a litigation and law enforcement agency like the Department of Justice, particularly one that has been found to have illegally employed partisan politics in the appointment of Immigration Judges. See Bruce J. Einhorn, Op-Ed., "Tainted Justice," *L.A. Times*, June 28, 2008, at A25. I would also elevate the Board of Immigration Appeals, which reviews the decisions of IJs, to a Court of Immigration Appeals that includes experienced and well-reviewed IJs from various regions of the country. Finally, I would eliminate the Board's policy of "streamlining [review of] routine [cases by] a single member adjudication process." See US Dep't of Justice, Board of Immigration Appeals: Final Rule 2 (2002), http://www.usdoj.gov/eoir/press/02/BIARulefactsheet.pdf. Cursory review of removal decisions, especially life and death decisions regarding asylum eligibility, should not trump a thorough appellate examination in the purported interests of efficiency. In a democracy, safety must always take precedent over efficiency.

31. Of course, adjustments in the number of new IJs assigned and appointed to each court should be adjusted to comport with rising and falling case loads.

32. Canada's Immigration and Refugee Board (IRB) functions as that country's USAC. The IRB has published an Assessment of Credibility in Claims for Refugee Protection available to both its judges and its practitioners, as well as to the public at large. See generally Immigration and Refugee Bd., *Assessment of Credibility in Claims for Refugee Protection* (2004), http://www.irb-cisr.gc.ca/Eng/brdcom/references/legjur/rpdspr/cred/Documents/credib_e.pdf. The Assessment calls for judges in asylum cases to consider "all the evidence, both oral and documentary [and] not just selected portions of the evidence." *Id.* at 11 (emphasis added). Adjudicators are admonished that they "should not selectively refer to evidence that supports its conclusions without also referring to evidence to the contrary." *Id.* The Assessment also warns that in cases "[w]here the claimant provides personal documentary evidence or medical reports, specific to and corroborative of his claim, it is not sufficient to simply make a blanket statement, without explanation, that no probative value was assigned to this evidence because of a general lack of credibility on the part of the claimant." *Id.* at 13. Finally, the Assessment cites a major Canadian appeals case, *Maldonado v. Canada* (Minister of Employment and Educ.), [1980] 2 F.C. 302, 305 (Can.), which held that "[w]hen [a claimant] swears to the truth of

certain allegations [of persecution], this creates a presumption that those allegations are true unless there be reason to doubt their truthfulness." *Id.* at 52 n.186. The Assessment is national in scope, and thus supports less deviation and eccentricity in judicial findings on credibility.

33. *Id.* at 83–84. It is high time that we in the United States abandon our parochialism and look for guidance, if not precedent, from the actions of asylum courts in other parts of the democratic world, particularly those within the Anglo-American legal tradition. As former US Supreme Court Justice Sandra Day O'Connor thoughtfully observed in a similar context: "I think that we . . . will find ourselves looking more frequently to the decisions of other constitutional courts, especially other common-law courts that have struggled with the same basic constitutional questions we have . . . All of these courts have something to teach us about the civilizing function of constitutional law." Sandra Day O'Connor, *The Majesty of the Law: Reflections of A Supreme Court Justice* 234 (Craig Joyce ed., 2003). What applies to constitutional questions should equally apply to asylum issues, which all arise out of the 1951 United Nations Convention and the 1967 Protocol Relating to the Status of Refugees. See generally Office of the UN High Comm'r for Refugees, UN GAOR, Convention and Protocol Relating to the Status of Refugees 5–7 (2007), http://www.unhcr.org/3b66c2aa10.pdf (providing the text of the 1951 convention and the 1967 protocol).

34. Stuart L. Lustig, "Symptoms of Trauma Among Political Asylum Applicants: Don't Be Fooled," 31 *Hastings Int'l and Comp. L. Rev.* 725, 730–31 (2008)

35. Adam Liptak, "Experts Hired to Shed Light Can Leave U.S. Courts in Dark," *New York Times*, Aug. 12, 2008, at A1.

36. Given that the REAL ID Act now allows for adverse credibility determinations based on "demeanor" and on an array of misrepresentations that may arise in asylum hearings, the need for extra care in crafting asylum decisions and the need for expert witness testimony have become even more critical to a balanced appraisal of a respondent. *See* INA § 208 (b)(B)(iii); 8 U.S.C. § 1158 (b)(B)(iii) (2006).

37. See *Gideon v. Wainwright*, 372 U.S. 335, 342–44 (1963); Ramji-Nogales et al., *supra* note 5, at 340 (reporting that based on their statistical analysis, the existence or absence of legal representation for asylum seekers in Immigration Court proceedings was the single most important factor affecting the outcome of their cases).

38. See 8 C.F.R. § 208.13 (a) (2009). In busy jurisdictions where asylum cases are sometimes complicated, poorly elaborated, and even more poorly represented (if at all), the burden of proof becomes a convenient and justifiable excuse for expeditious denials of relief. Like Pontius Pilate, an overworked and overwrought IJ may wash his or her hands of an alleged target of persecution where no spirited defense has been advanced on the respondent's behalf.

39. Since 2000, according to its current website, EOIR has had a Legal Orientation Program and Pro Bono Program that include a BIA Pro Bono Project and an unaccompanied Alien Children Initiative. US Department of Justice, Executive Office of Immigration Review, Pro Bono Program—Major Program Initiatives, http://www.justice.gov/eoir/probobo/MajorInitiatives.htm (last visited Nov. 8, 2009). While EOIR's efforts in this regard are commendable, there are no substitute for a paid public defender program that would guarantee counsel to every ingredient

respondent in Immigration Court proceedings, and thus ensure a more equal playing field for all asylum applicants.

40. "Top UN Refugee Official Wraps up Mission to Georgia, Russia," *U.N. Daily News*, Aug. 22, 2008, at 1, http://www.un.org/news/dh/pdf/english/2008/22082008 .pdf.
41. Pound, Roscoe, "Law in Books and Law in Action," *Am. L. Rev.* 44 (1910): 35–36.
42. Proverbs 4:7.

Bibliography

Cases

Agbor v. Gonzales, 487 F.3d 499 (7th Cir. 2007)
Fiadjoe v. Attorney Gen., 411 F.3d 135 (3d Cir. 2005)
Gideon v. Wainwright, 372 U.S. 335 (1963)
INS v. Cardoza-Fonseca, 480 U.S. 421 (1987)
INS v. Stevic, 467 U.S. 407 (1984)
Kebede v. Ashcroft, 366 F.3d 808 (9th Cir. 2004)
Maldonado v. Canada (Minister of Employment and Educ.), [1980] 2 F.C. 302 (Can.)
Mendoza Manimbao v. Ashcroft, 329 F.3d 655 (9th Cir. 2003)
Mousa v. Mukasey, 530 F.3d 1025 (9th Cir. 2008)
Lin v. Ashcroft, 385 F.3d 748 (7th Cir. 2004)
Paramasamy v. Ashcroft, 295 F.3d 1047 (9th Cir. 2002)
Tambadou v. Gonzales, 466 F.3d 298 (2nd Cir. 2006)
Tun v. Gonzales, 485 F.3d 1014 (8th Cir. 2007)
Zapata v. Canada (Minister of Employment and Educ.), IMM-4876-93, [1994] 1994 F.T.R. LEXIS 2121 (June 24, 1994)
Zhou v. Gonzales, 193 F. App'x 98 (2nd Cir. 2006)

Statutes

8 C.F.R. § 208.
8 C.F.R. § 208.13(a) (2009
8 C.F.R. § 208.16(a) (2009)
8 C.F.R. § 208.16(c)(2)
8 C.F.R. § 1003.10(a) (2009)
Immigration and Nationality Act (INA) § 101 (a)(3); 8 United States Codes (U.S.C.) § 1101 (a)(3) (2006)
INA § 101 (a)(42)(A), 8 U.S.C. § 1101 (a)(42)(A) (2006)
INA § 101(a)(43), 8 U.S.C. § 1101(a)(43) (2006)
INA § 208 (b)(B)(iii); 8 U.S.C. § 1158 (b)(B)(iii) (2006)
INA § 240 (a)(1), 8 U.S.C. § 1229 (a)(1) (2006)
INA § 240A(a)(1)–(3), 8 U.S.C. § 1229b(a)(1)–(3) (2006)
INA § 240A(b), 8 U.S.C. § 1229b(b) (2006)
INA § 240A (b)(1)(A); 8 U.S.C. § 1229b (b)(1)(A) (2006)

INA § 241(b)(3)(A), 8 U.S.C. § 1231(b)(3)(A) (2006)
INA § 242 (a)(5), 8 U.S.C. § 1252 (a)(5); 8 C.F.R. § 1003.1 (b)(1)–(3) (2006)
REAL ID Act of 2005, Pub. L. No. 109–13, 119 Stat. 302 (2005)

Books and Articles

Benedetto, M. "Crisis on the Immigration Bench." Brooklyn Law Review 73 (2008): 467.

Cheatham, H., A. Ivey, M. B. Ivey, P. Pedersen, S. Ragazido-Digilio, L. Simek-Morgan, and D. W. Sue. *Multicultural Counseling and Therapy II: Integrative Practice in Counseling and Psychotherapy.* 5th ed. Needham Heights, MA: Allyn and Bacon, 2002.

Einhorn, B. J. "Tainted Justice." *L.A. Times,* June 28, 2008.

European Council on Refugees and Exiles, "Guidelines on the Treatment of Iraqi Asylum Seekers and Refugees in Europe." *Int'l J. Refugee L.* 18 (2006): 452.

Forman, D. "Improving Asylum-Seeker Credibility Determinations: Introducing Appropriate Dispute Resolution Techniques into the process." *Cardozo J. Int'l and Comp. L.* 16 (2008): 207.

Frank, J. *Courts on Trial: Myth and Reality in American Justice.* Princeton, NJ: Princeton University Press, 1949.

Herlihy, J. "Evidentiary Assessment and Psychological Difficulties." In *Proof, Evidentiary Assessment and Credibility in Asylum Procedures* edited by Gregor Noll. Leiden/Boston: Martinus Nijhoff Publishers, 2005.

Immigration and Refugee Board. "Assessment of Credibility in Claims for Refugee Protection." Accessed 2004. http://www.irb-cisr.gc.ca/Eng/brdcom/references/legjur/rpdspr/cred/Documents/credib_e.pdf.

Kalin, W. "Troubled Communication: Cross-Cultural Misunderstandings in the Asylum-Hearing." *Int'l Migration Rev.* 20 (1986): 230.

———. "Cross-Cultural Misunderstandings in the Asylum Hearing." Special issue, *International Migration Review* 20, no. 2, special issue (1986): 230.

Kirmayer, L. J. "Failures of Imagination: The Refugee's Narrative in Psychiatry." *Anthropology and Medicine* 10, no. 2 (2003).

Liptak, A. "Experts Hired to Shed Light Can Leave US Courts in Dark," *New York Times,* August 12, 2008.

Lustig, S. L. "Symptoms of Trauma Among Political Asylum Applicants: Don't Be Fooled." *Hastings Int'l and Comp. L. Rev.* 31 (2008): 725.

O'Connor, S. D. *The Majesty of the Law: Reflections of A Supreme Court Justice.* New York: Random House, 2003.

Office of the UN High Commissioner for Refugees, U.N. GAOR. "Convention and Protocol Relating to the Status of Refugees 5–7." 2007. http://www.unhcr.org/3b66c2aa10.pdf.

Office of the UN High Commissioner for Refugees, UN GAOR. "Handbook on Procedures and Criteria for Determining Refugee Status Under the 1951 Convention and the 1967 Protocol Relating to the Status of Refugees." 1992. http://www.unhcr.org/publ/PUBL/3d58e13b4.pdf.

Pound, R. "Law in Books and Law in Action." *Am. L. Rev.* 44 (1910): 12.

Ramji-Nogales, J. "Refugee Roulette: Disparities in Asylum Adjudication." *Stanford Law Review* 60 (2007): 295.

Rights Monitoring News, May 30, 2011.

Sadowsky, G. R., E. W. M. Lai, and B. S. Plake. "Moderating Effect of Sociocultural Variables on Acculturation Variables of Hispanic and Asian Americans." *Journal of Counseling and Development* 70 (1991): 194.

Sue, D., D. W. Sue. *Counseling the Culturally Different.* 2nd ed. New Jersey: Wiley. 1990.

———. *Counseling the Culturally Different.* 3rd ed. New Jersey: Wiley, 1999.

Taylor, C. *Why Democracy Needs Patriotism.* Boston, MA: Beacon Press, 2002.

Tremblay, P. R. "Interviewing and Counseling Across Cultures: Heuristics and Biases." *Clinical Law Review* 9 (2002): 373.

"Top UN Refugee Official Wraps up Mission to Georgia, Russia," *U.N. Daily News*, Aug. 22, 2008, at 1, http://www.un.org/news/dh/pdf/english/2008/22082008.pdf.

US Department of Justice. "Board of Immigration Appeals: Final Rule 2." 2002. http://www.usdoj.gov/eoir/press/02/BIARulefactsheet.pdf.

US Department of Justice. Executive Office of Immigration Review, "Pro Bono Program—Major Program Initiatives," Accessed November 8, 2009. http://www.justice.gov/eoir/probobo/MajorInitiatives.htm.

Whelan, F. G. "Citizenship and Freedom of Movement: An Open Admission Policy." In *Open Borders? Closed Societies? The Ethical and Political Issues,* edited by Mark Gibney, 12–18. New York: Greenwood Press, 1988.

CHAPTER 12

Life, Liberty, and the Pursuit of Happiness

Human Rights and Immigration

*Richard H. Morgan**

From ancient times, the phenomenon of the migration of human persons from settled homelands to, from the point of view of the migrants, new and strange parts of the world has raised questions about the place, position, and treatment of newcomers into an existing, self-defined human community. "The United Nations (UN) defines as an international migrant a person who stays outside their usual country of residence for at least one year. According to that definition, the UN estimated that in 2005 there were about 200 million international migrants worldwide."[1] Koser summarizes the importance of migration to public policy and the close connection between migration and human rights: "Migration is inextricably linked with other important global issues, including development, poverty, and human rights. Migrants are often the most entrepreneurial and dynamic members of society; historically migration has underpinned economic growth and nation-building and enriched cultures. Migration also presents significant challenges. Some migrants are exploited and their human rights abused; integration in destination countries can be difficult; and migration can deprive origin countries of important skills. For all these reasons and more, migration matters."[2]

The previous chapters in *The Other People* have illustrated Koser's point about the opportunities and the tragedies associated with the global issues related to migration. In the introductory chapter, Meg Wilkes Karraker provides a

* Address correspondence to Richard H. Morgan, PhD, School of Social Welfare, HSC Level 2, Room 093, Stony Brook University, Stony Brook, NY 11794-8231. Email: Richard.Morgan@stonybrook.edu.

summary of the size and scope of migration in the twenty-first century in which "[i]mmigrants often face racial, ethnic, and national prejudice and discrimination as they enter new societies, and they (and their new countries) encounter a myriad of challenges around social inclusion and integration." Øystein S. LaBianca and Marcella Myers, in examining the challenges and opportunities present in teaching about migration, have suggested a pedagogy that focuses on the importance of experiencing the Other as "Other" rather than attempting to conform our conceptions of the Other to make them look more like ourselves. In addition, as we have seen in Part I of *The Other People*, the "everyday/everynight lives" of immigrants are significantly impacted by the ways in which they are, as Patti Duncan has said, "always already 'other.'" In both Duncan's chapter on the ways in which migration discourse is consistently racialized and gendered and Jennifer K. Blank's exposition of the tragic and criminal realities of the world of human trafficking (Chapter 4), we have seen examples of the kind of exploitation faced by immigrants in the areas of labor, transnational adoptions, and sexual trafficking. At the same time, it is clear from these chapters that immigrants typically face a dominant discourse that frames their experience in terms of oppressive and restrictive role definitions while characterizing them as victims in need of salvation. This kind of framing, of course, ignores the great resilience, energy, and drive that Koser talked about as the opportunities that immigrants bring to host nations. Likewise, Joanna Dreby, in Chapter 5 on "The Ripple Effects of Deportation Policies on Mexican Women and Their Children," has shown how immigrants and those who are close to them (including their children who may be citizens of the new country) live with an ongoing and pervasive sense of fear that they will be found out and how this tends to limit development and expression of individual or family strengths and the contributions these could make to their adopted communities. In Chapter 6, Xiong, Deenanath, and Mao have provided a window into the intergenerational struggles of immigrant families who not only face the tasks of finding their way in a new society but also find as part of that struggle the divide that erupts between older and younger family members who acculturate at different rates and experience the incongruity between the values of the new culture and the old culture. Similarly, in Chapter 7, Marianne S. Noh provided insights into the challenges that Asian immigrants in the United States and Canada face in living up to the dominant culture's labeling of them as "model minorities," by which they are allowed to almost pass as white while, at the same time, experiencing the kind of subtle racism this implies. This fractured kind of experience, ironically, has led them to seek out other second-generation Asian immigrants who have similar experiences for the support this provides and, ironically, to help them maintain a sense of their original ethnic identity (as in the case of the Korean immigrants the authors have described). And finally, in the last chapter in Part II, Marcella Myers has demonstrated the way in which immigrant vulnerability becomes highlighted during economic downturns in a host country (Germany in this case) as a question of social exclusion whereby immigrants are portrayed as a drain on resources by "taking advantage of welfare services to which they are not entitled." Again, the contributions and opportunities immigrants bring to a nation's labor market and economy are somehow lost when the discussion is framed in this way.

In Part III of this text, "Toward Justice," we have also seen how vulnerability and exploitation continues to place immigrants in situations that call into question basic human rights as they apply to immigrants. Susan Smith-Cunnien in Chapter 9 examined the recent history of xenophobic violence in South Africa against Zimbabwean immigrants and has urged a more migrant-centered approach to understanding the variety of causes for immigration and the way in which policy responses may be tailored to differences in motivation ranging from economic requirements to asylum seeking. In Chapter 10, Anthony Gray has detailed the way in which similar xenophobic reactions in France and other countries have led to the imposition of restrictions on religiously motivated dress codes. Such movements call into question what until recently would have been thought of as belonging to the sphere of the basic human rights of freedom of religion and conscience.

Finally, in Chapter 11, Bruce Einhorn has given us an insider's point of view into the variability that exists within US immigration courts on how asylum decisions are made and how these decisions are often subject to misunderstandings due to cultural differences (e.g., over how time and dates are remembered) between those seeking asylum and court officials (including judges, prosecutors, and defense attorneys) along with a lack of understanding of the ways in which trauma impacts asylum seekers' ability to recall and speak about the abuse they have experienced in their home countries or the threat that they would face if they were forced to return. Einhorn calls for an increase in cultural competency training and other clinical as well as financial resources for the courts if real human rights violations are to be avoided by enabling courts to make more informed and careful decisions on asylum. Moving forward then, by way of providing a summary and conclusion of the approach the authors of this book have taken to migration as a global concern, this chapter will examine the concept of human rights with an eye toward trying to understand how such rights may be thought of as applying to those in any society who are often viewed as "the Other People."

The question of human rights becomes particularly important in this discussion as immigrants are often seen as being guests in a country, invited or not invited, and often are not thought of as deserving the same protections as those who are considered citizens and/or native. Conversely, if human rights exist, they adhere to the individual human person as a member of the human race irrespective of their membership in any other subordinate societies. Human rights ought to "trump," so to speak, any other laws, regulations, restrictions, or policies that are contingent on the accidents of time or place as they appear in the history of local communities or nations. Without this priority of place in regards to human rights, the term itself seems to be vacuous. The human rights of immigrants then, particularly those who have entered another country without the required documentation, may be seen as something of a test case for this priority of human rights: the extent to which such rights would be honored or respected or recognized for a given resident of a society regardless of the legal standing of that person within the official polity would testify to the actualized priority of those rights that adhere to the person as a member of the human community.

The difficulty with this form of reasoning is that it seems to beg the question of the existence of human rights as such: in a very real way the discussion is getting ahead of itself because the case for human rights has not been established. We tend today, perhaps more so in Western cultures than other places in the world, to assume the givenness of human rights as part of the conceptual framework related to discussions of law, politics, policies, and international relations. It has been over sixty years, after all, since the UN General Assembly issued its famous Universal Declaration of Human Rights. On the other hand, the advent of human rights language is a relatively recent addition to the lexicon of politics and social ethics. It should be remembered in this context that the concept of life, liberty, and the pursuit of happiness—being among those inalienable rights with which members of the human community are endowed by their Creator is not yet 250 years old and that this represented a revolutionary departure from previous conceptualizations of human social relationships. The question then of whether a human being may expect to be treated in a certain way by other human beings is precisely that to which an argument for human rights must be addressed. The issue is particularly urgent in the lives of persons who have migrated from their original homelands due to the vulnerabilities that migration engenders. While in some situations migration itself has come to be seen as a fundamental human right,[3] such instances would still seem very much in the minority among nations in terms of immigration policies. The successful application of human rights language to the issue of immigration would seem to serve the purpose of strengthening the argument for human rights as such.

It is within this framework of the questioning of human rights that the philosopher and economist Amartya Sen (currently the Thomas W. Lamont University Professor at Harvard University) has devoted much of his attention studying the nature of social justice. First, in an article titled *Elements of a Theory of Human Rights* published in the journal *Philosophy and Public Affairs* in

2004 and later in his comprehensive book devoted to social justice titled *The Idea of Justice* (2009), Sen sought to provide a conceptual foundation for human rights language given what he recognizes as an intellectual atmosphere in which "many philosophers and legal theorists see the rhetoric of human rights as just loose talk—perhaps kindly and well meaning forms of locution—but loose talk nevertheless."[4] As an example of the long-standing nature of this form of opposition to human rights language, Sen holds up the utilitarian philosopher Jeremy Bentham's early (1791) denunciation of the concept of the rights of man that emerged from the French Revolution as nonsensical. The only rights that exist, according to Bentham, are those rights that proceed from legislation. All other concepts of natural rights remain a fiction. In this sense, as Sen points out, rights become the child of legislation—that is, rights only exist as laws exist, which create those rights following from the law.[5] Over and against his point of view, Sen cites another position that equally misses the mark in terms of the relationship between human rights and law. In the work of Herbert Hart, Sen sees a kind of opposite tendency in which rights are characterized as the parent of law, indicating that the only utility of rights language is in the extent to which it tends to inspire or generate legislation to codify and ground rights in the real world of implied sanctions.[6]

Against both of these extremes, Sen finds himself walking a golden mean: to exclusively tie rights language to legislation is to make a category mistake, since human rights are best understood in the realm of ethical obligations rather than legal statutes. As such human rights may lay claims on individuals that exist prior to and possibly in the absence of legislation. Not all ethical principles need necessarily become the stuff of legal sanction (e.g., fidelity in marriage), nor would legislation necessarily be the best route to take in promoting such principles within a community.[7]

For Sen, activism by itself is not enough: "The conceptual doubts must also be satisfactorily addressed, if the idea of human rights is to command reasoned loyalty and to establish a secure intellectual standing. It is critically important to see the relationship between the force and appeal of human rights, on the one hand, and their reasoned justification and scrutinized use, on the other."[8] Thus the need for a theory of human rights that Sen pursues in these writings. In this chapter I will examine Sen's conceptual framework for the grounding of human rights in a way that honors and promotes the necessarily universal nature of the concept as it is usually understood. After exploring Sen's framework for understanding human rights in general, I will then shift to considerations of how the model sketched out by Sen may be applied to the test case of immigration as described earlier.

A Conceptual Foundation for Human Rights

To begin exploring Sen's conceptual foundation for human rights language, it is first important to locate his approach within the broader context of the philosophy of social justice in general and human rights in particular. While there may be various approaches to establishing this context, Sen provides a very cogent summary of his own view of how his approach fits into the history of these discussions in an introduction he wrote to an edition of *The Theory of Moral Sentiments* by Adam Smith. Sen distinguishes here between two traditions in the philosophy of social justice, one he calls the "contractarian" approach and the other, the one in which Sen locates his own views, he calls "comparative realizations" approach.[9]

The contractarian approach Sen traces back to Hobbes, Locke, Rousseau, and Kant in the seventeenth century, all of whom contributed to the concept of the "social contract" as the foundational principal that underlies the notion of social justice within a society. Sen explains more specifically that "this approach concentrates on identifying 'just' institutional arrangements for a society, which would yield a corresponding—hypothetical—contract. The demands of justice are, then, seen in terms of those institutional requirements, with the expectation that people would behave appropriately to make those institutions entirely effective."[10] In modern social ethics, this point of view is best represented by the work of John Rawls in his classic work *A Theory of Justice*. Sen identifies this approach as a transcendental approach in that the goal here is to focus on the ideal of justice, what perfect justice, a perfectly just society, and perfectly just institutions within the society would look like. This "transcendental institutionalism," as Sen names it, seeks to create a priori institutions that would embody the perfect notion of justice and depends on "the assumption that people's behavior would be exactly what would be needed for the proper functioning of the chosen institutions."[11] The difficulty for this kind of idealism, of course, is that people have typically not always acted within institutional arrangements in the kind of selfless manner upon which the theory seems to hang (e.g., witness the complex of seemingly self-centered behaviors leading up to the economic collapse in 2008 following upon an environment of deregulation in the housing and mortgage markets). Sen also goes on later to point out that this approach presents particular difficulties for human rights language in that the concept of a social contract seems particularly difficult to extend to the universal level—that is, a contract to which all human beings are a party—without some form of institutional actualization in the form of world government.[12]

Over and against the contractarian approach, Sen provides what is perhaps the lesser known comparative realizations approach traced back to Adam Smith and other Enlightenment philosophers. This approach is decidedly not idealistic in that it does not set up a theoretical notion of what perfect justice would be and then seek to have everything measured against this ideal. Rather, comparative realizations would focus on what may be done in concrete social circumstances to make the lived social reality more just than it is now—that is, comparatively more just. As Sen explains, this approach is "concerned primarily with removing identifiable injustices in the world—such as slavery, or bureau-cracy-induced poverty, or cruel and counterproductive penal codes, or rampant exploitation of labor, or the subjugation of women. The focus is on what actu-ally happens to the lives of people, and the judgments are comparative—for example, how the world would improve if slavery were abolished."[13] By starting with what might be considered empirical instances of injustice and working toward comparative improvements in those situations (improvements that are also empirical as they are relative to the original circumstances), the comparative realizations perspective would seem to have the advantage of being grounded in the particular and local experiences of people wherever and whenever such injustices are identified.

The difference between the two approaches in terms of human rights seems to center for Sen around the place or importance of open dialogue in the attainment of a more just society. The Rawlsian approach is heavily dependent upon an a priori notion of the nature of justice, which is to be applied to all societies at all times and places. This would seem to have the consequence of shutting down all conversation about differences in percep-tion or culture since no one may argue with perfection (ignoring the pos-sibility that the very ideal itself is likely to be culturally bound in various ways). Smith, on the other hand, warned of the parochial nature of much social justice theorizing and urged the need for open dialogue with points of view that are not necessarily our own. Open dialogue is important according to Sen for two reasons that highlight the need to go beyond social contract language: "(1) the relevance of other people's *interests*—far away from as well as close to a given society—for the sake of preventing unfairness to those who are not party to the social contract for that society; and (2) the pertinence of other people's *perspectives* to broaden our own investigation of relevant prin-ciples, for the sake of avoiding under scrutinized parochialism of values and presumptions in the local community."[14]

Sen's Elements of a Theory of Human Rights

With the foregoing discussion of method in place, it is now possible to consider Sen's argument for how a theory of human rights may be founded. He accom-plishes this in *Elements of a Theory of Human Rights* in a series of steps that are posed as questions to be answered if a coherent theory is to be developed. What follows will be an overview of several of these key elements that are particularly important for the question of the human rights of immigrants.

The Nature of Human Rights Language

The first point to be considered in Sen's argument is the nature of the language involved in human rights talk: "What kind of a statement does a declaration of human rights make?" What he seems to have in mind here is the need to clarify the level of discussion involved when we speak of human rights and, specifically, to differentiate it from legal language. In fact, Sen argues, human rights language must be located primarily on the level of ethical discourse and the demands implicit in human rights declarations are necessarily in the nature of ethical claims. As an ethical claim, a human right carries a level of importance due to the fundamental subject matter that is involved in the right. The content of an ethical approach to human rights is taken up with notions of the *freedoms* to which the rights refer: "A pronouncement of human rights includes an assertion of the importance of the corresponding freedoms—the freedoms that are identified and privileged in the formulation of the rights in question—and is indeed motivated by that importance."[15] In other words, these freedoms form the content of the ethical claim and require people to consider their importance in ethical decision making.

As indicated earlier, ethical claims in the form of human rights language are to be distinguished from legal language in at least two ways. On the one hand, since rights language recognizes the importance of certain freedoms as fundamental characteristics of human life, they are not dependent upon the force of legislation. Laws do not create rights. Rights already exist whether recognized in law or not. Rights make a claim upon human ethical deliberation because of the importance attached to the freedoms involved.

Similarly, the ethical claims of human rights are not to be seen as existing only as inspiration for legislation. This is the second way in which rights are to be distinguished from law. While ethical concepts enshrined in human rights may serve to inspire legislation and legislation may be one avenue of activity that would help ensure that human rights are honored, it is not the only route and, in some cases, it might be a counterproductive way of promoting human rights. The fact that other means of promoting human rights are viable underscores the fact that rights are not dependent upon law nor do they exist only to inspire law but are in a different arena of concepts—namely, ethical discourse.[16]

The Importance of Human Rights

The second element in Sen's foundation for human rights is a further exploration of the nature of the freedoms indicated in human rights language. The importance of a human right is derived from the importance of the freedom to which it points. It is that freedom that is seen as an essential aspect of human life, and because of the importance of that freedom to any human life, the language of the right is crafted to express the inviolable character of that freedom. The freedom to live and the freedom not to be tortured are so critical to human existence that they take on the same level of importance for ethical deliberation. Sen points out that this focus on freedoms rather than some other aspect of the human condition allows for "a motivating reason not only for celebrating our own rights and liberties, but also for our taking an interest in the significant freedoms of others, not just their pleasures and desire-fulfillment (as under utilitarianism)."[17] Instead of focusing on maximizing everyone's pleasure or desires, a seemingly very elusive and hard to measure outcome, the focus on freedom enables the comparative realizations approach to differentiate levels of social justice in that different levels of reflect actual social conditions that might be altered through various means in order to achieve a comparative improvement. Sen also discusses how this approach avoids other problems involved in utilitarian approaches such as "valuational distortions resulting from the neglect of substantive deprivation of those who are chronically disadvantaged but who learn, by force of circumstances, to take pleasure in small mercies and get reconciled to cutting down their desires to 'realistic proportions.'"[18] Concentrating on freedoms rather than utilities as the fundamental component of the human condition would aid in avoiding this utilitarian trap of being happy with less. Less freedom in this context does not make sense because freedom is an all or nothing concept.

Sen goes on to explore the nature of freedom in more detail. Freedom in the form expressed in human rights is made up of two components: freedom of opportunity and freedom of process. Both aspects have a part to play in helping to define the nature of human rights. Freedom of opportunity indicates the kind of freedom associated with the capacities to "achieve valuable combinations of human functionings: what a person is able to do or be."[19] In this sense, the question becomes whether certain opportunities exist for a given person to achieve that which she or he values. Someone who is not able to achieve valued goals due to arbitrary limitations having to do with factors such as race or gender or due to characteristics of the individual that by their nature limit the options available (as in the case of physical or mental disabilities) is someone who is less free than she or he would be if those limitations were not in place. Process freedom, however, refers to the processes by which opportunities are actualized: it is, on the one hand, the way in which an individual may make a choice among options that are real and available; on the other hand, process freedom also involves the way in which social decisions are made in either the positive awarding opportunities (admission to college) or the negative denying of freedom (imprisonment) and the extent to which these decisions are subject to fair and open processes of deliberation. In either the positive or negative versions, the outcomes of the processes are not at issue in process freedom but rather the free nature of the process itself.

In both process freedom and opportunity freedom, real but different issues of liberty are at stake. Both forms of freedom are important to a theory of human rights that stresses freedom as the basis of rights. It would seem that, while both opportunities and process considerations may play a role in the first generation rights (free speech, freedom of the press and of association, trial by jury, freedom from torture or capital punishment, etc.), freedom of opportunity seems to be much more at stake in the second generation level of human rights (freedom from lack of medical treatment, freedom from illiteracy, freedom from unemployment, freedom from hunger, freedom from exposure, etc.). This question will be addressed later in Sen's fifth element regarding the viability of social and economic rights (i.e., second generation rights).

Before leaving Sen's consideration of the importance of freedom to a theory of human rights, it is important to note that he has set up a mechanism by which any proposed freedom being offered as a potential subject of a human right must be assessed. The mechanism consists of what Sen calls two "threshold conditions" that must be met for a human right to be seriously thought of as calling for recognition and support. The first of these threshold conditions has to do with the "*importance*" of the matter involved. By importance here Sen is indicating that there must be a kind of limit established as to what rises up to the level of concern necessary to qualify an opportunity as being important enough to warrant the kinds of activities invoked to promote human rights. The second criterion is what Sen calls that of "*social influenceability.*"[20] In this case he is arguing for the fact that society has to be able to do something to promote the freedom. Sen's own example serves best here to get the point of both across:

It is not hard to argue that some importance should be attached to all four of the following freedoms:

(1) a person's freedom not to be assaulted;
(2) her freedom to receive medical care for a serious health problem;
(3) her freedom not to be called up regularly by her neighbors whom she detests;
(4) her freedom to achieve tranquility.

However, even though all four may be important in one way or another, it is not altogether implausible to argue that the first (freedom not to be assaulted) is a good subject matter for a human right, and so is the second (freedom to receive necessary medical care), but the third (freedom not to be called up by detested neighbors) is not, in general, important enough to cross the threshold of social significance to qualify as a human right. Also, the fourth, while quite possibly extremely important for the person, is too inward-looking—and too hard to be influenced by others—to be a good subject matter for human rights.[21]

As threshold conditions, these criteria do not preclude discussion of any proposed freedom as a subject of human rights. Sen is simply saying here that within the context of this kind of open and informed deliberation, certain issues will not be found to be either important enough or influenceable enough to continue to inspire concerns over human rights.

Duties and Obligations

Any discussion of human rights is always closely associated with further discussion of the kinds of duties and obligations that such rights impose on members of the community. In social contract language, the members of the community (those bound by and to the social contract) have duties to establish and support the kind of just institutions needed to fulfill the ideal of a just society. A utilitarian approach requires the duty or obligation for each social actor to seek maximization of their own utility (desire fulfillment) while keeping as minimal as possible any interference in the same effort on the part of other members of society. In his third element of a theory of human rights, Sen also addresses the question, "What duties and obligations do human rights generate?"[22] This becomes an important question particularly when dealing with the social and economic human rights often referred to as second generation human rights. Although it may be somewhat obvious that a human rights claim over freedom to live (or to not have one's life taken away from her or him) generates duties or obligations in others not to take another person's life, it is not as obvious to discover the way in which, for instance, someone's right to be fed or given medical care or to have housing actually imposes a specific obligation on another member of the community. How is it that these ethical claims that form the basis of human rights language are able to impose requirements on other members of society? Why is it that those other members of society are not simply able to say, "Fine, you have your freedom to be employed, how does that involve me?"

It is hard to see, in the face of such questions, how social contract language can be avoided here. From that transcendental perspective, obligations are part of the social contract, and parties to the contract who expect to benefit from the contract are expected to hold up their end of the bargain in honoring the rights of others. Sen, on the other hand, was very clear (as described earlier in this chapter) in distinguishing his and Smith's comparative realizations approach from this kind of transcendental approach. Specifically, we have seen how Sen was concerned that the social contract approach is not practicable as a foundation for human rights since the social contract binds the members of a particular society and is not easily extended to a global level in such a way that would guarantee rights to all human beings.

As a way of coming to grips with the way in which social obligations can be generated from the ethical claims involved in human rights, Sen first recalls the assumption that, for a matter to have risen to the question of human rights, that matter involved must have already met the threshold conditions of importance and influenceability and is therefore a matter to be taken seriously. It is due a certain amount of careful consideration on the part of any actor as to the ways in which he or she may have a duty to assist in bringing about the realization of the right in question. This consideration, however, does not immediately leap to the level of an overwhelming command in which no account of specific circumstances and abilities are allowed:

> The recognition of human rights is not an insistence that everyone everywhere rises to help prevent every violation of every human right no matter where it occurs. It is, rather, an acknowledgment that if one is in a plausible position to do something effective in preventing the violation of such a right, then one does have an obligation to consider doing just that. It is still possible that other obligations or non-obligational concerns may overwhelm the reason for the particular action in question, but that reason cannot be simply brushed way as being "none of one's business."[23]

It is in this context that Sen introduces a distinction made in terms of obligations by Immanuel Kant as a useful way to conceptualize how different duties or obligations may be generated from the same concern for a human right depending on the factors involved. According to Sen, the distinction suggested by Kant in his *Critique of Practical Reason* is between *perfect obligations* and *imperfect obligations*. The former kind of obligation consists in what might be thought of as absolute or binding duties not to act directly to violate a human right. The duty not to kill or steal from someone imposes a perfect ethical obligation of the would-be murderer or thief. Such obligations are perfect in the sense that they take priority over other considerations, and deliberation about various obligations one might have does not come into play.

Informal obligations, on the other hand, are less specific and binding because they do not refer in this way to the person who may be contemplating (or in the act of) violating another's rights directly. Informal obligations refer instead to others who may be in some sort of a position to help protect or secure another person's freedom or to stop someone from directly violating another's rights. Obligation in this sense derives from the importance of the freedom implied in the right: in effect, the freedom is so important to human existence that everyone is drawn into a duty "to consider what they can reasonably do to secure the freedom."[24] The force of these obligations are less binding not due to the fact that the freedom is not important but due to the nature of the deliberative process that the other person must undergo as they assess (i.e., reasonably consider) what they are able to do given their own personal circumstances and after due consideration of the other obligations they have that are also important. A bystander on a city street who happens to see another person being attacked in an alley may have to consider calling the police on her cell phone, but the imperfect obligation to secure another person's right not to be attacked may not extend to her running into the ally and trying to break up the attack if it meant, for instance, that by doing so she would have to leave her baby in a stroller. Sen goes on to suggest the possible content of such deliberation:

> The person has to judge, for example, how important the freedoms and rights are in the case in question compared with other claims on the person's possible actions (involving other rights and freedoms, but also altogether different concerns that a person may, inter alia, sensibly have). Furthermore, the person has to judge the extent to which he or she can make a difference in this case, either acting alone or in conjunction with others . . . Also, since detailed reflection on what one should do is itself time consuming (and cannot even be actually undertaken for all the ills of the world), the duty of reasonable consideration will not, in a great many cases, translate into an obligation to take on an elaborate scrutiny— only a willingness to do just that, when it seems relevant and appropriate.[25]

The issue, then, is how this distinction of obligations pertains to the task of providing a conceptual foundation for human rights. Obligations become a necessary part of any declaration of human rights because rights language implies not only that someone has the freedom named by the right but also that the right itself calls for a corresponding form of support (obligation) from all people since all people would presumably want that freedom themselves (keeping in mind the two threshold criteria of importance and influenceability). The universal nature of the freedom calls forth the universal obligation to uphold the right associated with the freedom. The obligation will differ depending on the nature of the involvement and circumstances of the actor who incurs the obligation: some will be obligated to duties that are specific and unvarying (perfect) and others to obligations that vary with their circumstances (imperfect), but all are obligated one way or another. The introduction of imperfect obligations extends the reach of human rights to this universal level by involving "the demand that serious consideration be given by anyone in a position to provide reasonable help to the person whose human right is threatened."[26]

It is precisely this universal reach that is necessary for a theory of human rights since these kind of ethical claims are intended by the very definition of the term to be universal: they are to apply to all humans by virtue of their humanity. Recalling Sen's critique of the contractarian school of social ethics, it is noteworthy that this form of universalism cannot be supported by the concept of the social contract because in that line of reasoning, the rights extend only to those who are party to the contract—that is, those who belong to a particular society of "us" over against all other "thems." And yet the importance of universalism for the question of the human rights of immigrants is foundational and inescapable: people who are leaving their homes to go to other lands where they become the "foreigners" are uniquely invested in the firm existence of rights that belong to the human person at any time and in any place by virtue of his or her humanity. Without such universalism of freedoms and obligations, immigrants more than any other group are vulnerable to the whims of parochial notions of social justice. It would seem appropriate, then, that a conceptual framework for human rights would necessarily also call for development beyond the notion of a social contract in theories of social justice.

The Viability of Economic and Social Rights

In moving on to the next element in Sen's framework for human rights, we come to the point that seems crucial to that aspect of the debate on immigrant rights that seems most contested—that is, the foundation for the so-called second-generation rights. No one who has sincerely entered into the dialogue about the ethics of human rights (recognizing, of course, that there exist many situations in which ethics and human rights are simply ignored) would today try to make an argument about the existence of the first generation rights for immigrants or anyone else. These first generation rights such as the right to life, the right to freedom from torture or slavery, and the importance of basic civil rights such as due process of law are, for the most part, not debated despite the fact that they may be routinely violated (for immigrants more than others, perhaps). It may be important to recall that this was not always the case and that such recognition is a relatively recent phenomenon. For Sen, the concept of human rights only begins to receive a widespread hearing with the publication of the American Declaration of Independence and, soon after, the French Rights of Man in the late eighteenth century.[27] As indicated previously, social contract language does not provide support for the concept of rights that adhere to the human qua human. Prior to the development of the social contract concept, the place of the individual was subsumed under the priority of the community and the divine right of rulers in any way they deemed necessary for the welfare of the community (including summarily denying an individual continued life, liberty, or any other consideration of personal happiness). To the extent today that such cultural contexts exist in which the individual is considered of no importance next to the priority of the community, the question of first-generation rights as discussed here may still be in question.

However, it is in the realm of second-generation human rights—such as the right to medical care, the right to food, the right to education, the right to housing, and the right to work—that concerns about whether such "entitlements" can or ought to be considered under the rubric of rights language are still often expressed even by those who would acknowledge and grant the existence and importance of the first-generation rights. And yet it is particularly in the area of second-generation rights that immigrants may be most vulnerable. If medical care, education (for children, at least), food, shelter, and work are not seen as the subject of human rights, then migrants are made vulnerable in a way that almost makes support for the first-generation human rights vacuous: there is little good in saying that someone has the right not to be killed or tortured if their right not to starve or slowly die due to medical neglect are not also guaranteed. To what extent then can these so-called economic or social rights be thought of as inalienable human rights? To answer this question, Sen chooses not so much to make a positive argument for the existence of these social or economic rights as to consider the arguments that have been made against the inclusion of these kinds of rights within the human rights framework. These objections may be categorized, in Sen's view, into two major forms that are related yet distinct.

The first of these forms of objection is what he calls the "institutionalization critique."[28] In this case, the argument is made that the proclamation of a particular human right necessarily involves the incurring of a particular and specific obligation on the part of some party to meet the demand or entitlement specified in the right. The concept of "institutionalization" enters here because it is thought by those who make this objection that such rights only exist when institutional structures have been created that specify who has the duty to guarantee the fulfillment of those rights or, in other words, who incurs the obligation. This is reminiscent of the same form of argument that Sen cited earlier regarding the relationship of rights to law in which rights are not seen to exist unless a law granting (and enforcing) the right exists first (therefore, as discussed earlier, rights are children of the law).

As a means of answering this critique, Sen returns to the concept he has already developed about the different kinds of obligations a right establishes upon human agents, in particular, both perfect and imperfect obligations. In both cases, it is the importance and influenceability of the freedoms inherent in the right that call forth obligations on the part of the actors who are in some position to do something to uphold the freedom. The freedom may be so important, in fact, that it will call forth obligations upon certain members of society to seek ways of establishing institutional supports for the freedom: "The ethical significance of these rights provides good grounds for seeking realization through institutional expansion and reform. This can be helped through a variety of approaches, including demanding and agitating for appropriate legislation, and the supplementation of the legal demands by political recognition and social monitoring. To deny the ethical status of these claims would be to ignore the reasoning that motivates these constructive activities."[29] Sen is essentially claiming here that the institutionalization critique is putting the cart before the horse: rather than the institutions creating the right, the importance of the right calls forth modifications to institutional arrangements as well as other activities to ensure the protection of the freedom involved. In this context, it is important to remember that Sen has argued for a comparative realizations approach to social ethics. This approach is characteristically comfortable with recognizing that perfectly just institutions may not yet exist while at the same time arguing that it is possible to imagine improvements in our institutional structures based on the motivating desire to ensure greater freedom.

The second form of objection to seeing social or economic entitlements as human rights is what Sen calls the *feasibility critique*. This criticism essentially maintains that the concept of such entitlements cannot be put into the language of human rights simply because it would be impossible for some societies to come near to approaching the ability to provide for these rights due to lack of resources. In other words, such rights would simply not be *feasible* in many places and at many times. Such relatively poor societies would immediately be judged as violating the human rights of their citizens if they could not provide for the variety of social security measures guaranteed by the right. Whereas every society may be able to adhere to the freedoms related to first generation rights in that they cost very little to uphold, the kinds of entitlements claimed under the heading of the second generation human rights cannot reasonably demanded in many situations due to feasibility. It is, therefore, something of a category mistake to treat them as if they were inalienable entitlements granted by human nature.

In this case, Sen again sees a case of misplaced priorities: the importance of the freedoms involved (e.g., freedom from illness, freedom from unemployment, freedom from illiteracy) is not defeated by the fact that conditions do not yet exist to allow for the full realization of these rights in all places. "The understanding that some rights are not fully realized, and may not even be fully *realizable* under present circumstances, does not, in itself, entail anything like the conclusion that these are, therefore, not rights at all. Rather, that understanding suggests the need to work towards changing the prevailing circumstances to make the unrealized rights realizable, and ultimately, realized."[30] Once again, from a comparative realizations point of view, the challenge is to think about how the world could be comparatively better with changes that can be made to work toward actualizing their achievement rather than waiting around for the conditions to be just right in all times and places before a right may be claimed.

Sen does not go on to provide any further justification for the inclusion of these concerns within the concept of human rights. However, by suggesting that the typical arguments against these rights do not, in fact, take away from the importance of the freedoms involved, Sen does indeed provide a methodological framework for human rights activists. On the one hand, he has shown that these objections are misplaced in that they have only succeeded in demonstrating how much more work is necessary to improve institutions or circumstances to the point where such freedoms may be actualized for more and more people. On the other hand, he has also shown that the most important focus of any efforts to advocate for human rights must be on how important these freedoms are to any truly human way of life. The more agreement we have around the fundamental importance of these freedoms, the fewer objections there will be to including them in the list of human rights and the more motivation we will have for changing those conditions that militate against the freedoms. In itself, this would represent a significant contribution to the advancement of thought around the nature and place of the second generation rights.

Conclusions

The introduction to this chapter suggested that any theory of human rights faces perhaps its greatest test in the case of the rights of immigrants due to the difficulty of arguing for the rights of those who are quite literally strangers in a foreign land. In this chapter, I have tried to follow Sen's conceptual framework for a theory of human rights and to apply that framework to the question of the human rights of immigrants. While it may be too early to see yet how Sen's approach will survive his own call for open and informed public scrutiny and, thus, the extent to which it will stand the test of time, several key elements in his approach represent a genuine advance in efforts to conceptually ground the fervent rhetoric of human rights advocates. The comparative realizations approach, for instance, allows human rights advocates to take something of an empirical approach as opposed to the more theoretical approach of the transcendental school: Rawls and the social contract theorists. Comparative realizations does not hinge on an ideal set of institutional arrangements but allows for activists to examine concrete (empirically obvious) instances of injustice and to strive for changes that would lead to comparatively better—that is, more just—outcomes. Also, by focusing on the importance of the freedoms inherent in human rights language, Sen has provided a methodology for imputing these rights to all human persons by virtue of their common humanity rather than the more limiting and secondary concept of their participation in a social contract. Finally, the suggestion in Sen's approach that moral discourse in this area ought to take advantage of Kant's distinction between perfect and imperfect obligation allows for a more nuanced argument to be made by human rights advocates for the kind of "second generation" human rights such as those enshrined in the United Nation's Universal Declaration of Human Rights. It is because the freedoms involved in the second generation rights are so important to any human life—freedom from starvation due to lack of food, illness due to lack of medical care, ignorance due to lack of education, exposure due to lack of housing, and so on—that imperfect obligations may be said to apply to anyone who is in a position to further the process of actualizing these human rights in concrete circumstances, thus enabling a comparatively better realization of justice in the world. Such obligations would mean that all people would together be responsible for protecting the freedoms that all would claim to want for themselves. Ultimately, Sen is providing a philosophical rationale for the universal religious insight contained in the so called Golden Rule (in either its positive or its negative form): Do to others (or do not do to others) what you would have them do to you (or that you would not have them do to you).

What consequences follow from such philosophical speculations for what Duncan calls the "everyday/everynight lives" of immigrants? On the one hand, the arguments Sen has made for human rights being undergirded by basic freedoms would suggest that a certain floor exists in terms of a minimum standard of how any human being should be treated anywhere, the basic human rights that adhere to the person because of his or her humanity. So while immigrants might still experience themselves as "the Other People" in a new society, they should not have to fear for their lives or freedoms due to violence or human trafficking and they should be able to count on access to basic human needs such as food, shelter, and clothing but also to other basic needs such as health care, education, and appropriate legal representation.

On the other hand, it is hard to see how the guarantee of such basic human rights would change the climate of fear that exists among immigrant communities even though it may lessen the fundamental hardships that go along with that fear. As long as immigrants in other countries are seen as intruders rather than welcome newcomers who, as indicated by Koser cited earlier in this chapter, represent new potential and opportunity for the receiving country, as long as they are seen as a threat rather than a benefit, then it would seem they will continue to have to live with the fear of exploitation and deportation that have been described so well in the previous chapters of *The Other People*. It may be that the climate of fear will never disappear until the lessons have been learned from those countries like Argentina that have experimented with open immigration policies in recognition of the benefits that immigrants bring to the host nation. For an age in which conservative ideologies hold up free market processes as key to the most efficient and effective distribution of resources, perhaps it is time to start thinking of the distribution of human resources as a free market issue as well: allowing people to move freely to wherever they feel the best opportunities lie for them to achieve life, liberty and the pursuit of happiness. In short, as Hines has indicated in her article about the Argentine experience, it may be that the next horizon in the human rights debate may have to grapple with the possibility that "migration" itself ought to be considered a fundamental human right.

Notes

1. Kahlid Koser, *International Migration: A Very Short Introduction* (Oxford: Oxford University Press, 2007), 4.
2. Ibid., 1.
3. See Barbara Hines, "The Right to Migrate as a Human Right: The Current Argentine Immigration Law," *Cornell International Law Journal* 43 (2010): 471–85.
4. Amartya Sen, "Elements of a Theory of Human Rights," *Philosophy and Public Affairs* 32, no. 4 (2004): 315–16.
5. On Bentham and the concept of rights following upon legislation, see Sen, "Elements of a Theory of Human Rights," 324–26; Amartya Sen, *The Idea of Justice* (Cambridge, MA: Belknap Press, 2009), 361–62.
6. On Hart, see Sen, "Elements of a Theory of Human Rights," 326–27; Sen, *The Idea of Justice*, 363–64. Note: from this point forward these two primary sources will be referenced with the abbreviations: "ETHR" for "Elements of a Theory of Human Rights" and *TIJ* for *The Idea of Justice*.
7. Sen makes this argument in both primary sources: "ETHR," 327 and 342–45; *TIJ*, 368.
8. Sen, "ETHR," 317
9. Amartya Sen, "Introduction," in *The Theory of Moral Sentiments*, ed. Adam Smith (New York: Penguin, 2009), xv–xvi.
10. Ibid., xv.
11. Ibid., xvi.
12. Sen provides a more in-depth discussion of the limits of the social contract on a global scale in *TIJ*, 25–26 and 70–72; here he cites the inability of proponents of transcendental institutionalism—namely, Nagel and Rawles—to develop consistent global institutional frameworks (i.e., some form of world government) that would, from their point of view, be a prerequisite for perfect justice on a global scale.
13. Sen, "Introduction," xvi.
14. Ibid., xviii.
15. Sen, "ETHR," 321.
16. For Sen's differentiation of human rights language from these two extremes of relationship to law, see "ETHR," 324–28.
17. Ibid., 328.
18. Ibid., 329.

19. Ibid., 332.
20. On both criteria, see ibid., 329–30.
21. Ibid.
22. Ibid., 318.
23. Ibid., 340–41.
24. Ibid., 321.
25. Ibid., 340.
26. Ibid., 341.
27. See, for instance, ibid., 316.
28. See ibid., 346–48, for a summary of and Sen's counterarguments regarding objections to the inclusion of social or economic rights into the canon of human rights.
29. Ibid., 347.
30. Ibid., 348.

Bibliography

Hines, Barbara. "The Right to Migrate as a Human Right: The Current Argentine Immigration Law." *Cornell International Law Journal* 43 (2010): 471–85.

Koser, Kahlid. *International Migration: A Very Short Introduction.* Oxford: Oxford University Press, 2007.

Sen, Amartya. "Elements of a Theory of Human Rights." *Philosophy and Public Affairs* 32, no. 4 (2004): 315–16.

———. *The Idea of Justice.* Cambridge, MA: Belknap Press, 2009.

———. "Introduction." In *The Theory of Moral Sentiments*, edited by Adam Smith. New York: Penguin, 2009.

Appendix

Resources for Research on Global Migration

Jan M. Orf* and Mathew Vicknair

This appendix provides general resources useful to both students new to the field and specialists wishing to extend the scope of their research across disciplines. Both print and electronic resources are included, along with a brief annotation. The appendix is organized around the following:

- Dictionaries, Encyclopedias, and Handbooks
- Indexes, Abstracts, and Other Databases
- Subject World Wide Web Sites
- Professional Associations

Dictionaries, Encyclopedias, and Handbooks

Dictionaries, encyclopedias, and handbooks are often the best places to begin, as they identify terms used by those doing research in the field. The broadest sources (which will lead you to other sources on migration) are listed first, followed by two sources more specific to global migration.

Annual Reviews. Palo Alto, CA: Annual Reviews.
Available in both print and electronic formats, *Annual Reviews* publishes articles on current research across a wide range of fields of study.

Credo Reference. Boston, MA: Credo.
This online source references dictionaries, encyclopedias, and other sources on a wide variety of topics, including immigration and related topics from authoritative sources in anthropology, political science, race and ethnicity, religion, and other disciplines.

---

* Address correspondence to Jan M. Orf, reference librarian, University of St. Thomas Libraries, 2115 Summit Avenue, Mail #5004, St. Paul, MN 55105-1096,. Email: jmorf@stthomas.edu.

Flores, Juan, and Renato Rosado, eds. *The Blackwell Companion to Latina/o Studies.* Malden, MA: Blackwell, 2007.
> This source covers a wide range of topics in Latina/o studies, including employment, feminization, illegal and undocumented immigration, and immigration policy and legislation.

Gale Virtual Reference Library. Farmington Hills, MI: Thomson Gale.
> This collection of online resources includes migration and related areas in family studies, including geography, political science, race and ethnicity, religion, and sociology.

Gold, Steven J., and Stephanie J. Nawyn. *International Handbook of Migration Studies.* New York: Routledge, 2012.
> This brand-new resource is available in print but will soon be out in an online format. This publication includes information on both the country of origin and the country of settlement. All aspects of social, cultural, political, and economic impacts are included. The essays are written by international scholars and cover a wide range of subject areas affected by migration.

Ritzer, George, ed. *The Wiley-Blackwell Encyclopedia of Globalization.* Malden, MA: Wiley-Blackwell, 2012.
> Available in both print and electronic formats, this resource provides over six hundred articles covering a wide range of topics related to globalization. It includes historical information and several primary documents. Articles are written by experts in the field and include bibliographies, cross-references, and some recommendations for further reading.

Ritzer, George, ed. *Blackwell Encyclopedia of Sociology.* Malden, MA: Blackwell, 2007.
> Available in both print and electronic formats, this is a basic reference resource covering all aspects of sociology. Entries are written by leading scholars in the field and include a list of sources for further research. This encyclopedia includes detailed articles on migration and related topics of interest.

Indexes, Abstracts, and Other Databases

Because of the longer time required to publish books compared to journal articles and because most research is published in journal articles, indexes are the place to start your search for resources. Some index databases provide the full text of some journals. The following indexes and abstracts identify articles, book chapters, and occasionally books on a particular topic like migration. Most are available by subscription, but some databases are available free on the web. Most are updated on an ongoing basis.

Academic Search Premier. Ipswich, MA: EBSCO, 1975–present.
> This is an excellent resource for research on an interdisciplinary subject like migration. *Academic Search Premier* includes abstracts on a wide range of topics, as well as the full text for many.

AILA Link (The Affordable Immigration Law Library). Washington, DC: American Immigration Lawyers Association, 1993–present.
AILALink is a fully searchable, web-based immigration law library filled with practical guidance and authoritative resources regarding immigration law. This resource contains immigration-related statutes, cases, and regulations, as well as treatises and practice materials in immigration law.

CIAO: Columbia International Affairs Online. New York: Columbia University Press, 1991–present.
CIAO includes materials on theory and research in international affairs, including migration, published as books, conference proceedings, journal abstracts, policy briefs, and working papers.

CQ Researcher. Washington, DC: CQ Press, 2007–present.
This source includes in-depth coverage of global affairs from a number of international viewpoints. *CQ Researcher* offers focused, readable, single reports on vital world issues including migration and immigration. It also offers a version that includes the archives.

Expanded Academic ASAP. Farmington Hills, MI: Gale, 1980–present.
This electronic database not only identifies articles on specific topics but also provides the full text of many of them. This source covers a wide range of topics and includes some general periodicals as well as research journals. This resource is a good introduction for interdisciplinary topics like migration.

Family Studies Abstracts. Ipswich, MA: EBSCO, 1979–present.
Family Studies Abstracts includes bibliographic records covering essential areas related to family studies, including migration and its effects on the family.

Family & Society Studies Worldwide (FSSW). Ipswich, MA: EBSCO, 1970–present.
A companion database to *Family Studies Abstracts*, *FSSW* includes many full-text resources and covers anthropology, demography, economics, law, and other social sciences but with a worldwide scope.

Georgetown University Law Library. *Immigration Law (U.S.) Research Guide*. Georgetown University. Accessed August 29, 2012, http://www.law.georgetown.edu/library/research/guides/ImmigrationLaw.cfm.
This source provides information on federal statutes and legislation, including casework and proposed legislation on immigration; links to federal agencies, regulations, and rulings pertaining to immigration; and links to related journal articles.

Institute for Research on Poverty. "Poverty-Related Links by Category." *University of Wisconsin–Madison*. Accessed August 29, 2012, http://irp.wisc.edu/links/category.htm.
The Institute for Research on Poverty (IRP) at the University of Wisconsin, Madison, maintains a collection of poverty websites grouped by subject, including the intersections of migration and poverty.

Lexis-Nexis Academic. Dayton, OH: Lexis-Nexis, 1966–present.

Lexis-Nexis includes information from news and legal resources. The news section covers newspapers, wire services, and transcripts for television and radio news programs. The legal section searches full-text federal, state, and international legal materials including case law, statutes and regulations, legal news, and law reviews, including work pertaining to immigration, asylum, and other migration issues.

PAIS International. San Diego, CA: ProQuest, 1972–present.

This database indexes many different types of resources on public affairs topics, including migration. In addition to US government documents, *PAIS* indexes publications from many international organizations.

University of California, Los Angeles School of Law. *Immigration Law Research Guide.* Accessed August 29, 2012, http://libguides.law.ucla.edu/immigration.

This guide provides general and specialized sources for researching US immigration law, including online government resources, statutes, regulations, and case law, as well as general and specialized secondary sources and immigration-related organizations.

Social Sciences Abstracts. New York: EBSCO, 1983–present.

This resource identifies articles across the social sciences, including topics related to migration studies. *Social Science Abstracts* only provides abstracts but frequently identifies libraries that hold the journal in which the article can be found. An older version covers the years 1907–1983.

Social Services Abstracts. Bethesda, MD: ProQuest, 1980–present.

This resource identifies articles from social work, social policy, community development, and other areas relevant to global migration research.

SocINDEX with Full Text. Ipswich, MA: EBSCO, 1895–present.

SocINDEX with Full Text provides information on a wide range of resources in sociology, including some core resources back to 1895. *SocINDEX with Full Text* provides the full text for many of the resources and also provides many author profiles.

Sociological Abstracts. Bethesda, MD: ProQuest, 1963–present.

This first source for sociological research on a wide range of topics, including migration, includes citations and abstracts to articles from journals and books as well as to dissertations and research reports.

Westlaw. St. Paul, MN: Westlaw.

This is a comprehensive legal database that includes US federal and state cases, statutes, and regulations, including those related to immigration. Secondary materials include law review articles, encyclopedias, and treatises.

Subject Websites

Many subject websites provide research information on migration. The sites identified here are only a few of the many sites available on the web and many of the following websites are webliographies of other sources on the Internet. Note that websites come and go at an alarming rate. Therefore, although we have made every effort to ensure that each of the following are live at the time of publication, you may find that a few of following websites either no longer exist or have moved to a different URL.

European Research Centre on Migration and Ethnic Relations. "Homepage." Accessed August 29, 2012, http://www.ercomer.eu.
> This website offers comparative studies and publications on migration and ethnic relations within a European context.

International Organization for Migration. "Homepage." Accessed August 29, 2012, http://www.iom.int/jahia/Jahia/lang/en/pid/1.
> The International Organization for Migration (IOM) acts in partnership with other international bodies around international migration issues. The IOM website is an excellent source for statistics and policy on international migration.

Pew Research Center. "Homepage." Accessed August 29, 2012, http://pewresearch.org.
> The Pew Research Center is a nonpartisan "fact tank" that studies a wide variety of social and policy issues, including immigration. The Pew Hispanic Center (http://www.pewhispanic.org) casts light on the Hispanic population and Latinos' growing impact on the United States.

Population Reference Bureau (PRB). "Homepage." Accessed August 29, 2012, http://www.prb.org.
> The PRB is a private, nonprofit organization that provides data on key topics for the United States and worldwide. One of the PRB's core themes is migration and urbanization.

United Nations. "International Migration." Accessed August 29, 2012, http://www.un.org/esa/population/migration/index.html.
> This site provides links to United Nations research and policies and resolutions relating to international migration.

United Nations Population Division. "United Nations Population Information Network: A Guide to Population Information on United Nations Web Sites." Accessed August 29, 2012, http://www.un.org/popin.
> World population statistics collected and maintained by the Population Division of the United Nations Secretariat are available through this site.

US Census Bureau. *Statistical Abstract of the United States*. Accessed August 29, 2012, http://www.census.gov/compendia/statab.
> This annual resource is the first place to go for demographic and other statistical data on the United States. *Statistical Abstract* provides tables on immigrants, race and ethnicity, and related areas. In 2012, the United States government no longer supported this resource and Bernan Press and ProQuest took up publishing duties.

US Citizenship and Immigration Services. "Homepage." Accessed August 29, 2012, http://www.uscis.gov/portal/site/uscis.
This is the central source in the US government for finding the most recent information on immigration services and regulations.

US Department of Homeland Security. "Immigration Statistics." Accessed August 29, 2012, http://www.dhs.gov/files/statistics/immigration.shtm.
This is the central website for all government-based statistics on immigration and emigration related to the United States.

US Immigration and Custom Enforcement (ICE). "Homepage." Accessed August 29, 2012, http://www.ice.gov.
This site offers the most current statements on federal government policies on immigration and customs enforcement and provides the resources for obtaining legal entry into the United States.

Yale Center for the Study of Globalization. "YaleGlobal Online." Accessed August 29, 2012, http://yaleglobal.yale.edu.
This free online source covers many aspects of globalization organized by region of the world and by topic, including migration.

Associations

Many professional associations provide information and links to resources on topics of interest to scholars of global migration. Some also have sections organized around specific interest areas like migration; most have useful "search" indexes that link to specific sources on migration.

American Anthropological Association. "American Anthropological Association." Accessed August 29, 2012, http://www.aaanet.org.
The American Anthropological Association provides a variety of publications and bibliographies on migration-related topics.

American Immigration Lawyers Association. "AILA InfoNet: American Immigration Lawyers Association." Accessed August 29, 2012, http://aila.org.
The American Immigration Lawyers Association provides resources that allow access to all laws pertaining to immigration, as well as reviews of changing immigration practices. Many of the resources can be purchased online.

American Political Science Association. "APSA Section on Race, Ethnicity, and Politics." Accessed August 29, 2012, http://www.apsarep.org.
The American Political Science Association's section on race, ethnicity, and politics includes research resources and provides directories, links to other websites, and other teaching resources. This has several publications devoted to the intersection of immigration and American racial politics.

American Sociological Association. "Home Page." Accessed August 29, 2012, http://www.asanet.org.
　The American Sociological Association has several sections of interest to those studying global migration, including global and transnational sociology, international migration, and race and ethnic minorities.

Global Migration Group. "Homepage." Accessed August 29, 2012, http://www.globalmigrationgroup.org.
　This group provides news reports as well as research papers of interest to global migration. Watch for the *United Nations Global Migration Database,* which is in the development stages.

National Association of Social Workers. "NASW: National Association of Social Workers." Accessed August 29, 2012, http://socialworkers.org.
　The National Association of Social Workers provides materials on immigration policies for social workers and connects to various other sites and publications on migration. Many of the resources on migration can be found in several sections, usually the "practice" or "diversity" sections of the website.

Notes on Contributors

The Authors

Jennifer K. Blank received her master of arts in criminology from Middlesex University in London, England. Her research is among the first to interview human traffickers in a nonincarcerated setting. She has spoken on her research to a wide variety of audiences including the Gerald D. Vick Human Trafficking Conference, the Minnesota State Senate, and Soroptimist International. Her work is published in *Trends in Organized Crime* (Springer, 2008) and in *Global Families* (Sage, 2012).

Veronica Deenanath is a graduate student in the Department of Family Social Science at the University of Minnesota in St. Paul. She received her bachelor of science in family social science from the University of Minnesota. Her research interests include parent-child relationships, graduation and retention of first-generation college students, first-generation college student families, and financial socialization and management among immigrant families.

Joanna Dreby is assistant professor of sociology at the University at Albany, State University of New York. She studies the ways migratory patterns and families' decisions about work and child care affect children. In 2011 her book *Divided by Borders: Mexican Migrants and Their Children* (University of California Press, 2010) received outstanding book awards from both the Family and International Migration sections of the American Sociological Association and the Association for Humanist Sociology.

Patti Duncan is associate professor of women's studies at Oregon State University in Corvallis, Oregon. She specializes in transnational feminisms, women of color studies, and feminist media. She is author of *Tell This Silence: Asian American Women Writers and the Politics of Speech* (University of Iowa, 2004) and codirector/producer of *Finding Face*, a documentary about acid violence in Cambodia as a gendered form of violence. Her current research addresses motherhood in global contexts.

Bruce J. Einhorn is professor of international human rights, asylum and refugee law, and the laws of war and director of the Asylum and Refugee Law Clinic at Pepperdine University School of Law in Malibu, California. A retired US federal judge, he is the author of the modern US law of asylum and a former US Justice Department special prosecutor of fugitive Nazi war criminals. Judge Einhorn is preparing a work on the history and evolution of the legal and political term *citizen* in the West.

Anthony Gray is professor of law and deputy head of the University of Southern Queensland Law School, Australia. He specializes in constitutional and human rights law and has published extensively in international and national legal journals, including the *New Criminal Law Review*, *Common Law World Review*, and *European Public Law*.

Meg Wilkes Karraker is professor of sociology and family business fellow at the University of St. Thomas in St. Paul, Minnesota. She studies religious and civil networks among Catholic sisters serving migrants in the upper midwestern United States and Italy and family businesses serving the common good in their communities. Her publications include *Diversity and the Common Good: Civil Society, Religion, and Catholic Sisters in a Small City* (Lexington, forthcoming), *Global Families* (Sage, 2013), and *Families with Futures: Family Studies into the Twenty-First Century* (with Janet Grochowski, Routledge, 2012). She is president emerita of Alpha Kappa Delta, the international sociology honor society.

Øystein S. LaBianca is professor of anthropology at Andrews University in Berrien Springs, Michigan. His fieldwork in Egypt and Jordan has been supported by grants from the National Geographic Society, the National Endowment for the Humanities, the American Schools of Oriental Research, and Earthwatch Associates. He is the author or coeditor of ten scholarly books dealing with the archaeology of Jordan and numerous journal articles dealing with food system research and archaeology.

Dung Mao is a doctorate student in the Department of Family Social Science at the University of Minnesota in St. Paul. He received his bachelor of science in the Institute of Child Psychology at the University of Minnesota and his master of arts from the Department of Family Social Science at University of Minnesota. His research interests include parenting, finance, resiliency, and mental health.

Richard H. Morgan is assistant professor in the School of Social Welfare at Stony Brook University in Stony Brook, New York. In addition to masters and doctorates in social work and social welfare, he holds masters of divinity and masters of arts degrees in theology from Catholic Theological Union in Chicago. His teaching focuses on evidence-based social work practice.

Marcella Myers is assistant professor of political science and Fulbright Scholar at Andrews University in Berrien Springs, Michigan. Her primary interests are welfare states, public policy, and political parties. Her current research focuses on the possible relationship between austerity measures and income inequality. Her publications include *Important or Impotent? Radical Right Political Parties and Public Policy in Germany and Austria* (Lambert Academic Publishing, 2010).

Marianne S. Noh is a postdoctoral scholar in the Arthur Labatt Family School Nursing at the University of Western Ontario, Canada. Her research includes comparative analysis of ethnic and gender identity formations among Asian youth in the United States and Canada and multivariate analyses of depressive symptoms among immigrants living with chronic health conditions such as HIV/AIDS. Her recent work has been published in *Gender Issues* and *Journal of Immigrant and Minority Health*.

Jan M. Orf is a reference librarian at the University of St. Thomas Libraries in St. Paul, Minnesota. With master's degrees in library science and liberal studies, she has worked in the field for almost three decades, specializing in the social sciences. Her publications include reference guides for textbooks, including *Families with Futures* (Routledge, 2012).

Susan Smith-Cunnien is professor of sociology and criminal justice at the University of St. Thomas in St. Paul, Minnesota. Her research interests include both nonstate justice systems and formal criminal justice systems in the United States and Africa, including Ghana, Mali, and South Africa. She has led study abroad trips to both Ghana and Mali. She has also written about chiropractors and their movement from the medical margins to the mainstream in the United States.

Mathew Vicknair is an undergraduate sociology and economics major at the University of St. Thomas in St. Paul, Minnesota. He has worked with nongovernmental organizations in the United States and abroad and is a former Citizenship of the World counselor for the Boy Scouts of America. He is particularly interested in the social impact of nongovernment organizations programs and has studied the effects of microloans on female self-sufficiency in the Democratic Republic of the Congo.

Zha Blong Xiong is associate professor of family social science in the College of Education and Human Development at the University of Minnesota in St. Paul, Minnesota. He is coauthor of a highly respected, research-based parent education curriculum *Helping Youth Succeed: Bicultural Parenting for Southeast Asian Families* and serves on several boards, including the Center for Hmong Studies, Hmong National Development, and the *Journal of Southeast Asian American Education and Advancement*.

The Photographer

Wing Young Huie's work documents the dizzying socioeconomic and cultural realities of American society today, much of it focused on the urban cores of his home state of Minnesota. In public installations and in international museum exhibitions, he creates societal mirrors of who we are, seeking to reveal not only what is hidden but also what is revealed and rarely noticed. His most well-known works have transformed Twin Cities urban areas into public photo galleries, reflecting the everyday lives of thousands of its citizens in the midst of some of the most diverse concentrations of international immigrants in the country.

The author of five published books, including *The University Avenue Project: The Language of Urbanism, a Six-Mile Photographic Inquiry* (Minnesota Historical Society Press, 2010), Huie was named Artist of the Year by the Minneapolis Star Tribune in 2000.

Huie's the Third Place Photography Gallery is located at 3730 Chicago Avenue S, Studio B, Minneapolis, MN 55407. Further information about Huie's work can be found at http://www.wingyounghuie.com.

Index

Printed in the United States of America